D0968385

# THE GO-BETWEEN GOD

*The Holy Spirit and the Christian Mission*

*John V. Taylor*

ST FRANCIS SEMINARY
SALZMANN
LIBRARY
Milwaukee, Wis. 53207

OXFORD UNIVERSITY PRESS
New York

First Published in Great Britain in 1972
by SCM Press Ltd, 16 Bloomsbury Street, London

First Published in Paperback in the United States in 1979
by Oxford University Press Inc, New York

Copyright © 1972 by SCM Press Ltd

Unless stated otherwise, biblical quotations are from *The New English Bible*. © The Delegates of the Oxford University Press and The Syndics of the Cambridge University Press 1961, 1970. Reprinted by permission.

Library of Congress Cataloging in Publication Data

Taylor, John Vernon, 1914-
  The go-between God.

  Includes index.
  1. Holy Spirit. 2. Missions. I. Title.
BT121.2.T39  1979  262'.001  79-19919
ISBN  0-19-520125-6 pbk.

Printed in the United States of America

# CONTENTS

# LIST OF PLATES

# FOREWORD

In 1967, the Senate and Council of the University of Birmingham invited me to give the Edward Cadbury Lectures in Theology. For me it was an experience of stimulation rather than fulfilment and this book is very largely a rewriting of the original series of eight lectures. In the meantime some passages have already appeared in the *CMS News-letter* and a portion of Chapter 9 in a small book of essays entitled *Face to Face* (Highway Press). I apologize to all who while reading the pages that follow will have the sensation of having heard it before, and confess that very often the reason will not be the one I have just given, but the plain fact that I am a borrower and retailer of other men's ideas.

The contents of each chapter are indicated in the sub-titles. The schema of main chapter titles is one which I personally have found full of suggestion, but it is a counterpoint upon the main theme and should not be taken too seriously.

I have owed a great deal of my thought to the four pictures reproduced in this book, and I hope that readers may often turn to them, for they say it all better than I can hope to.

*Part One*

# FACTS OF LIFE

# I

# ANNUNCIATION

*The Intermediary Spirit and the Impulse of the Mission*

The chief actor in the historic mission of the Christian church is the Holy Spirit. He is the director of the whole enterprise. The mission consists of the things that he is doing in the world. In a special way it consists of the light that he is focussing upon Jesus Christ.

This fact, so patent to Christians in the first century, is largely forgotten in our own. So we have lost our nerve and our sense of direction and have turned the divine initiative into a human enterprise. 'It all depends on me' is an attitude that is bedevilling both the practice and the theology of our mission in these days.

That is precisely what Jesus forbade at the start of it all. They must *not* go it alone. They must *not* think that the mission is their responsibility.

> While he was in their company he told them not to leave Jerusalem. 'You must wait', he said, 'for the promise made by my Father, about which you have heard me speak: John, as you know, baptized with water, but you will be baptized with the Holy Spirit, and within the next few days' (Acts 1.4, 5).

They were not invited to deploy their resources or plan their strategy.

> 'It is not for you to know about dates or times, which the Father has set within his own control. But you will receive power when the Holy Spirit comes upon you; and you will bear witness for me in Jerusalem, and all over Judaea and Samaria, and away to the ends of the earth' (Acts 1.7, 8).

The very mandate to engage in this world-wide mission could only be given simultaneously with the gift of the Holy Spirit. This is made quite specific in the Fourth Gospel.

> Jesus repeated, 'Peace be with you', and said, 'As the Father sent me, so I send you.' Then he breathed on them, saying, 'Receive the Holy Spirit!' (John 20.21, 22).

And Luke makes the same point succinctly in the second verse of the Acts where he calls the apostolic mandate 'instructions through the Holy Spirit'. The marching orders and the gift of the Spirit come in the same package. How could it have been otherwise, seeing that Jesus himself received his mandate and his sense of mission only by being caught up into the operation of the Holy Spirit and dominated by him?

> At that moment heaven opened; he saw the Spirit of God descending like a dove to alight upon him; and a voice from heaven was heard saying, 'This is my Son, my Beloved, on whom my favour rests.' Jesus was then led away by the Spirit into the wilderness, to be tempted by the devil (Matt. 3.16–4.1).

> Then Jesus, armed with the power of the Spirit, returned to Galilee... He opened the scroll and found the passage which says, 'The Spirit of the Lord is upon me because he has anointed me; he has sent me to announce good news to the poor' (Luke 4.14, 17, 18).

If for Jesus himself both messiahship and mission were derived from his self-immersion in that flood-tide of the Holy Spirit, how could his followers possibly be involved in the same mission except through the same immersion? As Bishop Fison once said:

> The story of Acts is the story of the stupendous missionary achievement of a community inspired to make a continual series of creative experiments by the Pentecostal Spirit. Against a static Church, unwilling to obey the guidance of the Holy Spirit, no 'gates' of any sort are needed to oppose its movement, for it does not move. But against a Church that is on the move, inspired by the Pentecostal Spirit, neither 'the gates of hell' nor any other gates can prevail.[1]

But, while we piously repeat the traditional assertion that without the Holy Spirit we can get nowhere in the Christian mission, we seem to press on notwithstanding with our man-made programmes. I have not heard recently of committee business adjourned because those present were still awaiting the arrival of the Spirit of God. I have known projects abandoned for lack of funds, but not for lack of the gifts of the Spirit. Provided the human resources are adequate we take the spiritual for granted. In fact we have only the haziest idea of what we mean by resources other than human wealth, human skill and human character. This book is an attempt to interpret the meaning of the Christian mission for our contemporary world within the context of a fresh understanding of the Holy Spirit and his action in that world. What is it, essentially, that he adds to our natural human capacities, without which we cannot even begin to be witnesses for Christ? We say glibly that we need his power and his guidance: what sort of power are we to expect beyond that of ordinary men and by what kind of communication does he point out the way?

The whole of our uneasy debate about the meaning of the word 'God' for modern man cries out, I believe, for a recovery of a significant doctrine of the Holy Spirit. That is where we must now begin our talk about God – God working anonymously and on the inside: the beyond in the midst. If we had not relegated the Holy Spirit to the merest edges of our theology we might never have got ourselves into our present confusions – or, better still, we might have endured our present expansion of awareness without dismay. As it is, we seem to have rarified God out of existence. According to the most recent rules of the theological game, we must never again speak of him in the language of myth or in any other terms that 'objectify' him, for this suggests that our knowledge of·him is empirical, like our other experiences. And that must never be, lest our 'pure' faith run the risk of empirical contradiction – or confirmation – and, one way or the other, cease to be faith!

In this bleak view where the fact of God has nothing in common with any other kind of fact, we are stuck with a conflict between our acknowledgment of God existing in himself apart from the created universe and of God existing in and through all the facts; between our experience of a word of God given external to ourselves and a word speaking from within ourselves; between a system of moral ordinances and an intuitive recognition of certain values. These contradictions begin to resolve themselves when the Holy Spirit becomes so central to our thoughts about God and about man that whenever the name 'God' is used our minds go first to the Spirit, not last.

Martin Buber was one of the great interpreters of the Holy Spirit, though he rarely used that name for him. He marvellously grasped the manner in which God acts and is known 'through things temporal' yet remains transcendent.

> God's speech to men penetrates what happens in the life of each one of us, and all that happens in the world around us, biographical and historical, and makes it for you and me into instruction, message, demand. Happening upon happening, situation upon situation are enabled and empowered by the personal speech of God to demand of the human person that he take his stand and make his decision.[2]

Paul Tillich asserted that this is the clue to the reconciliation we seek, in a characteristic aside during a course of lectures he gave in 1963.

> If for a moment I may be allowed to be personal, you see this same conflict going on between my own theology and Karl Barth's, the one approaching man by coming from the outside (Barth) and the other starting with man. Now I believe that there is one concept which can reconcile these two ways. This is the concept of the divine Spirit. It was there in the apostle Paul. Paul was the great theologian of the divine Spirit. It formed the centre of his theology.[3]

In this study I take the position that the Spirit who is central to Paul's theology is the same being whom the Old Testament knew as the Spirit, or Breath, of God. In a later chapter I shall give my reasons for taking this view, which I know is challenged by some. The relationship of the Spirit to the Christian believer and to the church is without precedent, and this fact must be central to our understanding of the Christian mission. Yet the New Testament authors nowhere appear to infer from the uniqueness of their *experience* of the Holy Spirit that he himself had been quite unknown hitherto. The symbolism of the Pentecost experience – rushing wind, fire and ecstasy – linked the new experience with the familiar images of the Old Testament, as did the Johannine account of Christ's breathing the Spirit upon his disciples. The steady development of the Hebrew understanding of the Spirit of God shown in the Old Testament culminates in a leap into a new dimension in the New Testament. There is no discontinuity. If we want to understand in a fresh way what it was that possessed Jesus at his baptism, and what it is that we also need before we can engage in the Christian mission, we have to probe into the meaning of the ancient images – the breath of life, the hovering wings, the unpredictable winds, the fire in the mouth – for all this and far more is included in the gift that should be ours.

All is imagery. Or, rather, all is experience which only images can adequately convey. We do well, therefore, to remember that the word 'Spirit' itself is a metaphor, just as the words 'Father' and 'Son' are also metaphors. The Hebrew *ruach*, the Greek *pneuma*, the Latin *spiritus*, all mean 'wind 'or 'breath'. Even the north European *geist* and *ghost* are linked, according to Webster, with the Anglo-Saxon root *gast*, meaning 'breath'. In other words, we are dealing with a double analogy. Something in the physical world – the fierce wind of the desert, the breath of a living creature – is used as an image of an incorporeal element in man which cannot easily be named in any other way; and then this human 'spirit' is itself used as an image of another ineffable force which man feels working upon him and believes to be divine. Maybe he concludes that his own 'breath' is derived from this 'Breath of God', but with regard to his understanding and naming of things he has worked it out the other way round. So we too must think what we mean by 'the spirit of man' in order to see better what we mean by the Spirit of God.

In common with most animistic analyses of the nature of man, the Old Testament distinguishes between *nepesh*, or life-force, and *ruach*, or spirit. This always surprises me, for one might have supposed that the breath which man expires at death was an obvious image of the life-force. But in fact tribal peoples generally have associated the life-force not with breath but with blood, and the Hebrews were no exception. *Ruach* is a different kind of power inherent in man, associated not so much with his being alive as with his being a person. We might call it the power of his personhood, the power of his separate otherness, the power by which he is recognized as himself. But it is also his power to recognize, and to be impinged upon by, the otherness of the persons, things, realities which are not himself. For, as Hegel says, 'the truth of personality is just this: to win it through immersion, through being immersed in the other'.[4] My spirit, therefore, is never uniquely mine as are my body, my life, my individuality. It resides only in my relatedness to some other. Spirit is that which lies between, making both separateness and conjunction real. It generates a certain quality of charged intensity which from time to time marks every man's relationship with the world around him and with whatever reality lies within and behind that world.

The human infant has not yet learned to distinguish between himself and his surroundings. To grow up is to stand back from the rest of existence, to objectify, to negotiate a *modus vivendi* of control or acceptance. We have first to see every other being as an 'it' before we can meet it as a 'thou'. We must draw the sharp line between subject and object before that line can once again be blurred in an even more mature way of seeing. We must recognize the absolute otherness of the other in order to discover the mutuality of evocation and response.

But then comes the seeing which is not observation but encounter. When I was ten or eleven years old I had measles. I was kept back from school, and isolated from the rest of the family in our spare bedroom. My sisters came and sang on the other side of the door to cheer me up. I spent several hours a day with the wooden box gramophone which had been brought up to amuse me. The familiar tunes had always been enjoyable and I knew that the performers must be very clever people. But as I played one of them again a short passage affected me with a shock of excitement I had never felt before. It was musically trivial — a waltz by Delibes played as a piano piece, I remember – and its appeal was entirely sensual. But the surprise lay in my discovery that music could 'speak' – and I had not known that such a language existed.

Essentially the same, years later, was my first glimpse of Mount Kilimanjaro serenely shining high above the Tanzanian cloud line, 150 miles away. I knew then that I must climb it: that was a simple matter of fact; and only afterwards did I theatrically recall Mallory's reply when he was asked why he wanted to climb Everest: 'Because it is there'. But that is the point. That is what all such experiences have in common. The fact that something, or someone, is *there* suddenly becomes important. Instead of simply being part of the landscape, part of existence, it presents itself, it becomes present, it commands attention.

This happens most vividly when we fall in love. Across the

crowded ballroom Romeo catches Juliet's eye and one senses the almost electrical current of their mutual attraction. A moment later they are side by side, and the very lightness of their first contact, 'palm to palm' betrays the compulsive force that is drawing them together. Classical Hindu paintings of Lord Krishna and the beloved Radha portray what is called 'the meeting of the eyes', of which also our most intense western love poetry has spoken:

> *Our eye-beames twisted, and did thred*
> *Our eyes, upon one double string;*
> *So to' entergraft our hands, as yet*
> *Was all the meanes to make us one.*[5]

But these are only the more intense instances of something that is constantly happening to us, and I want to emphasize the ordinariness and frequency of these experiences. In a manner of speaking, we are falling in love at every turn of the road, with a fold in the hills, the mist over the lake, the stars tangled in the bare branches, the yellow chair in the sunlight, an old song at the peasant's fireside, a new thought flashing from the pages of a book, a lined face on a hospital pillow, a hair-ribbon from Ur of the Chaldees.

In his autobiography the poet Edwin Muir recalls such a moment during his wife's grave illness. Waiting one day by the doctor's door he

. . . glanced at a little tree a few steps away. A lamp above the door shone straight on it, illuminating it like a Christmas tree, and on one of the twigs a robin was sitting, looking at me, quite without fear, with its round eyes, its bright breast liquidly glowing in the light. As I stared at it out of my worry, which was a world of its own, the small glittering object had an unearthly radiance, and seemed to be pouring light into the darkness without and the darkness within myself. It astonished and reassured me.[6]

One of the best-known incidents of this peculiar type of confrontation is Wordsworth's boyhood escape on Derwentwater one summer night, when he rowed out across the lake in a little boat he had found.

*When, from behind that craggy steep till then*
*The horizon's bound, a huge peak, black and huge,*
*As if with voluntary power instinct*
*Upreared its head. I struck and struck again,*
*And growing still in stature the grim shape*
*Towered up between me and the stars, and still,*
*For so it seemed, with purpose of its own*
*And measured motion like a living thing,*
*Strode after me. With trembling oars I turned*
*And through the silent water stole my way*
*Back to the covert . . .*
*. . . for many days my brain*
*Worked with a dim and undetermined sense*
*Of unknown modes of being . . .*[7]

The quality of that kind of encounter is painfully contrasted with the inability to see in that way in a prisoner-of-war's account of the first day of his release.

We limped on; we wanted to see the camp's surroundings for the first time with the eyes of free men. 'Freedom' – we repeated to ourselves, and yet we could not grasp it . . . We came to meadows full of flowers. We saw and realized that they were there, but we had no feelings about them. The first spark of joy came when we saw a rooster with a tail of multi-coloured feathers. But it remained only a spark; we did not yet belong to the world. In the evening when we all met again in our hut, one said secretly to the other, 'Tell me, were you pleased today?' And the other replied, feeling ashamed as he did not know that we all felt similarly, 'Truthfully, no.' . . . One day, a few days after the liberation, I walked through the country past flowering meadows, for miles and miles, towards the market town near the camp. Larks rose to the sky and I could hear their joyous song. There was no one to be seen for miles around; there was nothing but the wide earth and sky and the larks' jubilation and the freedom of space. I stopped, looked around, and up to the sky – and then I went down on my knees.[8]

The core of these experiences is the mutual recognition of seer and seen. I can best call them 'annunciations'. I have in mind several renaissance pictures of St Luke's story which emphasize the mutually enraptured gaze of the angel and the Virgin, and the dove-symbol of the Holy Spirit spinning, as it were, the thread of attention between them. Edwin Muir caught this supremely in one of his poems on the theme which echoes Donne's timeless ecstasy.

> *See, they have come together, see,*
> *While the destroying minutes flow,*
> *Each reflects the other's face*
> *Till heaven in hers and earth in his*
> *Shine steady there . . .*
> *But through the endless afternoon*
> *These neither speak nor movement make,*
> *But stare into their deepening trance*
> *As if their gaze would never break.*[9]

Earlier in this century the German poet, Rainer Maria Rilke, saw the same significance in the familiar annunciation scene.

> *The angel's entrance (you must realize)*
> *was not what made her frightened. . .*
> *No, not to see him enter, but to find*
> *the youthful angel's countenance inclined*
> *so near to her; that when he looked, and she*
> *looked up at him, their looks so merged in one*
> *the world outside grew vacant, suddenly,*
> *and all things being seen, endured and done*
> *were crowded into them: just she and he*
> *eye and its pasture, visions and its view,*
> *here at the point and at this point alone:–*
> *see, this arouses fear. Such fear both knew.*[10]

I have quoted these meditations on a familiar story, not to turn the discussion into a 'religious' channel, but because they describe so clearly the kind of seeing I am talking about. I am not thinking of what is narrowly described as 'encounter with God', but of quite unreligious commonplace experiences. And if we try to remember them more carefully, I think we shall notice that what happens is this. The mountain or the tree I am looking at ceases to be merely an object I am observing and becomes a subject, existing in its own life, and saying something to me – one could almost say *nodding* to me in a private conspiracy. That, in fact, is the precise meaning of the word 'numinous', which comes from the Latin *nuo*, to nod or beckon. The truly numinous experience is not marked only by primitive awe in the face of the unknown or overwhelming, but occurs also when something as ordinary as a sleeping child, as simple and objective as a flower, suddenly *commands* attention.

There are actually two stages in my experience. First, I am forced to recognize the real *otherness* of what I am looking at: it does not depend on my seeing or responding; it exists without me. And, second, there is a *communication* between us which I am bound to admit, if I am not obstinately blind, has not entirely originated in myself. As Paul van Buren has said:

> The decisive point to be made is that some men are *struck* by the ordinary, whereas most find it merely ordinary. . . Seeing the ordinary as extraordinary, as a cause for wonder, is no more and no less in need of justification than seeing the ordinary as ordinary and as something to be taken for granted.[11]

Van Buren seems to limit this way of seeing to a minority whom he calls 'the strange ones'. I think he is wrong and that there are very few people, however unmetaphysical their minds have become, who do not see things in this way from time to time. But despite this emphasis, he describes most beautifully the kind of experience I have been trying to elaborate.

> Speech about God, or silence about God, for that matter, but in any case, the sort of speech and the sort of silence that marks off the strange ones from the masses, the deep ones from the superficial, appears within the context of a sense of wonder, awe, and joy before what is there for all to behold; the fact that we are alive, that there is anything at all. The mystical, as Wittgenstein put it, and he was surely one of the strange ones, is not how the world is, but *that* it is. This sense of awe and wonder occurs when one is *struck* by the fact that I am, and that I am I, that a tree is itself, that there is anything at all.[12]

'That I am I, that a tree is itself . . .' – these two phrases point to the heart of all the experiences I have been describing. The selfhood of the tree, the music, the girl, the mountain, confronts me in its absolute otherness, and also demands that I meet it in my own integrity. Its identity owes nothing to my seeing it, reflecting upon it, analysing it or reacting to it. Seeing it in this way does not endorse my former experiences and opinions but offers me the possibility of a new experience and a change of opinion. I am seeing 'with new eyes'. For now this other being meets me in its own authenticity, and I am face to face with the truth *of* it, not merely the truth *about* it.

The difference between those two kinds of truth is of the greatest consequence, as we shall see in later chapters. To learn the truth *about* Mount Kilimanjaro or Titian's 'The Death of Actaeon' or Jesus of Nazareth is a process of investigation and analysis which makes an object of what I am studying and puts me at one remove from its intrinsic reality. The 'facts' come between me and it, like over-intrusive interpreters at a conversation with a foreigner. But to encounter the truth *of* Mount Kilimanjaro or the truth *of* 'The Death of Actaeon' or the truth *of* Jesus is to submit to being the object of their impact. From one point of view this is a dangerously subjective way of knowing truth, but from another point of view it is the only way in which truth authenticates itself. It is the truth *of* Jesus which compelled men, and still compels them, to testify that he speaks not as the scribes but as one with authority; that is the impact of his intrinsic reality which transcends proof. And it is the truth *of* the Titian which comes out to meet me in such power that my direct response is a kind of 'Yes', not 'It swirls with movement' nor 'It reverses the positions in "Diana surprised at her bath".' Both these observations, and much more that I read or hear about the picture, may be true as facts and in due course my recognition of them will enrich my response; but my response will still consist simply in 'Yes'. Any truth *about* the picture, any informative truth, may affect the quality of my response to its intrinsic truth, but cannot give that intrinsic truth to me, for that can only come to me directly from the picture itself.

The truth *about* something is like a string of adjectives, but the truth *of* something must always be experienced as a noun or pronoun.

From a multitude of such experiences we come to understand that the source of a profound response of recognition, joy and wonder is not the responding person, myself, but the presence to which I am responding. What we call the object of our response is really the subject and activator. Or, to put it another way, the line we like to draw between subject and object, between that which calls and that which answers, grows faint and finally disappears. As soon as 'being' becomes 'presence' it has already become a part of that to which it is present.

Many people resolutely resist this fading of the line. They insist that the experience of being addressed by an object or event in the material world is a merely subjective fantasy. They admit that Juliet in the crowded hall may send signals that she herself is unaware of; so, perhaps, can the sleeping child and the dying patient. But to attribute any personal communication to inanimate nature is to revert, they say, to a primitive dynamism. And of course this is perfectly true; but it is only part of the truth. Our commonsense, objective way of looking at reality is necessary for our survival; but the more wondering, reciprocal way is equally valid. To say this is not an attempt to find a place for God in the gap of extra-sensory perception. For, as I have reiterated before, the second way of seeing, of knowing, of responding to reality, is as natural and as commonplace as the first.

The need to hold both these modes of perception in balance has nowhere been better expressed than by Martin Buber in his little masterpiece, *I and Thou*:

To man the world is twofold, in accordance with his twofold attitude. He perceives what exists round about him – simply things, and beings as things. . . It is to some extent a reliable world. . . It is your object, remains it as long as you wish, and remains a total stranger, within you and without. You perceive it, take it to yourself as the 'truth', and it lets itself be taken; but it does not give itself to you. Only concerning it may you make yourself 'understood' with others; it is ready, though attached to everyone in a different way, to be an object common to you all. But you cannot meet others in it. You cannot hold on to life without it, its reliability sustains you; but should you die in it, your grave would be in nothingness.

Or, on the other hand, man meets what exists and becomes as what is over against him. . . It comes even when it is not summoned, and vanishes even when it is tightly held. It cannot be surveyed, and if you wish to make it capable of survey you lose it. It comes, and comes to bring *you* out. . . Between you and it there is mutual giving: you say *Thou* to it and give yourself to it, it says *Thou* to you and gives itself to you. You cannot make yourself understood with others concerning it, you are alone with it. But it teaches you to meet others, and to hold your ground when you meet them. Through the graciousness of its comings and the solemn sadness of its goings it leads you away to the

*Thou* in which the parallel lines of relations meet. It does not
help to sustain you in life, it only helps you to glimpse eternity.[13]

In all such moments of intense mutuality the truth of that other
being calls to the truth of myself. 'It comes to bring *me* out.'
It demands, as I have already said, that I meet it in my own integrity. If I respond with pretention or begin to play a part, the other
withdraws, because my attention is now turned upon myself. As
soon as I dramatize myself as an aspiring Mallory I lose the truth of
the real Kilimanjaro and am left with a fantasy mountain of my own
creation. As soon as I pretend to see in the Titian the things other
people have said I ought to see, it ceases to speak with its own
authority, for the scribes have taken over. Annunciations, as I have
called these encounters, last only so long as truth faces truth.

But while, in these moments of mutual awareness, the other demands that I be truly myself, it demands also that I be all that I am
capable of being. There is nothing inert or passive about the mutual
giving; it is intense and exacting. Good art, for example, does not
have to be great art, and to respond to it one does not have to be
'highbrow'. It may be easy to like, but if it is good at all it will demand some self-giving and some stretching. Real listening and real
looking takes it out of one, though one only becomes conscious of
this afterwards.

I am aware that it is popular just now to decry Buber's thought as
too individualistic or, as Harvey Cox argued on a slightly different
tack in *The Secular City*, too idealistic:

> Often a nagging sense of guilt plagues the urban man with rural
> roots because he cannot possibly cultivate an I-Thou relationship
> with everyone.[14]

That betrays a misunderstanding which has become very common. The *I-Thou* experience Buber describes in the classic passage I
have quoted is not a relationship that one can 'cultivate'. It comes
unsummoned, that is its nature, and when it does not come no one
should feel guilty about the lack of it. Neither does Buber despise
the other attitude which sees the world and one's fellow men as the
objects of one's perception and which includes what Harvey Cox
calls the *I-You* relationship.

What I think needs to be added, however, is that there are some
people, probably very many, to whom this profound encounter with

another being comes most naturally as a group experience. I know several friends, in Britain and the U S A, who have entered into a new dimension of awareness and an experience of the significance of everything through being caught up into the mutual acceptance and open-ness and penetrating love of some group.

Sometimes it happens when, following the pain of conflict and self-discovery, they know themselves to be given to one another at a deeper level than ever before. What has struck me is that almost invariably any one of them, describing the moment of recognition says 'We saw', or 'It came to us', never 'I saw'. I believe this is accurate, and that the group in its togetherness was given moments of insight and liberation which no member could have received *singly* even in the company of others. The same can be said of the healing of certain mental patients, which it seems is only achieved in the context of a supportive community that will suffer with and for them. And this was clearly taught by Buber himself. 'We are waiting', he wrote, 'for a theophany about which we know nothing except its place, and that place is called community.'[15]

Whether corporately or individually experienced, these occasions are often the turning points in our lives when our old ideas are upset and forced to take a new direction. Gigadibs, in Browning's great poem, thought he had his sad sceptical philosophy all buttoned up, but then, says Bishop Blougram,

> *Just when we are safest there's a sunset touch,*
> *A fancy from a flower bell, someone's death,*
> *A chorus-ending from Euripides,*
> *And that's enough for fifty hopes and fears,*
> *As old and new at once as nature's self,*
> *To rap and knock and enter in our soul.*[16]

Now if it is these moments of recognition and awareness that change our minds and change our lives, if these can be the true turning points of human history, then something of enormous power must be at work in such commonplace experiences. One might say that a flash of recognition has a higher voltage than a flash of lightning, that the power that makes us suddenly aware is the secret of all evolution and the spark that sets off most revolutions.

But what is this force which causes me to see in a way in which I have not seen? What makes a landscape or a person or an idea come to life for me and become a presence towards which I surrender myself? I recognize, I respond, I fall in love, I worship – yet it was not I who took the first step. In every such encounter there has been an anonymous third party who makes the introduction, acts as a go-between, makes two beings aware of each other, sets up a current of communication between them. What is more, this invisible go-between does not simply stand between us but is activating each of us from inside. Moses approaching the burning bush is no scientific observer; the same fiery essence burns in his own heart also. He and the thorn-bush are caught and held, as it were, in the same magnetic field.

I have already started to talk about this force of influence in very personal terms. I am bound to do so because the effect of this power is always to bring a mere object into a personal relationship with me, to turn an *It* into a *Thou*.

So Christians find it quite natural to give a personal name to this current of communication, this invisible go-between. They call him the Holy Spirit, the Spirit of God. They say that this was the Spirit which possessed and dominated the man Jesus Christ, making him the most aware and sensitive and open human being who has ever lived – ceaselessly aware of God so that he called him, almost casually, Father, and fantastically aware of every person who crossed his path, especially the ones no one else noticed.

That is the Spirit which he promised to send to his friends and on the day of Pentecost that is the Spirit which came and possessed them just as he had possessed Jesus. And what was the first immediate result of his coming? – Communication. Awareness. They preached and everyone in that cosmopolitan crowd heard them speaking to him in his own language.

The prayer we call 'The Grace', taken from II Corinthians 13.14, is so familiar that we fail to notice what it really says. It points to the three absolutely basic qualities in the nature of the triune God. 'The grace our Lord Jesus Christ' – grace, or givenness, is the most characteristic quality of Jesus. And the essence of God in his unity is love – 'the love of God'. But then it does not say 'The power of the Holy Spirit', or 'the light of the Holy Spirit', or 'the purity of the Holy Spirit'; it says 'the Communion', the in-between-ness, of the Holy Spirit. It is often translated fellowship, but fellowship is the result which we can feel and see. What *causes* the fellowship is the gift of awareness which opens our eyes to one another, makes us see as we never saw before, the secret of all evolution, the spark that sets off most revolution, the dangerous life-giver, the Holy Spirit.

Every time I am given this unexpected awareness towards some other creature and feel this current of communication between us, I am touched and activated by something that comes from the fiery heart of the divine love, the eternal gaze of the Father towards the Son, of the Son towards the Father.

'God's love has flooded our inmost heart through the Holy Spirit he has given us' (Rom. 5.5).

'Ground of our being' has always seemed to me too static a concept of God. 'Ground of our meeting' is nearer the mark, and I think of the Holy Spirit as the elemental energy of communion itself, within which all separate existences may be made present and personal to each other. The first essential activity of the Spirit is annunciation. It is always he who gives one to the other and makes each really see the other.

Once more let me insist on the ordinariness of this kind of knowing. This is the sense in which the Bible says Adam knew Eve his wife, for sexual knowledge can be a supreme disclosure both of total otherness and of total in-each-other-ness between two persons. Such awareness, extended towards any part of reality, is the essence of that Wisdom which the later Hebrew poets extolled, the *Hagia Sophia* which is so nearly identified with the Holy Spirit, the Spirit of wisdom and understanding, the Spirit of counsel and knowledge.

The pre-requisite for ths kind of knowing is *attention*. Every good teacher knows the futility of rapping on his desk and calling: Pay attention, please! True attention is an involuntary self-surrender to the object of attention. The child who is absorbed is utterly relaxed. The adult mind, also, must be unstriving, receptive, expectant, before there can be any creative insight. Again and again this is the state of mind in which new truth dawns. We do not work it out or think it out; rather, we have the sense of waiting for the disclosure of something that is already there. Attention means being in attendance. It is the recognition of the real presence of the other, quite apart from one's own self or one's own mental processes. To be 'in the Spirit' is to be vividly aware of everything the moment contains, the twigs of the thorn-bush as well as the presence of God.

I am reminded of a passage in Bishop Anthony Bloom's book, *School for Prayer*,[17] in which he tells of an old lady who came asking for his counsel: though she had prayed continuously for fourteen years she had never sensed the presence of God. How could she learn the secret? He gave her wise advice, and later she told him of her first experience. She had gone into her room, made herself comfortable, and begun to knit. She felt relaxed and noticed with content what a nice shaped room she had, with its view of the garden, and the sound of her needles hitting the arm-rest of her chair. And then gradually she became aware that the silence was not simply the absence of sound, but was filled with its own density. 'And', she said, 'it began to pervade me. The silence around began to come and meet the silence in me . . . All of a sudden I perceived that the silence was a presence. At the heart of the silence there was Him.'

The fascination of that account lies in the woman's simple recognition that her awareness of God came together with her deeper awareness of the familiar things around her. It must always be so. The Holy Spirit is the invisible third party who stands between me and the other, making us mutually aware. Supremely and primarily he opens my eyes to Christ. But he also opens my eyes to the brother in Christ, or the fellow-man, or the point of need, or the heartbreaking brutality and the equally heartbreaking beauty of the world. He is the giver of that vision without which the people perish. We so commonly speak about him as the source of *power*. But in fact he enables us not by making us supernaturally strong but by opening our eyes.

The Holy Spirit is that power which opens eyes that are closed, hearts that are unaware and minds that shrink from too much reality. If one is open towards God, one is open also to the beauty of the world, the truth of ideas, and the pain of disappointment and deformity. If one is closed up against being hurt, or blind towards one's fellow-men, one is inevitably shut off from God also. One cannot choose to be open in one direction and closed in another. Vision and vulnerability go together. Insensitivity also is an all-rounder. If for one reason or another we refuse really to *see* another person, we become incapable of sensing the presence of God.

The spirit of man is that facility which enables each of us to be truly present to another. The Spirit of God is that power of communion which enables every other reality, and the God who is within and behind all realities, to be present to us.

It is in these terms, I believe, that we have to understand the necessity of the gift of the Holy Spirit for the Christian mission. The first apostles were strictly warned by the risen Christ that they must on no account start upon the mission until they had received this gift of the Spirit. In this Christ was bequeathing to his friends what had been his own experience. For he also was launched into his mission for mankind only through the coming of the Holy Spirit upon him at the time of the baptism. For him the descent of the dove was a moment of seeing and hearing, in which he realized in a deeper, clearer recognition, his own role both as Son of God and as Suffering Servant, and the identity of those two Old Testament images. He had to go into the wilderness to wrestle with the meaning of this vision for himself and for the world. Then, with the Spirit of the Lord upon him, he was ready to begin his mission.

So it was for the apostles afterwards. There can be no mission until eyes have been opened to see the living Christ. For the witnesses that were to go to the ends of the earth were witnesses of the resurrection. And the eye-opening which made this witness possible was the characteristic action of the Holy Spirit. Again and again, when they had first encountered the risen Christ, 'their eyes were holden so they could not know him'. There had to come the instant of recognition; and at any moment it might be given – in the garden, across the supper table, over the waters of the lake, on the road to Damascus. So, as I said at the start, the gift of a message and the gift of the Spirit are the same gift, for the one springs from the awareness that the other brings. Saul of Tarsus becomes an apostle at the moment when Ananias says to him: 'The Lord Jesus has sent me to you so that you may recover your sight and be filled with the Holy Spirit' (Acts 9.17).

It is no different for us. Our interchange between church and church, our massive programmes of aid, our technical skill, even our compassion, are no part of the Christian mission until and unless some of those who take part in them have known that miraculous opening of the eyes whereby the figure of Jesus in history and in the church encounters and accosts us as the living Christ, knowing and known, calling and answered. After that we have a message, however many doubts may intervene, however many difficulties may dishearten.

All faith in God is basically a way of 'seeing the ordinary' in the light of certain moments of disclosure which have been the gift of the Holy Spirit. In his poetical and heartening small book, *A Rumour of Angels*, Peter Berger suggests that a recovery of faith may come to our generation only through a re-opening of eyes.

A rediscovery of the supernatural will be, above all, a regaining of openness in our perception of reality. It will not only be, as theologians influenced by existentialism have greatly over-emphasized, an overcoming of tragedy. Perhaps more importantly it will be an overcoming of triviality. In openness to the signals of transcendence the true proportions of our experience are rediscovered. This is the comic relief of redemption; it makes it possible for us to laugh and to play with a new fulness.[18]

But no less necessary to the Christian mission is the opening of our eyes towards other people. And this also is the gift of the Spirit. A Christian can never be the means of communicating Christ to another until what we might call the current of communication has been switched on. The scales fell from the eyes of the convert in the city of Damascus precisely when he heard one of those whose very lives he had been threatening say: 'Saul, my brother, the Lord Jesus has sent *me to you*'. I-Thou.

I am certain also that it is by design that St Luke follows his account of Pentecost with the encounter of Peter and John with the lame man at the Beautiful Gate of the Temple. Notice how the interlocking of eyes is central to the story.

Seeing Peter and John about to go into the temple, he asked for alms. And Peter directed his gaze at him, with John, and said, 'Look at us'. And he fixed his attention upon them (Acts 3.3–4).

And a little later the account goes on: 'And all the people saw him walking and praising God, and recognized him' (Acts 3.9).

Without this ability to see the truth of the other man – we call it empathy today – the missionary of any colour may do more harm than good. The person in the hospital bed is not a case; he needs to be seen, even more than he needs to be cured. The mass of children in the classroom are not just pupils; they need to be recognized and accepted as themselves individually, even more than they need to be filled with information.

Perhaps the most distressing moment in Samuel Beckett's play *Waiting for Godot* is the second appearance of the boy to announce, as he has done before in the first act, that Mr Godot won't be coming that evening. He asks one of the tramps, Vladimir, what he should say to Godot, and Vladimir, desperately searching for words, replies: 'Tell him . . . tell him you saw me and that . . . that you saw me. You're sure you saw me, you won't come and tell me tomorrow that you never saw me!'[19]

In these days more and more people are sick and lost because they do not know with any certainty who they are or what they are. They can find their identity and their role only when someone else sees them with love. It is useless to call for repentance or commitment until we have first given acceptance. No one can change until he can first of all *be*. No one can give himself until he has a self to give. The first step in mission, therefore, is that of Jesus Christ with the first disciples: 'You are Simon, the son of John, you will be called Peter.'

'You are': 'You will be' – the actual and the potential. Both must be seen equally clearly, and both must be seen together. For, as I have already said, when the truth of the other confronts the truth of myself it demands that I be myself but also that I be all that I am capable of being. But an I-Thou encounter with one's self is almost unbearably painful, for in the light of what might be, or what might have been, what one is appears so twisted, so unlovable, so crushingly disappointing. The potential accuses the actual; the actual defies the potential. Each tries to deny the truth of the other. The good self is idolized and becomes the tyrant on the pedestal, the bad self is exiled and becomes the enemy at the gates – the man with the black or the yellow skin, perhaps, or the man with long hair, or the man in uniform. During the second World War Michael Tippett brought this out in his oratario *A Child of Our Time*. As the young Jew on the run from the Nazis reaches the climax of his despair the narrator states flatly 'He shoots the official', and the alto adds the comment: 'But he shoots only his dark brother, and see – he is dead.' As the work moves towards its close and the dawn of a new hope for mankind the tenor sings with the chorus: 'I would know my shadow and my light, so shall I at last be whole.'

That is the gift of the Go-Between God, the Spirit. Just as he opens my eyes in recognition of some other being and generates a current of communication between us, in the same way he can open my awareness towards the reality of myself, my shadow and my light, and give me an empathy towards both. This sudden recognition in a single vision of what is and what might be is, as we shall see, the gift he imparts to the prophet. This also is his essential act of creation – either in the cosmos or in the self. It begins with the recognition of absolute otherness and goes on to the interplay of communion. It begins with the separation of darkness from light, of the waters above from the waters below, of my shadow from my light, of Simon from Peter, accepting and welcoming each in its distinct truth. But his act of creation is consummated in the gathering up of all things, the day and the night, the good son and the dark brother, the Jew and the Gentile, all the hated selves, the banished loves, the dead babies, in him who holds all things together.[20]

In the following chapters what is said about the cosmos will be equally true, if it is true at all, of the innermost heart of man, and of our human communities and vice versa; for when you speak of the Spirit you are dealing with him in whom there are no differences of scale. It would become intolerably tedious to make this point continuously, so he that hath ears to hear, let him remember that all things are done in parables, for that is the nature of reality.

## NOTES

1. J. E. Fison, *Fire upon the Earth*, Edinburgh House Press 1958, p. 79.
2. Martin Buber, *I and Thou*, T. & T. Clark, paperback ed. 1966, p. 136.
3. Paul Tillich, *Perspectives on Nineteenth and Twentieth Century Protestant Theology*, SCM Press 1967, p. 20.
4. G. W. F. Hegel, *Lectures on the Philosophy of Religion*, Humanities Press, NY 1962, Vol. III, p. 25.
5. John Donne, *The Extasie*.
6. Edwin Muir, *Autobiography*, Hogarth Press 1954, p. 227.
7. Wordsworth, *The Prelude*, Book I, 377–93.
8. Viktor E. Frankl, *Man's Search for Meaning*, Hodder & Stoughton 1964, pp. 88–90.
9. Edwin Muir, *Collected Poems*, Faber & Faber and OUP, NY 1960, pp. 223–4.
10. Rainer Maria Rilke, *The Life of Mary*, trs. N. K. Cruikshank, Edinburgh 1952, p. 17.

11. Paul van Buren, *Theological Explorations*, SCM Press 1968, pp. 170–71.

12. Ibid., p. 169.

13. Buber, op. cit., pp. 31ff.

14. Harvey E. Cox, *The Secular City*, SCM Press 1965, p. 48.

15. Martin Buber, *Between Man and Man*, Collins Fontana Books 1961, p. 24.

16. Robert Browning, *Bishop Blougram's Apology*.

17. Anthony Bloom, *School for Prayer*, Darton, Longman & Todd 1970, pp. 6of.

18. P. L. Berger, *A Rumour of Angels*, Allen Lane the Penguin Press 1970, p. 119.

19. Samuel Beckett, *Waiting for Godot*, Faber & Faber, 1965 ed., p. 92.

20. Gen. 1.4, 7; Eph. 1.10; Col. 1.17.

# 2

# CONCEPTION

## *The Creator Spirit and the Range of the Mission*

Our modern, inductive patterns of thought have made us concentrate inescapably upon the material universe as the only object
we may confidently claim to know. Hence it follows that if we are
to rediscover God's reality for ourselves we must start with his
relation to this knowable universe. For that also was conceived by
the Holy Ghost. He did not abhor the Virgin's womb that was to
bring forth the Son of God: neither did he abhor the womb of
creation which groans and travails in pain until all the other sons
of God are revealed.

The involvement of the Spirit, or Breath, of God in the processes
of creation is a theme that occurs in several places in the poetry of
the Old Testament. 'By the word of the Lord were the heavens
made and all the host of them by the breath (*ruach*) of his mouth'
(Ps. 33.6). That is the Revised Standard Version: the New English
Bible has only the meagre paraphrase, 'at his command'. But it
deals magnificently with the great verses in Job recalling the
Babylonian myth of Marduk slaying the water-dragon of chaos and
making earth and sky out of her divided body.

> With his strong arm he cleft the sea-monster,
>     and struck down Rahab by his skill.
> At his breath (*ruach*) the skies are clear,
>     and his hand breaks the twisting sea-serpent
> These are but the fringes of his power;
>     and how faint the whisper that we hear of him! (Job 26. 12–14).

All one seriously misses in that translation is the force of the verb
in verse 13, part 1, which the Revised Version translates: 'By his

spirit (*ruach*) the heavens are garnished.' This is reminiscent of those artists and craftsmen who, under the impulse of the same Breath of God, were said to have designed and *embellished* the tabernacle in the desert and the temple in Jerusalem.

> See, I have called by name Bezalel the son of Uri ... and I have filled him with the spirit (*ruach*) of God, in wisdom and in understanding and in knowledge and in all manner of workmanship (Ex. 31.2, 3 R V).

> Then David gave to Solomon his son the pattern of the porch ... and of the place of the mercy seat and the pattern of all that he had by the spirit (*ruach*) for the courts of the house of the Lord (I Chron. 28.11, 12 R V).

But the most profound and evocative image of the Creator Spirit is that which is given at the opening of the Genesis story. The words can be interpreted in two ways. The one, as given in the New English Bible, takes up the literal sense of the noun: '... the earth was without form and void, with darkness over the face of the abyss, and a mighty wind that swept over the surface of the waters' (Gen. 1.2). We shall meet that symbol of the Holy Spirit many times again. But the more familiar translation takes its cue from the Hebrew verb, which suggests not the gale force of a great wind but an oscillating movement more like the fluttering of wings, as in Deuteronomy 32.11: 'As an eagle ... hovers above its young.' So we are given the image of the Spirit of God brooding over the formless deeps in which nothing exists because nothing is separated, overshadowing them as one day he will overshadow a girl in Nazareth. The great wings of his otherness are outstretched in the primal dark and dimly reflected in the face of the waters below. Out of those depths of undifferentiated chaos all the multitudinous forms of existence are going to be beckoned into being by call and response. But in that timeless moment nothing is present except the ardent, cherishing love, the irresistible will for communion, of the Go-Between Spirit.

To envisage creation in terms of life-giving energy and inspiration is a far profounder insight than the earlier image of God the potter or builder who remains outside and essentially separate from his handiwork. The poets and mystics have always been aware that the whole earth is full of his glory. 'We are all in him enclosed', said Julian of Norwich, 'and he is enclosed in us!' And the pagan Plotinus anticipated the same thought: 'We must not think of ourselves as cut off from the source of life; rather we breathe and consist in it, for it does not give itself to us and then withdraw itself, but ever lifts and bears us.' Creation, providence and redemption are aspects of one action.

This is the essential feature of the doctrine of the Creator Spirit: creation is still going on in ceaseless renewal and development.

Thou sendest forth thy Spirit, they are created; and thou renewest the face of the ground (Ps. 104.30 R V).

The Spirit of God has made me, and the breath of the Almighty is giving me life (Job 33.4 R V).

For my life is yet whole in me, and the Spirit of God is in my nostrils (Job 27.3 R V).

This was the bone of contention between Jesus and the legalists. They attacked him for healing on the Sabbath on the grounds that the day should be one of inaction to commemorate God's resting after he had completed the work of creation. But that is an interpretation of the story that Jesus rejects outright. 'My Father', he retorts, 'has never yet ceased his work, and I am working too' (John 5.17).

The Spirit of Life is ever at work in nature, in history and in human living, and wherever there is a flagging or corruption or self-destruction in God's handiwork, he is present to renew and energize and create again. Whenever faith in the Holy Spirit is strong, creation and redemption are seen as one continuous process.

*And for all this, nature is never spent;*
*There lives the dearest freshness deep down things;*
*And though the last lights of the black West went*
*Oh, morning, at the brown brink eastward, springs—*
*Because the Holy Ghost over the bent*
*World broods with warm breast and with ah! bright wings.*[1]

So Gerard Manley Hopkins takes us back to the old image of the Spirit at the dawn of creation and shows that it is an image of an action and a relationship which never ends. Paul's great passage in the eighth chapter of Romans endorses this view of a process still going on, still struggling in travail.

Whatever else this means, it affirms quite clearly that, if we think of a Creator at all, we are to find him always on the inside of creation. And if God is really on the inside, we must find him in the processes, not in the gaps. We know now there are no gaps, no points at which a special intervention is conceivable. From first to last the process has been continuous. Nature is all of a piece, a seamless robe. There is no evidence of a break, as we once imagined, between inorganic matter and the emergence of the first living organisms; nor between man's animal precursors and the emergence of man himself. If the hand of God is to be recognized in this continuous creation, it must be found not in isolated intrusions, not in any gaps, but in the very process itself.

That seemed to be impossible as long as we still thought of the universe as a mechanism. But today a respectable and respected minority of physicists, chemists and biologists – or several such minorities, since more than one 'school' agree on this point – are suggesting that it is truer to think of the universe as a life, with a disconcerting spontaneity and non-determinism in the most elementary components but an equally disconcerting force of organization in each combination of components. Sir George Thomson said in his presidential address to the British Association in 1960: 'We have been forced, some of us very unwillingly, to believe that at bottom the laws of physics are not statements of what *must* happen, but of the relative chances of a variety of alternatives.'

So much for randomness and freedom at the lowliest level. But that is not the whole of the picture. For nearly twenty-five years a theory of 'systems' or of 'organizing forces' has been quietly built up. It is closely related to the insights learnt from sociology, business management, cybernetics and computer science, but the theory has received its greatest impetus in the field of biochemistry. A molecule is a system of atoms arranged in an invariable pattern which may be as complex a structure as that of the nucleic acids which are the basis of living organisms. A cell is a system comprising a nucleus with its chromasomes, and the cytoplasm with its various organelles – mitochondria, sacs, tribules, cilia and so on – sliding and squirming, breaking up, fusing and re-forming, in a freedom that would be chaotic if the separate units were not somehow being brought into obedience to the pattern of the whole. An organ like a hair or an eye or a brain is a superior system controlling as its component parts tissues which are systems in themselves. The body of any animal is a yet greater system, and the whole species in its evolving continuity is a greater system again. Organic life, therefore, is seen to be a towering hierarchy of systems, neither the upper nor the lower limits of which have yet been disclosed, in which each system, autonomous in its own right at one level, takes its place as a sub-unit in another system at a higher level. Professor Ludwig Bertalarffy, contributing to a symposium of academics from various scientific disciplines in 1968, said:

> We are forced, in all fields of science, to deal with complexities, wholes, systems, organizations, or whatever terms you choose to express the problems. . . The conventional categories, concepts and models of physics and chemistry do not deal with the organismic aspects that I have mentioned.[2]

One can take a machine to pieces, infer from the structure of each piece its function in relation to the rest, learn from this how the machine works, and put it together again. That is exactly what physicists have thought they could do with atoms and biologists with living organisms. But Professor Paul Weiss, speaking at the same symposium, asserted that that is just what cannot be done with a 'system' at any level in the hierarchy:

> A living system is no more adequately characterized by an inventory of its material constituents, such as molecules, than the life of a city is described by the list of names and numbers in a telephone book. Only by virtue of their ordered interactions do molecules become partners in the living process. . . All living phenomena consist of *group behaviour*, which offers aspects not evident in members of the group when observed singly.[3]

So it seems that some kind of awareness and response towards 'the other' is basic to the most elementary forms of physical existence. Apart from their behaviour *as a collective* the individual components amount to nothing. Eddington said some years ago: 'We often think that when we have completed our study of *one*, we know all about *two*, because "two" is "one and one". We forget that we have still to make a study of "and".' It seems that we have touched the Go-Between again. Here it may be apt to point out that Martin Buber did not normally omit the word 'and' as is done by those who, misquoting him, talk about the 'the I-Thou relationship'. Whether betokened by a word or a hyphen, however, it looks as if nothing can emerge from chaos without that mediation between one and another which I have suggested is the action of the Holy Spirit.

But, furthermore, which I find enormously significant, the mediation has to be not only between one and one, but between each one and the whole. Somehow or other the whole communicates to its parts a pattern which is not written into their individual structures. A system such as a human brain is not determined by the operation of the thousand million million macromolecules that it contains; on the contrary it is the whole – its memories, established patterns and constant identity – which imposes direction and order on its ceaselessly changing and reconstituted parts. Or, to take another example, instanced by Professor C. H. Waddington at the same symposium, 'there is a determination of regions of the egg to become some general part of the organism, such as the foreleg, or the head and so on. This is decided long before it is settled whether this particular portion of the egg will become part of the bones or the muscles in the foreleg, or exactly which part of the brain it will turn into.'[4] This is an astonishing example of 'partners in the living process' co-ordinating their autonomous lines of development in accordance with some superimposed programme. The same is equally true of the life of any single cell. Professor Paul Weiss commented:

> The only thing that remains predictable amidst the erratic stirring of the molecular population of the cytoplasm and its substructures is the overall pattern of dynamics which keeps the component activities in definable bounds of orderly restraint. These bounds again are not to be viewed as mechanically fixed structures, but as 'boundary conditions' set by the dynamics of the system as a whole.[5]

Another aspect of the programming of the erratic parts by the system as a whole was touched upon in an enchanting 'aside' made by W. H. Thorpe during one of the discussions. 'That wagtail (Motacilla) there in the garden was here before the Himalayas were lifted up. This constancy is so extraordinary that it seems to demand a special mechanism to account not for the evolution but for the fixity of some groups.'[6]

Charles Birch, Professor of Biology at Sydney University, may have had in mind this mysterious communication from the whole to the part when he affirmed that there is something in the nature of the elementary organisms which escapes analysis in the laboratory. And he, like others, fastened upon the concept of 'awareness' or 'recognition', though granting that these anthropomorphic terms are at best only models.

Biology is the study of the larger 'organisms', and physics is the study of the smaller 'organisms'. And every organism, large or small, is a perceiving entity . . . a perceiving, responding being.[7]

In another small book, *Nature and God*, Birch quotes Agar, Sewell Wright, Dobzhansky, Thorpe, and Heisenberg to argue that everything, down to the primary particles of matter, seems to be capable of 'awareness' (not consciousness, of course) and of response, not only towards the wholeness of the system of which it forms a part, but also to the upward pull of unrealized potentiality. When there was still no life on earth the hidden unrealized potentiality for life seems to have acted as a spur upon the inorganic crystals. With the appearance of the first living organisms, the inherent, unattained possibility of man seems to have thrust the emerging species into greater and greater sensitivity and perception. Birch suggests:

In his primordial nature God is 'the absolute wealth of potentiality' of the universe. God confronts the world in his primordial nature which is the lure of unrealized possibility. The world experiences God as the world is created.[8]

As a believer in the Creator Spirit I would say that deep within the fabric of the universe, therefore, the Spirit is present as the Go-Between who confronts each isolated spontaneous particle with the beckoning reality of the larger whole and so compels it to relate to others in a particular way; and that it is he who at every stage lures the inert organisms forward by giving an inner awareness and recognition of the unattained.

I realize that I am using verbs that can strictly be used only of human action and response, but this is simply a communication device, an analogy, as when one speaks of genes 'transmitting coded information' or even of a computer 'remembering'. One is saying that the behaviour of the other entity resembles one's own behaviour when doing this or that, not that it is experiencing the human experience of transmitting information or of remembering.

It is impossible for me to imagine the inner experience of an amoeba's or even a bird's response. The only experience of responding I can ever know from the inside is that of a human being, so from that I must draw the vocabulary with which I speak of the experience in other creatures.

The idea of a blind compulsive urge towards more complex and sensitive responses advancing towards personhood has become familiar to us through the writings of Pierre Teilhard de Chardin. Sir Alister Hardy, in his momentous double series of Gifford lectures, counselled caution in the use we make of his scientific arguments. It is all the more impressive, therefore, that Hardy, with his guarded and objective approach, staked his reputation on a fundamentally similar conclusion.

The stages of his exposition are particularly important because they draw attention to a second aspect of the age-long creative activity of the Holy Spirit, namely the stimulation of initiative and choice. Having shown how astonishingly creative has been the blind, non-purposive hit and miss of natural selection, he goes on to elaborate the theory of *organic* selection. This is the proposition that evolutionary change may be caused *initially* by a spontaneous change in behavioural habits. An animal's choice to act out of character, either adapting to changed circumstances or exploring a new way of life by change of habit, may be copied by others in the species. In recent years the new habit of opening the metal tops of milk bottles has spread through the tit population of Europe! Sir Alister goes so far as to surmise that the existence of something like a group mind may become the depository of such new behaviour patterns and ensure their continuance into the next generation.[9] Paul Weiss's concept of 'systems' and their inherent dynamic may come nearer the mark. Be that as it may, once the new habit is established among a sufficient number of the species, the process of natural selection would take over again, variations in the gene complex favourable to the new habit would persist, and the new physical characteristic would become established over the millenia.

I am not in any way belittling the force of the external type of selection . . . but I would suggest that the behavioural influence, particularly in the higher group, may often be the more fundamental in determining the animal's make-up. . . It is adaptations which are due to the animal's behaviour, to its restless exploration of its surroundings, to its initiative in seeking new sources of food when its normal supply fails or becomes scarce through competition, that distinguish the main diverging lines of evolution.[10]

This means that, as the Quantum Theory hinted long ago in the realm of physics, spontaneity and choice are at least as important as chance through the whole physical structure of the universe. It is certain that choice plays increasingly the greater part as life advances from lower to higher forms. With the appearance of human reason, choice consciously takes over from chance the direction of the evolutionary process.

In Christian terms this means that the Creator Spirit works from the inside of the processes not only by startling his creatures into awareness and recognition and luring them towards ever higher degrees of consciousness and personhood, but also by creating the necessity for choice in one situation after another. And that choice arises always from the contrast between the actual and the potential, between things as they are and things as they might be. It is as though his ceaselessly repeated word to every detail of his creation is: 'Choose! I have set before you life and death, the blessing and the curse; therefore choose life. Stay as you are and drop out; change, however painfully, and move towards life.' Whenever I learn a little more of the processes of creation I am amazed afresh at the unbelievable daring of the Creator Spirit who seems to gamble all the past gains on a new initiative, inciting his creatures to such crazy adventure and risk.

I cannot emphasize this element of risk too strongly. To embark upon a change of milieu, a change of habit, always feels like a 'little death'. Every step forward into a fuller dimension of life is a kind of dying. It must have been that quite literally, for example, for birds that lost their forest feeding grounds and ventured into the edge of the lake, initiating a habit that was to launch a new species of spoonbill. Certainly for us who are so much more *conscious* of the choices we make and the habits we change, real advance never feels like self-fulfilment, though that is what it is; it is always experienced first of all as self-surrender. This fact is perhaps rather closely linked to a third principle of creative development.

For I believe that, as Christians, we can detect a third principle at work in the evolutionary process. I say deliberately 'as Christians', because I doubt whether we would ever had detected it unless the clue had been provided for us when the Creator Spirit at the heart of all being emerged incarnate in the manhood of Jesus of Nazareth, just as we might never have guessed at the element of sentient responses in the lower orders of the physical world if we had not first met it in man. This third principle of creativity or, if you like, this third characteristic of the Holy Spirit, can best be summed up in the word 'sacrifice'.

Creation has not been a series of clear, authoritative fiats but an innumerable number of hit-and-miss experiments involving un-believable waste and suffering. 'The misfits', says Charles Birch, 'are part of the creative process. They are part of the cost of creation.'[11] It could not be otherwise if, in fact, God's creativity is to be identified wholly and solely with persuasive love. For love must insist upon the element of freedom, of a potential reversion towards chaos, not only at the highest, but at the most elementary level of matter. As St Paul saw so clearly, the unfinished processes of creation are like an agonizing childbirth of struggle and cruelty and pain. The lure of the unfulfilled has been exercised in a context of murderous competition. Progress has thrived upon the law of the wolves: 'Each for himself, and the devil take the hindmost.'

Yet ruthlessness is not the last word. It is not the Word that was made flesh at Bethlehem. That birth, and the life and death and resurrection which followed, provide the clue by which we can detect this other law at work in the processes of the universe, one which lies at a deeper level than the stimulus of rivalry and self-preservation. It is the law of self-oblation. Without that clue we might never have suspected its existence, but once it is pointed out to us we find evidence of it on every side. The pelican pecking its breast to feed its young with its own blood may be only a myth but its use as a symbol of Christ shows how readily the church took it for granted that these 'lesser calvaries' could be found in the natural order. Laurens van der Post has told of a female ostrich, sur-prised with her mate by his truck's sudden arrival over a ridge of the desert.

Knowing how ostriches hate and fear men, I do not think I have ever seen a braver deed. The bird was desperately afraid. Her heart beating visibly in her throat, she advanced towards us like a soldier against a machine-gun post. With the afternoon sun making a halo round her feathers, which stood erect with the fearful tension in her, she came on pretending to be mortally hurt, limping badly and trailing one great wing as if it were broken. . . Meanwhile the male, in the shining black dress of a bountiful summer, hurried the other way in a zigzag fashion like a ship tacking into the wind. . . When his rushes had presently taken him into a bare patch of sand higher up on the ridge, we saw the cause of it all: the male was trying to hustle out of danger nineteen little ostrich chickens, while the female distracted our attention by doing all she could to entice us into capturing her instead.[12]

We need no moral evalution of such phenomena to see them as instances of a principle of life-through-death, of individual self-immolation in the interests of a larger claim, which is at variance with the principle of self-preservation. How, indeed, *could* the law of the jungle alone lead men out of the jungle? How could an inherent ruthlessness lift men into sensitivity? The immanent Creator must have been of another temper. And in the humility of Jesus, his pureness of heart, his forgiveness, his courage and sacrifice, his infinite concern for all men persisting even in the throes of death, we meet that eternal, persuasive love which through the countless aeons has been striving, suffering, going under, yet ever rising to new life, within the fabric of his universe.

> *His crown of thorns is twined with every thorn,*
> *His cross is every tree.*

The saga of cosmic evolution is now seen to resemble the old Roman hippodrome where the chariots raced down one length, then swung in a sudden, perilous turn before beginning the run home to the starting point. Self-interest was the drive which carried all forms of life on to the end of the first lap. We speak of turning points in history, but the living and dying of Jesus has, in fact, been the only one. Up to that point history ran straight on. But the-man-for-others reversed the old law of 'each for himself', and revealed the deeper principle which from the beginning was always at work in the midst: that in order to continue to be one must be a gift, an offering. If men are to remain human and go on to those higher levels of sensitivity towards which the Creator Spirit is inexorably drawing them they must learn to 'range themselves with God in his suffering', as Bonhoeffer put it.

'Behold', said Jesus, 'I send you forth as sheep among wolves' – to live for others in a world that still lives for itself; to follow the law of the Lamb in the midst of the law of the wolves. It is as though, along this homeward lap, the Creator, now incarnate, and those who will follow his way must make amends to the universe for the appalling cost of that first outward drive. The principle of persuasive love which has worked in secret for such immeasurable time has, from the coming of Jesus, entered man's consciousness and demands his assent as the only way forward. If man will not choose to live by this way he is in grave danger of losing his hard-won humanity.

Walking down the long gallery of the Academy of Fine Arts in Florence one meets three of Michelangelo's supreme statements in marble which seem to present a progression of insight. First comes the group of four slaves, unfinished giants struggling to emerge from the raw stone that still imprisons them. Next one's attention is caught and held by the gigantic David which, as one studies the face from different angles, presents all the conflicting emotions of a moment of decision, doubt, resolution and terror. And the third, also unfinished, is the Palestrina Pieta, which some find theatrical; but the monumental grief of the Virgin and the peace of total abandonment in the dead Christ combine to speak the ultimate word about sacrifice. These are the three aspects of the creative activity of the Holy Spirit, the Lord, the Giver of Life, to which I have drawn attention in this chapter. From within the depths of its being he urges every creature again and again to take one more tiny step in the direction of higher consciousness and personhood; again and again he creates for every creature the occasion for spontaneity and the necessity for choice, and at every turn he opposes self-interest with a contrary principle of sacrifice, of existence for the other. And, in the fulness of time, all of this was perfectly disclosed in Jesus Christ, who was conceived by the Holy Spirit and to whom the Holy Spirit has been directing men's attention ever since. It is not difficult to see how this must affect our understanding of that mission which is the continuing Christ-centred activity of that same Holy Spirit.

As a first step we must begin to see our engagement in mission as a participation in the continuing work of creation and not simply in the redemption of that which was long ago created. In fact, we shall no longer be able to make such a clear-cut distinction between creation and redemption. The fall of man will be seen as his continuing falling short of the glory of God, his missing the mark of what it might mean to be a man, his failure to respond to the patient lure of the unattained, his refusal, which has become endemic, of the pain of self-giving and the cost of becoming personal. An on-going creation involves a continuous restoration and though the cost of restoration was the historical death on the cross, the one who died on it was the Lamb slain before the foundation of the world. Mission, therefore, means to recognize what the Creator–Redeemer is doing in his world and try to do it with him.

> Like his relationship to his work partner, man's relationship to God derives from the work they do together. Rather than shutting out the world to delve into each other's depths the way adolescent lovers do, God and men find joy together in doing a common task.[13]

In the same vein, Professor Leonard Hodgson often argued that Jesus challenged the basic religious conviction of his time, and, indeed of most times, that man's highest good is to be accepted into a pure face-to-face communion with God free from the intrusions of the world.

> The following that Jesus wanted was not that of man drawn by personal devotion to himself, or of those who were concerned about their own salvation, but of those who would share with him in his devotion to the finding and doing of the Father's will. To Jew and gentile alike this was so utterly incredible that they simply could not take it in. . . It never occurred to them that he could possibly think of religion as not involving concern for God's favour and the soul's salvation, or of these not being the blessings promised to God's elect.[14]

Of course that does not mean that personal forgiveness and reconciliation to God can be omitted from the Christian scheme of salvation. The very opposite is true. But the soul's salvation is to be seen more as a by-product, or as a step towards a much greater objective. So Hodgson adds a little later:

> Let a man's eyes be opened to catch a glimpse of God's will for his creation as revealed to us in Christ. Let him be moved to answer the Lord's call to share in his work of overcoming and

casting out whatever in it hinders it from embodying and expressing the goodness and glory of its Creator, of setting forward its latent possibilities of such embodiment and expression. Then he will discover for himself how much there is in himself from which he needs to be cleansed and set free, if he is to share in the life of him who was, and is, the wholly free man for others and for God.[15]

One is reminded of George McLeod's great dictum that it is only those who commit themselves to live out the prayer 'Thy Kingdom come, thy will be done', who will ever know the absolute need to pray 'Give us our daily bread', because they may not know where their next meal is coming from, and to pray 'Forgive us our trespasses' because they are certain to make such fearful mistakes!

We can see now the enormous breadth and range of the mission of the Creator Spirit. It embraces the plant-geneticist breeding a new strain of wheat, the World Health Organization team combating bilharzia, the reconstruction company throwing a bridge across a river barrier, the political pressure group campaigning for the downfall of a corrupt city council, the amateur dramatics group in the new cultural centre, the team on the new oil-rig, the parents' committee fighting for de-segregated schools in the inner city. The missionaries of the Holy Spirit include the probation officer and the literacy worker, the research chemist and the worn-out school teacher in a remote village, the psychiatrist and the designer, the famine-relief worker and the computer operator, the pastor and the astronaut. Our theology of mission will be all wrong unless we start with a song of praise about this surging diversity of creative and redemptive initiative.

What, for example, should one make of the college notice-board in a theological seminary in the autumn of 1966? In a prominent position was the caption, *This Week's Project in Mission*, and below it the current notice: 'The chapel offertories this week will be used for the restoration of art treasures damaged in the recent floods in Florence.' I am not instancing this as a joke or an absurdity. It raises serious questions. If God is concerned for our greater sensitivity may we not see him at work in the restoration of Renaissance pictures? May we not work with him and call it mission? If we are looking for a really sound theology of mission I think it is better to start by being too inclusive rather than too narrow. And a passionate concern for the human-ness of man makes a good beginning. For our human-ness is under attack as never before, and the evolutionary process as such holds out no guarantee that man, the crown of creation, will remain human. For evolution has turned to decline before now and, as spontaneity and choice play an ever more determinative part in the process, we see how often the greatest promise is blighted by the wilful irrationality of free will and the irretrievable blunders of moral impotence. This is the point at which mission turns into battle. For there are many aspects of technological society which are tending in the opposite direction to sensitiveness and fuller personhood. This is where modern man must be saved if he is not to be totally lost. And the missionary of the Holy Spirit learns how to recognize these issues and knows how to fight for the truly personal values in himself and in others. These are the things the religious press ought to be telling us about.

Of course there is a great deal more to the Christian mission than this; in later chapters I shall try to examine other aspects and some of them will appear to be more recognizably 'religious' in the accepted sense. But the basis I want to establish at the start is that we need to come off our religious high-horse and get our feet on the lowly, earthy ground of God's primary activity as creator and sustainer of life. We must relinquish our missionary presuppositions and begin in the beginning with the Holy Spirit. This means humbly watching in any situation in which we find ourselves in order to learn what God is trying to do there, and then doing it with him.

Note well that even such a broadly inclusive definition of mission is far from being indiscriminate. Already in these two chapters we have seen that there are characteristic marks by which we can recognize the action of the Holy Spirit. If it were not so we should fall into the trap of identifying every movement that seems exciting and new, or everything that falls out according to our own ideas, as the mission of God. There are criteria by which we can judge, and I have suggested three of them already: Which factors in this situation are giving people the more intense awareness of some 'other' who claims their attention or of some greater 'whole'? Which factors are compelling people to make personal and responsible choices? Which factors are calling out from people self-oblation and sacrifice?

To make this concrete let me give three thumb-nail sketches.

'One thing I advise you to do', said the organization and method man to the management of a chain of city snack-bars, 'is to rebuild all your lunch counters on a curve. It will cost you a lot initially, but at a straight counter every customer eats by himself and broods over his troubles. Experiments have shown that if you make them curved even the loneliest man will find himself talking to his neighbour.' After a long tussle the organization and method man got his way.

In 1964 the Council of Churches in Rochester, New York, voted to donate 100,000 dollars to a militant community organization among poor blacks, despite the local radio station's decision to cancel the Council's weekly religious programme if it did so. It was a choice between an evangelism of action and an evangelism of words.

'I am afraid I have to tell you, doctor,' said the ward sister, 'that I am not prepared to follow your instructions in this case. I intend to let this patient know that she is dying. She's got it in her to rise to this and I'll not rob her of her dignity.'

In each of these cases it is easy to identify the three characteristics of the Creator Spirit – the enhanced awareness, the necessity to choose and the 'little death' of sacrifice. In each of the examples I have chosen the Spirit was in fact working through Christians, but it need not be so, for the church depends on him, not he on the church. And even when these three clues are given you may easily miss him if you have any preconceived ideas, for he may be working at a carpenter's bench.

## NOTES

1. Gerard Manley Hopkins, *God's Grandeur*.
2. *The Alpbach Symposium, Beyond Reductionism*, ed. Koestler and Smythies, Hutchinson 1969, pp. 57f.
3. Ibid., p. 8.
4. Ibid., p. 328.
5. Ibid., p. 21.
6. Ibid., p. 393.
7. L. Charles Birch, 'Creation and the Creator', *Science and Religion*, ed. Ian G. Barbour, SCM Press 1968, p. 211.

8. L. Charles Birch, *Nature and God*, SCM Press 1965, p. 94.

9. Sir Alister Hardy, *The Living Stream* (1st series of Gifford Lectures), Collins 1965, pp. 257ff.

10. Ibid., p. 192.

11. Birch, art. cit., p. 214.

12. Laurens van der Post, *The Heart of the Hunter*, Hogarth Press 1961, pp. 99–100.

13. Harvey E. Cox, *The Secular City*, SCM Press 1965, p. 264.

14. Leonard Hodgson, *Sex and Christian Freedom*, SCM Press 1967, p. 29.

15. Ibid., p. 30.

# 3

# GESTATION

*The Power of the Spirit and the Violence of the Mission*

In the essay which I quoted in the last chapter Charles Birch opposes the view of neo-orthodoxy, and of Emil Brunner in particular. In that view God is so absolutely distinct from his creation that nothing can be known of him by inference from the facts of the world, but only by revolation pure and simple; therefore the scientist and the theologian must look for no correlation between their spheres of study. Says Birch:

> Some of us who are scientists and Christians have, rightly or wrongly, an earnest desire to bring the learning of our specific discipline into the light of Christian convictions and vice versa. We are unable to believe that the one part of our lives has nothing to do with the other.[1]

That sets him (with Pierre Teilhard de Chardin, Sewall Wright, Theodosius Dobzhansky, Max Planck, Sir Alister Hardy and others among the scientists, and with Whitehead, Hocking and Hartshorne among the philosophers) against the existentialists and the language analysts as well, for these also have insisted on the isolation of religion from empirical knowledge. The battle is an old one.

> Against the deistic principle of God existing beside the world, either never interfering with it, as the rationalists said, or occasionally interfering with it, as the supernaturalists said, we now have the principle of *deus sive natura* (God or nature) coming from John Scotus Eriugena, the great theologian of the ninth century.[2]

So Tillich, like Pope John XXIII, reminds us of a great master who may be particularly apt for our times.

The synthesis that Charles Birch longs for, overcoming the disconnection of God and nature, of finite and infinite, is waiting to be rediscovered in the concept of the Holy Spirit. The Baron von Hügel, who was anything but a pantheist, found no difficulty in writing:

> Spirit and spirit, God and the creature, are not two material bodies, of which one can only be where the other is not; but, on the contrary, as regards our own spirit, God's Spirit ever works in closest penetration and stimulation of our own; just as, in return, we cannot find God's Spirit simply separate from our own spirit within ourselves. Our spirit clothes and expresses His; His Spirit first creates and then sustains and stimulates our own.[3]

That is an expression of what Charles Williams called the 'co-inherence' of God and man through the operation of the Holy Spirit.[4] I am daring to make a small but, I believe, important distinction, which Williams and von Hügel do not make, between the immanent God of whose presence we are made aware and the Spirit who makes us aware; or – lest I seem to speak of two gods – between that aspect of God which I can feel and know, and that aspect which makes me feel and know. We can never be directly aware of the Spirit, since in every experience of meeting and recognition he is always the go-between who creates awareness. The woman in Anthony Bloom's story was conscious of God in the silence of her room; she was not conscious of the Holy Spirit. You cannot commune with the Holy Spirit, for he *is* communion itself. It was he who made her so vividly aware of the ticking clock and the trees outside as well as of the pervading presence of God. He made her recognize the otherness of these things as well as their intimacy, the otherness of God as well as his co-inherence. But you can never know the otherness of the Holy Spirit, only the aliveness that his presence brings, the inertness that comes from his absence. He acts anonymously and unnoticed.

> *You see a wind in its signs but in itself not.*
> *You hear a spirit in its motion, in its words, even*
> *In its stillness, but in itself not. Know it here in the stance*
> *Of a prophet, and his beard blown in a door-way.*[5]

That is why prayer addressed to the Holy Spirit is unknown in the Bible and rare in the prayers of the early church. Prayer *in* the Spirit, not *to* the Spirit, is the pattern of the New Testament. He is 'a Spirit that makes us sons, enabling us to cry "Abba! Father!" In that cry the Spirit of God joins with our spirit in testifying that we are God's children' (Rom. 8.15, 16). So, however close I feel God to be – nearer to me, as Luther said, than I am to myself – the Spirit is closer still. I am not, of course, speaking of space but of relation.

If we are to visualize him as a force or element in which all things not only are sustained but also meet and touch, the best metaphor or image for our use is that of water. Remember the startling intimacy of the almost weightless intertwining when two people, swimming under water, clasp each other. Remember the strange familiarity of the skin-diver's casually brushing contact with the marine life around him. In just such a way the Holy Spirit brings us into more vivid contact with one another and with God while remaining imperceptible himself.

Life in the womb is water-life in which the foetus can know neither separateness nor otherness. Afterwards we are born into air-life in which growth can only come through separateness. The male element in our human nature is a creature of the air, good at making definitions, keeping the lines clear and distinct and establishing public relations. The female element in us is of the water-life, so our dream symbols tell us, and is more conscious of the underlying unities, more intuitively aware of the real presence of things. Our first birth brings us into the air and its clarities.

It can be argued that I am confusing the second birth with a return to the womb, as Nicodemus did. I am. For in that most simply profound of all the conversations in the Bible Jesus never contradicted the Pharisee's supposition; he only pointed out that the rebirth must be spiritual, not physical. In fact, not only was there to be a return to the womb, but birth *of* water and Spirit was to be the start of a new life *in* water and Spirit as its permanent condition. Baptism has so often been treated simply as a *rite de passage* which, having been passed through, is left behind, that the church has largely forgotten to see in its waters the symbol of that element in which the Christian lives and moves and has his being, namely the Spirit himself. 'I baptize you with water', John had said; 'he will baptize you with the Holy Spirit' (Mark 1.8). The point about the Christian's baptism is that he remains in that element into which he is baptized – 'into Christ' (Gal. 3.27); 'in the Holy Spirit'

(Acts 11.16); 'into union with Christ Jesus, into his death' (Rom. 6.3). He does not leave those waters behind but lives on in their meaning. 'There are three witnesses, the Spirit, the water, and the blood, and these three are really one' (I John 5.8: Bishop Wand's translation of οἱ τρεῖς ἐις το ἔν εἰσιν). We may, then, and indeed we must, allow the awesome archetypal resonances of the water symbol to fill out our understanding of our baptism and of that life in the Spirit which it represents.

To accept the primitive meanings in the symbols of our religion calls for a boldness which has been sadly lacking in Christian thought through the centuries. Though she proclaims the victory of her Lord, the church stays permanently afraid of paganism's power of recuperation. I am writing this book out of a conviction that nothing is more needed by humanity today, and by the church in particular, than the recovery of a sense of 'beyond-ness' in the whole of life to revive the springs of wonder and adoration. And, oddly enough to our distorted view, our retrieval of mystery is dependent on our reinstatement of the body, with its rhythms and dreams and ways of knowing. Of course we cannot hark back to a pre-rationalistic approach to reality. We must learn to meet the supernatural, if at all, not in discontinuous, 'vertical' interventions, but in a universal, 'horizontal' pervasion. 'Supernatural' will no longer be the right word; 'sacramental' better conveys the idea of another dimension if it can only be freed of its narrowly ecclesiastical frame of reference. But, when all is said and done, what we desperately need is not so much to discover a word as to discover a vision: a vision of the many-splendoured glory of God within everything, the missing of which has turned our 'estrangèd faces' hard and tense.

But the glory of God in everything is not going to shine out like a gentle nimbus around the commonplace. To discover it will be more like suddenly catching sight of the volcanic inferno beneath our earth's familiar crust. Horrors! So *that* is our milieu! The Holy Spirit is totally primordial. His is the elemental force beyond all other forces, and to call it, correctly, the force of love is not to temper its intensity but to increase fearfully our estimate of love's fervour.

I said in the first chapter that our flash-points of recognition have a higher voltage than a flash of lightning. The impact with which awareness of another being breaks in upon us can be catastrophic even when it is quiet. One can recall many examples of revolutionary changes that flowered from a single moment of vision faithfully followed through. By way of illustration I choose a great love affair, but it could just as well have been young Marie Slodowska's overwhelming conviction in the chemistry laboratory of the Warsaw lycée, or the impact of Bartholdi's sculptured negro upon the boy Albert Schweitzer.

Dante Alighieri was less than nine years old when at a May-Day revels he met his host's daughter, Beatrice, a child some months younger than himself, 'dressed in rich and subdued red, girded and adorned in a manner becoming to her very tender age'. In that instant, he avers, his heart trembled and said: 'Behold a god stronger than I that is come to bear rule over me.' During an adolescence as filled with intellectual and social activity as that of any other young Florentine of his day, he used to wait at places where he might catch sight of her, but it was not until he was eighteen that she first spoke to him, wearing a white dress in the street on a May morning. On another day she refused to salute him because of some report she had heard of him and, shortly after, she seemed to join the other girls at a party in making fun of him because he was so overcome by his feelings for her. When she was twenty-one she married a banker, and three years later she died.

That slender handful of brief encounters was fraught with stupendous power – power enough not only for the orientation of his whole life, power enough not only to stamp his vision upon the whole of western thought, but, as he claimed, cosmic power itself.

> *Already my heart and will were wheeled by love,*
> *The Love that moves the sun and the other stars.*[6]

After his second critical meeting with Beatrice, Dante dreamed of 'a lord of terrible aspect' who carried the sleeping girl in his flaming arms. That fiery figure is usually named love, but it would not be amiss to call him the Holy Spirit. For he it is that *presents* the girl to the boy in such an intense current of communion and vision that he will never be the same again. Charles Williams, in his account of Dante's first meeting with Beatrice, quite clearly makes this identification: 'Certainly that first communication of charity and humility, that first sensible coming of the Holy Ghost, is, in terms of time, unique. But terms of time are not the only measurement.'⁷ And he specifies the action of the Go-Between in almost the same terms as I have used earlier.

> The lord of terrible aspect then has so far defined himself. He is the image of a quality by which the truth of another image is seen, and that other image is a girl in Florence, as it might be in London or San Francisco, in the thirteenth century or in the twentieth.⁸

Dorothy Sayers also uses the same language of recognition and awareness.

> Beatrice thus represents for every man that person – or, more generally, that experience of the Not-self – which, by arousing his adoring love, has become for him the God-bearing image, the revelation of the presence of God.⁹

All the marks of the Spirit's activity which we have previously distinguished are present in this classic example: the creation of greater sensitivity, the compulsion to choose and the call to sacrifice – but especially the compulsion to choose. For even as a boy at the beginning of his apprenticeship in love, Dante seems to have recognized that he could either let this terrible divine power carry him on to transfiguration and beatitude, or draw back to something cheaper and shallower.

> Nothing will ever be the same again; *he* will never be the same again – if he takes another step. There is about him an agony of choice.¹⁰

> It is a choice between action and no action, intellect and no intellect, energy and no energy, romanticism and pseudo-romanticism. . . But the temptation to turn aside is immediate, swift, subtle, and very sweet. It is only to linger in the moment, to desire to be lost passionately and permanently in the moment, to live only for the recurrence of the moment.¹¹

Few are they who, after the first enraptured steps on the path of love, stick to it all the way to its heroic conclusion, allowing its power to humble, to discipline, to purify, to let in truth, to toughen with responsibility, and so enable the lover, in Charles Williams' words, 'to become the perfection he has seen'; but there are many who cannot bear to let love grow, and either deny that it ever began, or flit from one re-enactment of its beginning to another. Few are they who follow through to its logical conclusion a truth newly conceived in their imagination, for its unorthodoxy scares them, and to work out and verify all its implications is too exacting a task; but there are many who will dine out on their new discovery for a week or two and may even give a journalistic semblance of weighing it up, for these cost nothing and commit no one. Few are they who, after their first awakening, dare trust the Spirit to carry them by way of the wilderness and the dark night into a widening freedom and availability until the manhood of Christ himself is formed in them; but there are many who will either settle for religion without miracle, or try to live by a regular recurrence of the moment of their conversion. And all these drab infidelities are committed not because too little power is available to us, but because the power so far exceeds the petty scale we want to live by. He has made us little lower than gods, while our highest ambition is to be a little above the Joneses. We are looking for a sensible, 'family-size' God, dispensing pep-pills or tranquilizers as required, with a Holy Spirit who is a baby's comforter; no wonder the lord of terrible aspect is too much for us!

There can be no recovery of vital belief in the Holy Spirit and, consequently, no true theology of mission, unless we are prepared to have dealings with the great deeps of an elemental energy. There is a passage of splendid writing in Bishop Fison's little book *Fire upon the Earth* which well conveys the mystery and power with which we have to deal.

> There is no possibility of contact with the Divine without running the risk of being destroyed by the demonic. That is why Biblical religion at its best is the deadly enemy of the false 'safety, certainty and enjoyment' of mother-possession. It is always either bliss or perdition, salvation or damnation, the greatest curse or the most wonderful blessing in life. It cannot be the one without running the risk of the other; promise and peril must always co-exist. So long as we refuse that total commitment to the Creator by the creature, that humbling awareness of the Infinite by the finite and that hazardous encounter between the Holy and the sinful, which are only possible when the great deeps of the unconscious as well as the shallows of consciousness are broken up – for just so long we shall have no reality in our conscious experience to correspond with the words, Holy Spirit.[12]

It is this incalculable and sometimes violent aspect of the Holy Spirit which the Hebrew word *ruach* conveys in its primary meaning. It is the sudden scorching wind of the desert which often presages storm and rain. It is the breath of life, the breath of God himself. In the last chapter we concentrated on the image of the *ruach* of God brooding over the face of the waters at creation. It was the same *ruach* of God which swept over the waves of Noah's flood and began to dry them up. It was the gale-force of the great *ruach* which held back the waters of the Red Sea to let the children of Israel escape from Egypt. After Elijah's dramatic triumph on Mount Carmel it was the sudden uprising of the *ruach* which blackened the sky with clouds and brought the torrential rain through which Ahab drove back to Jezreel. And the last of the disasters on that calamitous day of Job's trial was the great *ruach* from the wilderness which smote the four corners of the house so that it fell and killed all his sons. These were the associations on which the Hebrews drew to convey their experience of the Holy Spirit. In Psalm 104 (R V) the word occurs four times and the combination of its meanings is significant.

v.3 who maketh the clouds his chariot
who walketh upon the wings of the *ruach*;
v.4 who maketh *ruach* his messengers
his ministers a flaming fire.
v.29 Thou hidest thy face, they are troubled;
Thou gatherest in their *ruach*,
They die and return to their dust.
v.30 Thou sendest forth thy *ruach*, they are created;
And thou renewest the face of the ground.

We are familiar with the fact that in the primitive period of Hebrew history this incalculable wind of the Holy Spirit seems to have come upon men as a form of possession and the experience, while it lasted, was a state of ecstasy. This is the inspiration of the craftsmen, the super-human strength and wisdom of the great heroes, the power of divination by which dreams are interpreted, and the extraordinary insights by which prophets can see the things that are hidden from other mortals. It is highly significant that all these gifts belong to a kind of knowledge which is not bestowed, as it were, like a crown upon the highest reaches of rational thought but which wells up through the depths of the unconscious and the subliminal group mind.

In a later lecture of the series I have previously quoted, Tillich warned his pupils against defining the common factor in God and men in terms of 'mind'.

> If you speak of absolute mind, then you have to think of some highest intellect somewhere, a bodiless intellect, so to speak, a mind without power. However, according to the religious tradition, both Jewish and Christian, as well as many other religions, God is the first of all the Almighty. He is power. He is unrestricted. He is infinite power. He is the power in all other powers, and he gives them the power to be. This element of power belongs to the concept of spirit.[18]

It is vital for our understanding of the Holy Spirit to recognize that the spirit in a man is not the most rarified element, lying beyond 'mind' in the spectrum of his being. It is the power of his personhood which holds body and mind in unity. We, who suffer from the long unnatural divorce we have imposed upon the two, need desperately to learn that the Holy Spirit is just as likely to speak through our bodies as through our minds. The Greek philosophers supposed that pure reason was the only element in man that could aspire to know absolute reality, which was why they found it virtually impossible to believe in a total incarnation of God. But the mystery religions kept alive an older, truer and more dangerous knowledge of the meeting of God with man. There is more of Dionysus than Apollo in the Holy Spirit.

Beneath the high altar of St Peter's, Rome, at the level of the pre-Constantinian cemetery, there is a mosaic depicting Christ as the young Apollo in the chariot of the sun. It was a natural choice of imagery for that Graeco-Roman world, but one that was fraught with danger for the church. It was one thing to proclaim Christ as the Logos and Light which enlightens every man, and to experience the Holy Spirit as the Spirit of Truth, for these are concepts deeply rooted in the prophets' faith in the God who has acted. It is quite a different thing to identify either Christ or the Spirit with the philosophers' abstraction of rationality and enlightenment.

In the Levantine world the masculine Apollo had won his long struggle for supremacy over the older cult of the Great Mother. It was the victory of a god who is above and beyond, over a god who is deep within, the victory of the sunlight over the subterranean mystery, of a patriarchal over a matriarchal society, of an urban over an agricultural way of life, of analytical thought over ecstatic insight, of consciousness over the unconscious.

Of course there was a reaction. Apollo was said to have slain the ancient female dragon, the Delphine or Python. Yet it was to the Python spirit, speaking through an entranced priestess, that men had recourse when they consulted Apollo's oracle at Delphi. And in later times the younger god Dionysus, travelling through all the lands of the Middle East, won back the devotion which the Great Mother had lost. He represented a resurgence of irrationality and ecstasy, a recognition of the instinctual power in nature, of the bi-sexual elements in every person, and of the tragic irreconcilables in every life – was he not the patron of the Greek tragedies? An affronted puritan conscience will be quick to point out that he was merely the god of intoxication. But we would do well to remember that that was the charge levelled on the day of Pentecost. 'These men are full of new wine' (Acts 2.13) were some of the truest words ever spoken in jest.

I am not suggesting that we can safely identify the movement of the Holy Spirit with the upsurging of the unconscious. But I am saying that this is very often the medium in which he works; for this is the sphere from which our sudden recognitions and 'annunciations' seem to arise. We first meet him in the scriptures hovering over the great deeps of chaos, the dragon of the older creation myths, preparing not to bind or eliminate it like Apollo, but to open it up and release what was potential in it. The Spirit is not averse to the elemental world of our dreams, the raw emotion of our fears and angers, the illogical certainties of our intuitions, the uncharted gropings of our agnosticism, the compulsive tides of our history. These are his *milieu*.

In his book *The Savage and Beautiful Country* Alan McGlashan asks the questions, 'Who, or what, is the Dreamer within us? And to whom is the Dreamer talking?' He concludes:

In my analogy the psyche appears as a mirror image of the Christian Trinity; the Self emerges as an aspect of the Father, the conscious mind as an aspect of the Son, and the Dreamer – an aspect of the Holy Ghost. The Dreamer as an aspect of the Holy Ghost, the Comforter, the Paraclete within the individual . . . is this merely and ignorantly blasphemous? It could be so – but it could be otherwise.[14]

The beyond-in-the-midst is ceaselessly luring creation towards graciousness and 'civilization', but his influence does not make one polite. He is found most of all in human corporateness, and hence in the miraculous corporateness of the church; yet his is an *esprit de corps* that leaps out at Ananias and Sapphira like a flame. Bishop Fison insists that any study of the Holy Spirit must take seriously the uncanny outbreaks, ecstasy and power recorded in the books of Judges and Samuel.

> Of course, this uprush of the primitive, the elemental and the unconscious, this 'possession' by the Spirit, is not the be-all and end-all of the biblical evidence for the doctrine of the Holy Spirit. But it is the starting point of that doctrine, and only if we are prepared to start where the Bible starts are we likely to know in experience anything of the higher reaches of the Spirit's work. We cannot jump the queue.[15]

In the history of our religion we find a tendency to pendulum between the Apollonian and the Dionysiac preferences. This pattern and its sociological causes were brilliantly exposed in Tillich's course of lectures from which I have already quoted. He showed that the Age of Enlightenment glorified a religion of reason and harmony because bourgeois man could not tolerate anything that might disturb his calculating and controlling activities in relation to reality.

> Thus the existential elements of finitude, despair, anxiety, as well as of grace, were set aside. What was left was the reasonable religion of progress, belief in a transcendent God who exists alongside of reality, and who does not do much in the world after he has created it. In this world left to its own powers moral demands remain, morals in terms of bourgeois righteousness and stability. Belief in the immortality of the soul also remains, namely, the ability of man to continue his improvement progressively after death.[16]

Then came the reaction in the so-called Romantic philosophies of Schelling and Schleiermacher, leading on to Hegel and Nietzsche. Paul Tillich argues that the pivot of their teaching was the rediscovery of the principle of the infinite within the finite, of the 'within-each-otherness' of God and nature. In other words the Holy Spirit was reinstated, even at the risk of releasing demonic as well as life-giving energies from the restraints of the rational.

Of course these romantic philosophies of the co-inherence of God and man had to be challenged in their turn by Marxism and Existentialism, both of them doctrines of the Fall without a doctrine of the Spirit, posing instead of the question, What is man?, the question, Where is man now? But what particularly interests me in all this is the coincidence of a new missionary dynamic with each recovery of faith in the immanent spirit of God. The Celtic church, whose monks carried the gospel across north-western Europe, enjoyed an almost animistic sense of the divine presence in all nature. The same was true of the Franciscans, some of whom later developed the extravagances of pentecostalist schism. The great Jesuit movement which carried the Christian faith to East Asia was attacked by the Inquisition in its early days as savouring of the heresy of the inner light. This was because it rejected the monastic idea that a transcendent God could only be reached through a complete withdrawal into contemplation and offered to ordinary lay people a devotional method which, as St Francis de Sales claimed, 'is suited to all vocations and professions'. And, last but not least, the modern missionary movement flowered directly from the 'enthusiasm' of the eighteenth-century revival.

Mission is often described as if it were the planned extension of an old building. But in fact it has usually been more like an unexpected explosion. By recording the growth of the church in mainly institutional terms we have suggested a slow, even expansion and maturing, whereas the great leap forward and the equally sudden collapse have been such common features of the story that we should have had the modesty to recognize that the Breath of God has always played a far more decisive part than our human strategy. It should not surprise us that the most rapidly growing Christian communities in the world today are the Pentecostal Churches of Latin America. A recent sociological examination of the movement in Chile ends with this conclusion.

Here lies the key to the difference in the effectiveness of traditional Protestant forms of religion and Pentecostalism in South America; both are, broadly speaking, tied to the same credo;

both have before them the same potential market. The first, however, affects only very small groups and are stagnating; the second seems like a tidal wave. . . To create trust in the national or regional churches, their members and leaders, trust in their fitness to help themselves and to solve their own problems – that, I think, is what the Pentecostalist example urges upon us. . . To create trust in the national churches – is that not, at the end of the day, to create trust in God?[17]

The spontaneous spiritual awakening of congregations all over India in 1905–6, stimulating directly the first wave of peoples' movements and the formation of the National Missionary Society under the secretaryship of V. S. Azariah, probably represents the greatest advance of Christianity in the sub-continent in this century. The same could be said of the revival in Korea in the same decade. In Africa today it seems that the incalculable Spirit has chosen to use the Independent Church Movement for another spectacular advance. This does not prove that their teaching is necessarily true, but it shows they have the raw materials out of which a missionary church is made – spontaneity, total commitment, and the primitive responses that arise from the depths of life.

The presence of those three elements in a church will not ensure what we choose to call success. At times faith will spread like a prairie fire; at other times it will be frustrated and opposed, and the only glow will be the flame of suffering. But one way or the other we should expect the church to burn. If it does not it is nonsense to talk about its mission.

To say these things is not to undervalue the faithful plodding of Christian witness in the institutions of the church or in the daily work of lay people, but rather to remind ourselves that 'ever since the coming of John the Baptist the Kingdom of Heaven has been forcing its way forward and men of force are seizing it' (Matt. 11.12). Ever since the Baptist's heroic opposition, the Kingdom has withstood 'the powers' in a spiritual warfare that is nonetheless incarnate. So the violent and spasmodic quality of the mission's advance is not limited to statistics but marks its impact on human society as well. 'They that have turned the world upside down have come here also' (Acts 17.6 R V). When the *ruach* of God sweeps into a situation change cannot be smooth. Whether or not one accepts Jacques Ellul's absolute veto on Christian resort to violence, one must not evade the challenge of all he says about the higher violence of love.

> We must demand entrance to the powerful because, in virtue of representing the poor, we are ambassadors of Christ. I hold that in every situation of injustice and oppression, the Christian – who cannot deal with it by violence – must make himself completely a part of it *as representative of the victims*. . . Provided we reject human means, our spiritual intervention may become effectual spiritual violence. Of course, this involves risk. But if we do not take the risk, we can only take the middle way, and even if we plunge into armed, violent, extremist revolution, we are still among the lukewarm.[18]

But the controversial nature of Ellul's main thesis forces on us a question which has been lurking unanswered since my first chapter and which we can no longer avoid – the question of discernment. If it is the Holy Spirit who stands between me and the other, making us mutually aware, can we hold him responsible for every obsession, every love affair? And if not, was our mistake that we did not follow him far enough, or that it was some other spirit in the first place? If mission means finding out what God is doing and trying to do it with him, how, apart from the three pointers I have suggested, can we be sure that it is God we see at work and not simply the fever of activity? If the Spirit moves in the elemental depths how may we distinguish him from the demonic or merely sensual? And what is the difference between coinherence and pantheism?

The very fact of our feeling the need of criteria suggests that we are on the right track, for the church of the New Testament clearly lived with these risks and was regularly concerned with 'testing the spirits' (I John 4.1; I Thess. 5.19–21; I Cor. 12.10; 14.29; Heb. 5.14; Rev. 2.2).

Whether the hazards of surrendering to this primitive Spirit allure or appal any one of us is largely a matter of temperament and upbringing. But in either case we need to recall that he is the Spirit of Truth. Whenever he generates the current of mutual awareness the truth of some 'other' summons and confronts the truth of oneself. To respond to that beckoning, even along irregular and unorthodox paths, is the way of life and freedom, but on one condition: that one holds to the truth of what one is and the truth of what that other is. But as soon as one begins to falsify or romanticize or deceive oneself then it is time to beware of a will-o'-the-wisp of one's own creation.

> *... Look, with what courteous action*
> *It waves you to a more removed ground :*
> *But do not go with it.*[19]

Two examples may help to make this clearer.

George Seaver's biography of Albert Schweitzer tells of an 'annunciation' which was certainly one of the thrusts which brought that supremely great man to Africa.

> Not far distant from his native Grünsbach, in the Champ de Mars at Colmar, stands the great sculptor Bartholdi's statue of Admiral Bruat. At the foot of the statue rests the figure of an African negro, whose wistful expression embodies the very soul of the perpetual suffering of his race. It is this look of haunted sadness that first startled Schweitzer as a boy, and which has never ceased to haunt his mind. On every visit to his homeland, fresh from the scene of his life's work for the African, he goes again to Colmar and gazes at it.[20]

In that initial and oft-repeated 'annunciation' the truth of African suffering, expressed in the statue, met the truth of Schweitzer's compassion and sense of responsibility, and one might say this was one of the most creative encounters of this century. But, though I shrink from finding fault in so great a man, an element of fantasy was allowed to distort both the 'I' and the 'Thou' of that confrontation. Seaver quotes from Schweitzer's *On the Edge of the Primeval Forest* where he wrote: 'Anything we give them is not benevolence but atonement . . . and when we have done all that is in our power, we shall not have atoned for the thousandth part of our guilt.'[21] But even allowing for a proper sense of collective responsibility, such a burden of guilt was out of line with the actuality of Schweitzer. It was romanticism of a sort, and it demanded a further garbling of the truth of the other, the African. Pseudo-guilt needed a pseudo-victim to whom to make amends. So Schweitzer could never come to terms with self-reliant, educated Africans, and those of them who have told me of their visits to his hospital have invariably regretted the paternalism they met there.

My second example is the love of a married man and an unmarried girl. Their falling in love was a moment of profound recognition, and the gladness of their infrequent meetings was such an unsought gift they had no urge to grasp it. For them to say either 'This cannot happen' or 'This ought not to happen' would have been forcing the truth into a prefabricated mould of unreality. There should have been a way by which they could say 'Yes' to what was given to them without violating any part of the truth of their situation. Charles Williams envisages this 'freedom' in a passage arising out of Dante's love for another woman besides Beatrice.

> The second image is not to be denied; we are not to pretend it is not true, or indeed to diminish its worth; we are only asked to free ourselves from concupiscence in regard to it.[22]

That might be far easier than our calloused imaginations can allow if only the love of husband and wife were more daring and trustful. Williams goes on:

> Natural jealousy and supernatural zeal – the zeal of the officers of the supernatural rather – have brought us to regard that great opportunity of the second image rather as a sin than as a goodness. If it were possible to create in marriage a mutual adoration towards the second image, whenever and however it came, and also a mutual limitation of the method of it, I do not know what new liberties and powers might not be achieved.[23]

In the case I am recounting, however, the possibilities of the relationship were destroyed at the point where the husband began to offer less than the truth of himself. He knew, and had never concealed the fact, that he was indissolubly and at the depth of his being 'married' to his wife. But he found he was unwilling, or genuinely unable, to entrust her with the knowledge of his new love and a share in deciding how to take account of its reality. That inability also was part of the truth of him. And it was this which he would not face. He allowed the girl to believe that his wife knew and accepted more of their relationship than was the case, yet, while in her company, he gave more and more rein to the fancy that the marriage did not exist. The more he had to pretend and conceal, the more the affair lost its innocence and became for him a simple temptation to infidelity. She, with greater integrity, grew confused and hurt. In the end, when they decided to stop seeing each other, it was she who gave the verdict: 'If you had only been true to the facts, our delight in each other could have lived under any condition those facts demanded . . . But now it's gone.'

The Spirit, then, is quite likely to lead us into a savage and beautiful country but he will not lead us astray so long as we dare to live with the truth – our particular truth. That is our only guarantee of discernment by which we can 'test the spirits'. That, I believe, is what lies behind the frequent juxtaposition, throughout the Bible, of the parallel concepts of Spirit and Word. If the term Spirit (*ruach*) suggests the undifferentiated, all-pervading power of awareness and mutuality, the other term 'word' (*dabar*) expresses particularity and form, meaning and purpose.

We ought not to make too much of this, for the two are as closely related as breath is related to voice. In the parallelism of Hebrew poetry *ruach* and *dabar* are virtually synonyms.

By the word of the Lord were the heavens made:
and all the host of them by the *breath* of his mouth (Ps. 33.6 R V).

He sendeth out his word and melteth them:
he causeth his *wind* to blow and the waters flow (Ps. 147.18 R V).

It is this same combination of Spirit and Word that God imparts to men in that unique phenomenon we call prophecy, the nearest thing to creation which man can ever experience.

The *Spirit* of the Lord spake by me:
and his *word* was upon my tongue (II Sam. 23.2 R V).

This, says the Lord, is my covenant which I make with them: My *spirit* which rests on you and my *words* which I have put into your mouth shall never fail you from generation to generation of your descendants from now onward for ever. The Lord has said it (Isa. 59.21).

In many of the narrative passages also these two words seem almost interchangeable. The divine interventions in the oracles of Balaam, for example, are described either as 'the Lord put *words* in Balaam's mouth' (Num. 23.5) or as 'The *Spirit* of God came upon him' (Num. 24.3). God's rejection of King Saul is affirmed identically in the two phrases: 'You have rejected the *word* of the Lord' and 'The *spirit* of the Lord had forsaken Saul' (I Sam. 15.26; 16.14).

The strict trinitarianism of orthodox Christian doctrine has probably led the church to draw too sharp a distinction between the Word or Logos and the Holy Spirit. In the minds of the earliest Christian apologists the two were inextricable. Charles Raven, in the first series of his great Gifford Lectures, claimed that it was the near-identification of the two terms which enabled the early apologists to present the first coherent and convincing theology of creation and redemption for that Graeco-Roman world.

> The Logos was at once the divine agent in the giving of the Torah and the inspiration of the prophets, the rational principle whose guidance could be traced in the cosmos and in the ways of the animal creation, the reason which distinguished man from the irrational beasts, the Son of God incarnate for us in Jesus and thus made Man, and the indwelling Spirit by whose presence the body of the Church was constituted. The simplest of all theologies, belief in a transcendent and 'wholly other' Deity manifested by an ever-present all-sustaining cosmic Representative was thus brought to the service of the Christian Gospel.[24]

So Raven went on to deplore the theological developments of the fourth century.

> When the Holy Spirit was separated from the Logos, no attempt was made to define his relationship to the Word or the particular character and sphere of his activities. . . . As a result the Spirit, whose indwelling had been regarded as the essential and constitutive element in the life of the Church and the source of all value and virtue, became restricted in his operation implicitly, if not expressly, to certain ecclesiastical rites, baptism, confirmation, ordination and the like, which it was the privilege of the hierarchy to bestow.[25]

Raven argued that these theological changes were inevitably accompanied by a separation of the secular from the sacred, and a restriction of religion to ecclesiastical and almost to monastic areas of life. God's sphere of activity had become limited to the church, the experience of the Holy Spirit was the prerogative of pietism, and Christ, having died for the world, was to have no more to do with it until he came again to be its judge. We needed the revolt of the renaissance and the blossoming of inductive and experimental enquiry to restore the biblical doctrine of creation as the universal and continuous activity of the divine energy.

And yet, though we do not want to fall back into the old error of exaggerating the distinction between Word and Spirit, we need to recognize the particularity of each, and their subtle interplay, in order to be confident enough to run the risks of life in the Spirit. The Hebrews were not unaware of the spiritual dangers of tapping such dynamic springs. They would never deny that their heroes and prophets owed their unquenchable fire to a direct encounter with, and possession by, the Spirit of God; yet they were at pains to assert that there was always another element in the experience. That which was encountered was not simply energy but also form; not simply drive but also direction; not only holy but also righteous. The hand of God was upon them, aweful and overwhelming, but it was a hand which pointed, a hand which wrote. They were dealing not only with vision but with a voice.

I believe that there is an important difference between those of our dreams in which sight predominates and those in which a word is spoken, and in fact frequently wakes us up. Martin Buber, for whom 'seeing' was such an important element in the I-Thou encounter, records such a dream, which in his case recurred many times.

The dream begins in very different ways, but always with something extraordinary happening to me. . . The strange thing is that this first part of the dream story . . . always unrolls at a furious pace as though it did not matter. Then suddenly the pace abates: I stand there and cry out. . . Each time it is the same cry, inarticulate but in strict rhythm, rising and falling . . . and very long, a cry that is a song. When it ends my heart stops beating. But then, somewhere, far away, another cry moves towards me . . . not repeating mine, not even in a weakened form, but corresponding to mine, answering its tones – so much so, that mine, which at first had to my own ear no sound of questioning at all, now appears as questions, as a long series of questions, which now all receive a response. . . But now, as the reply ends, in the first moment after its dying fall, a certitude, a dream certitude comes to me that *now it has happened.* Nothing more. Just this, and in this way – *now it has happened.*

After this manner the dream has recurred each time – till once, the last time . . . my cry died away, again my heart stood still. But then there was quiet. There came no answering call. I listened, I heard no sound. . . And then, not from a distance but

from the air round about me, noiselessly, came the answer. Really
it did not come; it was there. It had been there – so I may explain it – even before my cry: there it was, and now, when I laid
myself open to it, it let itself be received by me. . . When I had
reached an end of receiving it, I felt again that certainty pealing
out more than ever, that *now it has happened*.[26]

In all these experiences in which the Spirit opens our eyes and
gives us a deep awareness of some other, our attention is held and
we feel we are being addressed. But a word, given or received,
commits us like a pledge. A word is an injunction or a promise of
something particular. Bonhoeffer has written:

> The word conveys unequivocal clear meaning. Clarity and
> straight-forwardness are part of its make-up. It explains itself.
> Clarity and straight-forwardness are the basis of its universal
> validity. Clarity and straight-forwardness are part of the make-
> up of the Word of God. The divine Logos is truth and mean-
> ing.[27]

So perhaps after all there is a slight but significant difference of
meaning in the two phrases applied to the tragedy of King Saul.
The withdrawal of the Spirit speaks of a general state of abandonment by the divine power while the rejection of the Word of God
refers to some specific act of disobedience. This would endorse the
distinction I have already drawn, that the Spirit represents the
divine action in its total impact, while the Word represents the
specific direction and form which the divine action takes at one
point of time. Spirit is experienced as inspiration, Word as revelation. *Ruach* is the eternal lying in wait in every moment, but *dabar*
commits itself to the uniqueness of a particular moment. That is
why it was not the Spirit but the Word which was made flesh and
dwelt among us.

Henceforth he is the criterion which makes it safe for us to trust
the Spirit's unpredictable promptings. Whatever else he is up to
the Spirit always points to Jesus and makes us see him more clearly
(which is not the same as saying 'in a more orthodox light'). So it
was in Dante's passion for Beatrice, in Edwin Muir's vision of
beauty. 'This is how we may recognize the Spirit of God: every
spirit which acknowledges that Jesus Christ has come in the flesh is
from God, and every spirit which does not thus acknowledge Jesus
is not from God' (I John 4.2–3).

But if our life of response to the Spirit needs the clarity and particularity of the Word made flesh to give it discrimination, our life in Christ needs the Spirit's gift of awareness to ensure that it is indeed the *living* Word we are responding to. Bonhoeffer continues:

> Christ as the Logos of God . . . is the Word in the form of living address to men, whereas the word of man is word in the form of the idea. . . An idea is universally accessible, it is already there. Man can appropriate it of his own free will. Christ as idea is timeless truth; the idea of God embodied in Jesus is accessible to anyone at any time. The Word as address stands in contrast to this. Whereas the Word as idea can remain by itself; as address, it can only be between the persons. Address leads to answer and it is answerable. . . Christ as Word in the sense of address is thus not timeless truth. He is truth spoken in the concrete moment.[28]

But once that safeguard is given to us then timidity is inexcusable. If the Spirit is making Jesus more real, neither caution nor convention nor reputation nor love for any other creature ought to make us resist his possession of us. More than once the disciples were unsure whether the figure they saw was Jesus or some phantom. No less than Hamlet they believed that if the apparition were false its intent might be hellish. Yet we and our whole church stand in need of that audacity of love that cried out in Peter: 'Lord, if it is you, tell me to come to you over the water' (Matt. 14.28).

## NOTES

1. L. Charles Birch, 'Creation and the Creator', *Science and Religion*, ed. Ian G. Barbour, SCM Press 1968, p. 195.

2. Paul Tillich, *Perspectives on Nineteenth and Twentieth Century Protestant Theology*, SCM Press 1967, p. 94.

3. Quoted by Evelyn Underhill in *The Golden Sequence*, Methuen 1932, p. 26.

4. Charles Williams in *The Descent of the Dove*, Faber & Faber, 2nd ed. 1952.

5. W. S. Merwin, *The Isaiah of Souillac* from *Poems of Doubt and Belief*, Macmillan, NY 1954. Reprinted by permission of David Higham Associates, Ltd.

6. The final lines of *The Divine Comedy*, in the translation given by Dorothy L. Sayers in her introduction to volume 1, *Hell*, Penguin Books 1949, p. 9.

7. Charles Williams, *The Figure of Beatrice*, Faber & Faber 1943, p. 47.

8. Ibid., p. 29.

9. Sayers, op. cit., p. 68.

10. Williams, *The Figure of Beatrice*, p. 25.

11. Ibid., p. 123.

12. J. E. Fison, *Fire upon the Earth*, Edinburgh House Press 1958, p. 9.

13. Tillich, op. cit., p. 120.

14. Alan McGlashan, *The Savage and Beautiful Country*, Chatto & Windus 1966, p. 132.

15. Fison, op. cit., p. 1.

16. Tillich, op. cit., p. 48.

17. Christian Lalive d'Epinay, *Haven of the Masses*, Lutterworth Press 1969, p. 223.

18. Jacques Ellul, *Violence*, SCM Press 1970, pp. 151–2, 169.

19. *Hamlet*, I. iv.

20. George Seaver, *Albert Schweitzer—the Man and his Mind*, A. & C. Black 1951, p. 54.

21. Ibid., p. 55.

22. Williams, *The Figure of Beatrice*, p. 49

23. Ibid., pp. 49–50.

24. Charles E. Raven, *Natural Religion and Christian Theology* (1st series), CUP 1953, p. 42.

25. Ibid., p. 51.

26. Martin Buber, *Between Man and Man*, Collins Fontana Books 1961, pp. 17–18.

27. Dietrich Bonhoeffer, *Christology*, Collins 1966, p. 50.

28. Ibid., p. 51.

# 4

# LABOUR

*The Spirit of Prophecy and the Historical Perspective
of the Mission*

So far we have been thinking of the Holy Spirit as that unceasing, dynamic communicator and Go-Between operating upon every element and every process of the material universe, the immanent and anonymous presence of God. And we have seen that the true ground of all mission is this creative-redemptive action at the heart of everything. But if the Holy Spirit were confined, as it were, within the continuum of progressive evolution we could never know him or consciously experience him. We do not experience the growth of cell structure in our own bodies, unless it has become malignant, nor are we aware of the beating of our own hearts unless for a short period something brings it to our attention. In the same way, our conscious recognition of the Holy Spirit comes to us not through the ceaseless pressure of his presence upon us but at particular moments of encounter which he initiates.

If there is any uniqueness in the biblical revelation of God this is where it is to be found. The Bible is consistent from beginning to end in its understanding that God works always through the moments of recognition when mutual awareness is born. It is a history of encounters. I shall be discussing in a later chapter the reality and truth of the encounter-experiences of other religions. At the moment I am concerned only to point out the absolute centrality of this experience of encounter to the biblical witness.

In his comparative study, *Buddha, Marx and God*, Trevor Ling argues that what distinguishes Judaism and Christianity from the great religions of Asia is what he calls 'the nature of the prophetic experience'.

The prophet is one who at certain times has had an overwhelmingly strong awareness of the presence of a personal, transcendent reality, to whom, as yet, maybe, no name has been given . . . Here and there certain men receive a new, dreadful, challenging kind of knowledge, the knowledge of God. . . Revelation in the theological sense, is the unsuspected and unforeseen entry into the processes of human consciousness of a wholly new element, a 'breaking in' from 'elsewhere', that is from the outside of the whole field of human consciousness in which every individual shares . . . the prophet, in the experience of revelation, is made aware of the *personal* nature of the transcendent reality which has taken hold of him.[1]

Later in the same chapter, Ling dismisses the suggestion that the so-called prophetic experience is self-induced, that the God whom man encounters is a projection of his own parentally conditioned super-ego, a god made in man's image.

The God of whom men thus became aware was not one whose description they could have fabricated, nor was he by any means a projection of their own nature. One of the most usual features of revelation is the disturbing or unwelcome or challenging new insight which it brings. Characteristic of the experience of the Hebrew prophets is the reluctance or inadequacy which the prophet feels in face of the burden which is laid upon him of declaring to his contemporaries the revelation he has received. . . Why does prophet after prophet so *reluctantly* declare the revelation of a God he has fabricated?[2]

The objective fact that men everywhere and in every age have experienced this overwhelming encounter with him who is both within and beyond them deserves the most serious and thorough examination. This is the thesis of Sir Alister Hardy's double series of Gifford Lectures to which I have already referred and these are so important for my own theme that I want to quote them at some length.

In one fascinating lecture in the first series, Sir Alister examines a little of the evidence for the existence of extra-sensory perception and telepathy. He suggests that perception and communication of this kind are functions of the sub-conscious mind and sees the possibility of some direct link between the sub-conscious of one individual with that of another. He takes up Whately Carrington's idea that a whole species may share a common reservoir of experience on which the individual draws in an instinctive way and, as I have said already, relates this to the spread of a new behaviour pattern. It might be nearer the mark to posit something like Jung's theory of a group unconscious or to apply here Weiss's concept of a hierarchy of 'systems'.

Be that as it may, Sir Alister believes that it is through the powers of perception which we possess at this sub-conscious level that men encounter God – and not men only but any organism in which what may be called consciousness resides.

> It is in this field that I believe science will come to make its second great contribution to natural theology by shewing the reality of part of the universe outside the world of the physical senses. It is in this *apparently* non-material part of the world that the power we call God must lie: some source of influence to which Man can have access in an extra-sensory way by the communicative act we call prayer. I have suggested that the power we call God may well have some fundamental link with the process of evolution. In saying this I hope I shall not be thought to be belittling the idea of God; I would rather appear to be saying that the living stream of evolution is as much Divine as physical in nature, which is what I believe.[3]

At first sight this looks like one more attempt to discover a gap into which God can be fitted. But Sir Alister's deeply rational conviction that the divine element is part of the natural process – not strictly supernatural, as he says but para-physical – leads him to assert in his second series of lectures that a universal response to the experience of encounter with God is just as much a natural response as any other that may be studied by the biological sciences.

> It is an act of devotion to some fundamental element beyond the self which we may rightly call God. And this mystery, I believe, is as much part of the natural world as is the psychic side of animal life; it is part of the biological system, and as important as sex. If in our private lives, or in a place of worship, we feel we can approach this hidden Power with a greater sense of divine reverence in a physical act of obeisance, as on our knees, we should not, I believe, feel it to be a childish act. Religion is not

rational, it is essentially emotional; if it is to be real and to work, it must be as deep and sincere as human love. Without much sincerity, or emotion, faith, if you like, it makes *no* response at all; with the right approach, however, lives can be transformed, seemingly impossible tasks achieved, and the drabness of the world turned to joy.[4]

I cannot leave these magnificent lectures of Sir Alister's without quoting a more general plea which he makes as the conclusion of his argument in the earlier series of lectures.

I believe that a truer biology, one which will not sell its soul to physics and chemistry for quick results, will emerge and tackle the more important and more difficult aspects of life about whose nature we are almost as ignorant as when physics and chemistry began. I say more important because in this field lie consciousness, the nature of memory, the feeling of purpose, love, joy, sorrow, the sense of the sacred, the sense of right and wrong, the appreciation of beauty – indeed of all the things that really matter in life. . . If only one per cent of the money spent upon the physical and biological sciences could be spent upon investigations of religious experience and upon psychical research, it might not be long before a new age of faith dawned upon the world. It would, I believe, be a faith in a spiritual reality to match that of the Middle Ages; one based not upon a belief in a miraculous interference with the course of nature, but upon a greatly widened scientific outlook.[5]

But let us not be too quick to take comfort at finding ourselves on familiar ground and forget some of the more weirdly disturbing things in this scientist's analysis of encounter with God. For he also reminds us that it is in the depths of our being more than in the reasoning mind that God meets and possesses us.

My experience of divination as practised by mediums in Africa leads me to believe that, when they induce a state of trance in which the voices of what they call the ancestors diagnose the problems of the present, what is actually being made articulate is the subconscious awareness of the community. The whole village has in fact known at the hidden levels of perception that this particular man is cutting himself off inwardly from his parents or that particular woman has allowed her brooding envy to reach the pitch of

animosity which boils over into witchcraft; but the clues and hints
have been too subliminal, or the conclusions to which they pointed too
painful for the knowledge to be verbalized in the conscious thought
of any individual. So the trance, and sometimes the dance, must be
used to prise up the normal barriers and release the springs of
hidden awareness. Both trance and dance were used by the early
prophets of Israel and there is every reason to believe that their
methods of achieving insight were the same. Nor need we feel in
saying this that the Holy Spirit's part is excluded, for as I cannot
say too often, that *is* the sphere in which he so often operates.

But in the writings of the eighth and seventh centuries B C we
may detect a certain revulsion from the more irrational and potentially amoral manifestations of spiritual power. Too much has perhaps been made of the disclaimer of Amos: 'I am no prophet
neither am I one of the sons of the prophets', which was a protest
against phoney professionalism, not against ecstatic utterance as
such. A clearer note of disapproval, however, appears early in the
preaching of Jeremiah where he records the scoffers of the city com-
plaining that the prophets are nothing but *ruach*, with no *dabar* in
them (Jer. 5.13). And possibly the most striking of such criticisms
is concealed in the account of Elijah's meeting with God on the
mountainside of Horeb. 'Behold the Lord passed by, and a great
and strong *ruach* rent the mountains . . . but the Lord was not in
the *ruach* . . . not in the earthquake . . . not in the fire: and after
the fire a still small voice' (I Kings 19.11-12).

Yet in spite of this note of caution the prophets in general
affirmed that the experience which made them what they were was
an encounter with both *ruach* and *dabar*. 'I truly am full of power
by the Spirit of the Lord', claims Micah in contrast to the false
seers (Micah 3.8 R V). 'Now the Lord God hath sent me, and his
Spirit', says Isaiah of Babylon (Isa. 48.16 R V). Ezekiel speaks often of
the Spirit of the Lord who 'falls upon him', 'enters into him' or
'takes him up' (Ezek. 2.2; 3.12; 11.1, 5, 24). This overwhelming yet
intensely personal meeting between the spirit of a man and the
Spirit of God seems to be the source from which a prophet derives
both his compelling sense of call and his penetrating gift of insight. And this is a phenomenon which deserves our very serious
thought.

We belong to a generation for which communication has become
a technique. We are fascinated by means and methods, uneasily

aware of their power over men's minds. We hire professional communicators for our case, knowing they would just as soon sell their skill to any other. So our scepticism towards the message – any message – grows in proportion to our faith in the media. We are more ready to admit the cleverness of a presentation than the truth of what is presented. So, for example, if Marxism is gaining ground anywhere in the world, the governments of the western nations attribute this invariably to some feat of propaganda and seem unable to imagine that a revolutionary idea might carry conviction on its own account. To us it is simply a matter of matching knack against knack: the power of the persuaders against the power to resist.

But in a madly competitive world the question of power touches our most sensitive spot. Incompetence causes us more shame than sin. Success is the only credential we know, and unless a belief is widely accepted we soon start to doubt the truth of it. This makes us latter-day Christians nervously anxious about the effectiveness of our proclamation of the gospel. The prophets and apostles were obsessed by divine revelation or the lack of it; we are obsessed by human response or the lack of it.

Marshall McLuhan has taught us to see our whole apparatus of communications as an extension of the human body – from the motor car, which puts seven-league boots on our feet, to the radio which gives us voices to penetrate every home in the land. But it is significant that all these 'extensions' of man are extensions only of his reasoning and assertive consciousness, extensions of the Apollonian self. The computer makes us fantastically more able to calculate and analyse; it does not help us to meditate. We have instruments to enable us to see everything from the nebulae to the neutron — everything, except ourselves. We have immeasurably extended our gift of sight, but not of insight. For that we have the same equipment as the eighth-century prophets. Potentially the same, but actually far poorer, for while we have been so busy extending one aspect of the knowing and telling self, we have allowed other aspects to atrophy. We have built ourselves up into powerful transmitting stations, but as receiving sets we are feeble.

What turned a man into a prophet was not eloquence but vision, not getting the message across but getting the message. Prophecy is essentially an act of recognition by which one sees the significance of an event as a revelation which must be passed on.

That is what Christian preaching is also. The hallmark of the apostles was that they were *autotypes*, men who had seen for themselves, not merely in the sense of having been physically present at the crucial events, but as those upon whom the meaning of the events had burst as a revelation. It was not enough to have talked with the risen Christ as long as 'something held their eyes from seeing who it was' (Luke 24.16). Things had to 'come together' as they do in flashes of insight – the horrible death, words from the Old Testament, sayings of Jesus, a broken loaf – until they crystallized in an instant of disclosure, when 'their eyes were opened and they recognized him' (Luke 24.31). In that moment they were launched into mission, and hurried out again to tell 'how he had been recognized by them' (Luke 24.35).

No wonder the disciples must wait for the promise of the Spirit before setting out on their mission. For it is he alone, working in the deepest recesses of our being, who arranges the meaningless pieces of reality until they suddenly fall into shape. So the Spirit opens the inward eyes of the prophets to recognize God, the inward eyes of the apostles to recognize Jesus. There could be neither mission nor preaching until they had *seen*.

This is something that men have always understood until our own day. In many of the traditional communities of Africa the tribal spokesmen and instructors of the young, the 'bearers of the word', have been placed in the same category as the mediums or oracles through whom the ancestors speak. The special endowment which sets such men apart is not the gift of utterance but the gifts of sight and hearing.

The main concern, therefore, of any missionary training should be to help people to become more receptive to the revelations of God. The primary aim of all sermon preparation should be to recognize Jesus Christ, somewhere, as though for the first time. And since preaching is so much more than sermons and includes, as Canon Douglas Webster has said, 'the song, the dialogue, the conversation, the silent witness of Christian integrity, the personal confession of faith in Christ before men, the selfless acts of service inspired by love for Jesus, the total life and thrust of the Christian community in a particular place',[6] the church's perennial need is for him whose inward stirring can make her sons and daughters prophesy, her young men see visions and her old men dream dreams.

How secondary, indeed how futile, are all the means of communication unless they are actually born out of the very truth they are meant to convey. That is, of course, what happens when an artist communicates his vision. He does not first conceive an idea and then devise the most effective play or picture or story to express it. He sees the idea *as* a picture or a play; there is no other way of seeing it in his particular situation and moment of history. The medium *is* the message, as McLuhan has shown us, which is another way of saying that the medium is the artist, or that the artist, like the prophet and the preacher, is the medium, the oracle, the channel of a Spirit and a Word which has utterly possessed him.

It would be pretentious to claim that the vocation of a modern missionary is as overwhelming and transforming an experience as the call of a prophet. The decision to be an agent of the gospel in this or another country can be as matter-of-fact as the transfer from one branch of a firm to another. But I believe we are in danger today, especially in the more firmly established Protestant churches, of carrying matter-of-factness too far, and altogether losing sight of the possibility that in dealing with a man who feels he has been called we are dealing with the Holy Spirit. He may, it is true, need help to discern more truly the direction in which he is being called and the precise word which the Lord is speaking to him, especially if he is labouring under some fantasy about himself or about the situation to which he hopes to go. There is a place for careful direction by the church which may send him, by the missionary fellowship to which he may belong, and by the authorities under whom he is going to work. But when all this has been said I would still maintain that, at the present time, there is far too little recognition by all these parties of the 'fire in the bones' of the person they are handling. It is time we recalled the terms in which so many of the great missionaries of the past have spoken of their own call, and ask ourselves how many of them would have become great if their guidance had been discounted or frustrated as we and the churches overseas discount and frustrate that of many missionaries in these days. A theology of mission based upon a truer understanding of the Holy Spirit is bound to challenge that hardening of our structures and that institutionalizing of our inter-church relationships which has been going on for the past half century.

But to return to the doctrine of the Spirit, we should consider what it means that this disclosure-experience which gives the religion of the Bible its uniqueness is invariably brought about by the anonymous Go-Between, the Holy Spirit. It certainly means, as we saw in the last chapter, that the one whose spirit is so met by the Spirit of God will find himself drawn towards recognizing some 'other' beyond himself and some larger whole to which he must relate, will find himself confronted with the necessity for choice, and will find himself involved in a new degree of sacrifice. But he will also find that, in one way or another, the springs of his own creativity will be let loose.

Those who have read Arthur Koestler's fascinating study *The Act of Creation* will remember that he analyses the vision of any original artist or thinker as a process of what he calls 'bisociation'. By this he means the ability to perceive, usually in a flash of intuition, some unsuspected link between two completely unrelated objects or ideas. He quotes several instances of breakthrough in scientific understanding being achieved in such an instantaneous 'vision', sometimes emerging from the subconscious depths in dreams, which places side by side two facts which no one had previously seen together. Any insight which make us exclaim: 'Oh, now I see the connection!' is potentially a new revelation. These experiences are of exactly the same kind as those moments of 'I-Thou' recognition I was considering in the first chapter.

This is the reason for the explosive force of symbols and metaphors compared with plain statement. 'No man is an Island' has fifty times the voltage of 'No one is self-sufficient'. Presumably this is why Jesus chose to teach in parables. So the prophet Amos suddenly finds himself *seeing*, as though for the first time, an ordinary mason's plumbline and its connection with the state of Israel. Hosea *sees* the breakdown of his own marriage super-imposed, as it were, upon the spiritual infidelity of the people. Jeremiah *sees* in a single vision the upset cooking-pot and the gathering hordes in Scythia. Jesus *saw* at one and the same moment the seed falling here or there from the sower's hand and that Kingdom of God which was never absent from his thoughts. It belongs to the very nature of such creative insight that up to that moment the two elements in the analogy have never been associated in the mind of man, unless it were at some subconscious level. But, once the link has been made, more and more people find it so obvious that it is hard to remember there has ever been a time when it was not a common-place. Yet anyone who has ever tried to write a modern parable of the Christian faith knows that the sheer genius of Christ's prophetic vision is not something that can be reproduced to order.

It is by the same process of bisociation that a prophet suddenly sees the connection between a historical event and the spiritual condition of a people, or between a past event and the present situation. So the young Isaiah sees in a single, merged vision the corrupt, easy-going, racketeering life of his own city, and the quiet mustering of hard-faced, disciplined battalions along the northernmost reaches of the Euphrates. And a century later Jeremiah's compassionate imagination conjures up the scene of despair in the concentration camps on the banks of that same Euphrates. But are these, in fact, the waters of Babylon, or is it the ancient Nile? From that moment of confusion, the fusion of two captivities a thousand years apart, springs the certainty that there will be another exodus.

Putting two and two together seems simple to those who are wise after the event; but at the time it is a gift granted to very few and it rarely comes except in a flash of inspiration. It is this gift which still distinguishes the great from the ordinary in political journalism today. The prophetic experience is a sudden encounter with the meaning behind events.

But such an encounter is inevitably fraught with frustration. To see and then to realize that no one else is capable of seeing is a kind of dying. To see what is, superimposed upon what might be, is a kind of dying. This is the inescapable burden of anyone who truly encounters the Creator Spirit for, as we saw in the second chapter, every step forward into new growth feels like a death. To be lured by the Spirit who is ceaselessly drawing all existence towards higher development, is to be made acutely aware at any moment, in terrible bisociation, of both the actual and the potential. George Adam Smith's marvellous commentary on Isaiah has a passage which describes this fused vision.

The next verses . . . stand in strong contrast to those which have described Israel's ideal. There Zion is full of the law and Jerusalem of the word of the Lord, the one religion flowing over from this centre upon the world. Here into the actual Jerusalem they have brought all sorts of foreign worship and heathen prophets; *they are replenished from the East and are soothsayers like the Philistines and strike hands with the children of strangers.*

There are all nations come to worship at Jerusalem; here her thought and faith are scattered over the idolatries of all nations. The ideal Jerusalem is full of spiritual blessings, the actual of the spoils of trade. There the swords are beat into ploughshares and the spears into pruning-hooks; here are vast and novel armaments, horses and chariots. There the Lord alone is worshipped; here the city is crowded with idols. The real Jerusalem could not possibly be more different from the ideal, nor its inhabitants as they are from what their prophet had confidently called on them to be.[7]

This unique and authentic opening of the eyes by the Spirit of creativity within the heart of all things produces that double exposure by which what is and what might be are seen together in a single vision. The fire with which he burns is the fire of judgment precisely because it is the fire of creation. Possessed by such a Spirit, the prophet is bound to criticize and protest. His experience is directly responsible for that doctrine which I would single out as perhaps the most peculiarly biblical insight in our faith, namely the doctrine of the Fall.

For the myth of man's first disobedience and its cosmic outcome is, above everything else, a ringing assertion that the nature of ultimate reality cannot be deduced from the totality of existence as we know it. This is the great divide between the religions of Asia and those which have sprung from the Old and New Testaments. The saints and sages of India, brooding upon the unresolved contradiction of good and evil, generation and destruction, have argued that God, if he is God at all, must be eternally ambiguous and indefinable, embracing all opposites and ultimately submerging all differences in the ocean of homogeneity. 'This also is Thou; neither is this Thou.' In contrast to this stands the biblical assertion that what is is not the same as what God intends. There is a divine Will, and there is antagonism to it. There is conflict, choice, process and final fulfilment.

I vividly remember the point at which this difference emerged after a long conversation I enjoyed with the devout and sympathetic abbot of a Buddhist monastery in Japan. I had made a passing reference to the purposes of God, and the old man fastened upon that phrase. 'There lies the real gulf between us', he said. 'You Christians talk a lot about the will of God. That is why you also make so much of human will and human choice. But to us the idea is actually inconceivable. If God's will is such that some phenomena are in accordance with it and some are outside it, then God is less than the whole. And to us that seems to be a contradiction in terms.'

The doctrine of the Fall is derived directly from the prophetic experience which grasps what is and what might be in a single vision. It is not altered by our knowledge of the evolutionary process for, if we no longer think of it as a historical falling back, we must think of it as a falling short. And, since the arrival of consciousness in the situation introduced a new element of responsibility and choice, it has been a *deliberate* falling short. It gives birth, both in the individual person and in our human solidarity, to what H. R. Mackintosh called 'that painful sense of accountability and self-contempt which may broadly be designated "guilt"'.[8] Such conscious and guilty falling short is a rebellion from which the only way forward is by repentance and faith, a dying into life. So far from being a negation, then, this doctrine of the Fall is a redemptive break-through. Offering a realistic diagnosis of sin, it is the source of that philosophy of discrimination, of purposive development, of history and eschatology, which has successively given form to Judaism, Christianity, Islam (to a lesser degree) and Marxism.

To be confronted by the Holy Spirit as both creator and restorer, and to be committed to his mission, means that thereafter we look upon the present with the pain of judgment and upon the future with the certainty of consummation. But the judgment and the hope are not successive but superimposed in one single image of reality, since both reflect the Spirit who inspires them.

This means, I believe, that whoever looks at the historic process from the point of view of the Christian mission will never be able to see it simply as a progressive evolution towards higher and higher spiritual attainment. At every point in the story the Creator Spirit presents the opportunity for advance by creating the occasion for choice; but to the end of time it is always, as it were, a choice between bliss or perdition, salvation or damnation, the greatest curse or the most splendid blessing. Any view, therefore, of the Christian mission which anticipates a gradual expansion of the church to embrace more and more of mankind, or a gradual improvement of man's knowledge and power to perfect human society, or the development of more and more sensitive forms of consciousness such as Pierre Teilhard envisaged, must mislead and finally disappoint because it leaves out of account what might be called the ambiguity of the prophets' vision of history. That ambiguity has never been better expressed than in St Paul's Epistle to the Romans:

> The created universe waits with eager expectation for God's sons to be revealed. It was made the victim of frustration, not by its own choice, but because of him who made it so; yet always there was hope, because the universe itself is to be freed from the shackles of mortality and enter upon the the liberty and splendour of the children of God (Rom. 8.19–21).

Judgment and fulfilment, a sense of progress and an in-built frustration – such is that double vision with which the Spirit of creativity compels us to see everything, including his own mission in the world. One need only look a few simple facts in the face to realize how true this is. It is certainly possible, for example, that more and more of the world's population will become Christian, especially if one accepts Dr Latourette's pattern of successive waves of advance and regression, each new advance gaining on the one before. It is certainly worth working for. But the contrasting rates of population growth in the predominantly Christian and non-Christian areas of the world are working strongly against such a pattern. Or, again, when one considers the fantastic acceleration in man's control and self-knowledge and the immeasurably longer period of time which physically may remain for his further development it is possible to allow for a great deal of self-destruction and still to believe that we are living only at the initial stage of God's eventual rescue of all creation in time and space. But it takes a lot of believing, and the prophets of the Bible, whose sense of truth has been found not unreliable, predict a more ambiguous story.

Judgment and promise, then, go hand in hand to the end of the story. And which of the two predominates depends entirely on the way we look at time. To take the familiar image of the living stream of history and ourselves somewhere in mid-river, do we picture ourselves facing downstream so that our 'now' is flowing from behind us with all the drift and debris of the past, or do we picture ourselves facing upstream so that our 'now' is always coming to meet us? Is the source behind us or ahead? If the present is always coming towards us out of the future then we must travail over the contradiction between what is and what might be. But if the present is given by the past we are condemned to the contradiction between what is and what might have been. The first is the pain of birth, the second the agony of death. The first was supremely expressed by St Paul in Romans 8: 'Up to the present, we know, the whole created universe groans in all its parts as if in the pangs of childbirth. Not only so, but even we, to whom the Spirit is given as firstfruits of the harvest to come, are groaning inwardly while we wait for God to make us his sons and set our whole body free.' The second view of time St Paul expressed no less vividly in the previous chapter. 'The good which I want to do, I fail to do; but what I do is the wrong which is against my will. . . When I want to do the right, only the wrong is within my reach. . . Miserable creature that I am, who is there to rescue me out of the body doomed to this death?'

Of the two views the second is the more realistic, for experience seems to teach that the actual has more toughness and tangibility than the potential and that to think otherwise is romantic subjectivity. The feebleness of what might be matched against the solidity of what is makes it impossible to believe that tomorrow will be any different from today. Judgment therefore outweighs hope, and we are condemned to live either with the unredeemed guilt of all our might-have-beens or with the meaninglessness and absurdity of an existential 'now', shut off as much from the past as the future.

But this backward-looking view of time which cannot imagine the present arriving from the future reminds me, by analogy, of those earlier mechanistic theories of biology which thought that an organism must be explainable by an analysis of its components and could not conceive that, on the contrary, they might be shaped and directed by the system as a whole. But supposing what Jesus called 'the Kingdom of God' is the ultimate 'system' in terms of time, then we should expect the present to be moulded by the unprecedented which is arriving from the future rather than by the normal and typical which has been established by the past. This would certainly be a complete reversal of our assumptions about chronological cause and effect, in favour of the eschatalogical cause and effect which the prophets took for granted. This is exactly how Jürgen Moltmann treats the resurrection of Jesus.

The resurrection of Christ is without parallel in the history known to us. But it can for that very reason be regarded as a 'history-making event' in the light of which all other history is illumined, called in question and transformed.[9]

The New Testament speaks of the risen Christ not as the crown of man's development through the past millennia but as the first-fruit of a new creation. If that is what he is, then the resurrection was historically unprecedented and its credibility cannot be judged by comparing it with what history has shown to be possible. On the contrary what is possible in history has henceforth to be judged in the light of the resurrection of Christ and the outpouring of the Spirit.

But even the resurrection would not suffice by itself to turn us around so as to see our existence stemming from Christ's future instead of from our past. Something must first break the entail of the past, for our 'painful sense of accountability and self-contempt' is no childish fantasy but a profound recognition of responsibility. That past which so dogs us that we feel it hanging over us like a curse needs to be remembered in order to be forgotten, which is how Tillich once defined forgiveness.[10] The resurrection will not set us free for the future unless the cross also sets us free from the past. The rock must be smitten before the living water of the Spirit can flow. Easter is significant for the world – beyond being a nine days' wonder – because he who was raised had died for the world.

It is the revelation of the potentiality and power of God in the raising of the one who was crucified and the tendency and intention of God recognizable therein, that constitutes the horizon of what is to be called history and to be expected as history. The revelation of God in the cross and resurrection thus sets the stage for history, on which there emerges the possibility of the engulfing of all things in nothingness, and of the new creation.[11]

The capacity to see history being shaped by the future rather than the past is not exclusively Christian inasmuch as the Hebrew prophets, and all that stemmed from their vision, looked at time in this way. The messianic age or the classless society are both seen as having a dynamic that works upon things as they are now to determine their development. These, however, were the promises; the risen Christ was the onset of what had been promised, which some claimed to have seen for themselves. What is new in the Christian experience is the happenedness of that which is to come. But if new creation is, as it were, the invisible 'system' which is even now dictating the pattern of the world's unfolding history, we who have such a hope must stick by that history, and not opt out of it into any *cultus privatus*. The prophetic vision never permitted that.

> Because of this universality, the new hope of the kingdom leads us to suffer under the forsakenness and unredeemedness of all things and their subjection to vanity. It leads us to solidarity with the anxious expectation of the whole creation that waits for the liberty of the children of God (Rom. 8.22), and thus it perceives in all things the longing, the travail, and the unfulfilled openness for God's future.[12]

Suffer we must with the rest of creation in one respect at least. For at the heart of all our awareness of the flow of time stands the irremediable frustration, on which exponents of secular theology have remained signally silent, the fact that each of us is going to die.

Some will object that to obtrude this thought is to allow concern for the individual to outweigh concern for the whole race. But we can't have it both ways. If the true development of the race is towards more sensitive personhood, then value must be found more and more in the person and less and less in the abstraction. In any case the real problem of death does not lie there. Most people, probably, are prepared to face personal extinction if only their children's lives can be more fulfilled than their own. But that way lies tragedy, as the psychiatric clinics bear witness. The man who looks for fulfilment and a kind of omnipotence in the lives of his children will end by robbing both his own life and theirs of the happiness and value they might have. And the pathos of that is writ large in any ideology which tempts the living to seek their fulfilment in the unborn. Truly to face death is to accept non-fulfilment and non-omnipotence as the very data of existence.

In his classic *Christianity and History*, Herbert Butterfield wrote of the goal of human history in a manner which still has very great significance for those who think seriously about the Christian mission in the world.

The generations of the past are not to be dismissed as subordin-
ate to the later ones, mere stepping-stones to the present day,
mere preparations or trial shots for an authentic achievement that
was still to come. . . The technique of historical study itself demands that we shall look upon each generation as, so to speak, an
end in itself, a world of people existing in their own right. . .
So the purpose of life is not in the far future, nor, as we so often
imagine, around the next corner, but the whole of it is here and
now, as fully as ever it will be on this planet. It is always a 'Now'
that is in direct relation to eternity. . . If atomic research should
by some accident splinter and destroy the whole globe tomorrow
. . . it would be an optical illusion to imagine that God's purposes
in creation would thereby be cut off unfulfilled and the meaning
of life uprooted as though the year A D 2,000 or 40,000 had a closer
relation to eternity than 1949.[13]

And he went on to offer the analogy of a Beethoven symphony to
bring home this existential dimension of history.

The point of it is not saved up until the end, the whole of it is
not a mere preparation for a beauty that is only to be achieved
in the last bar. And though in a sense the end may lie in the
architecture of the whole, still in another sense each moment of
it is its own self-justification, each note in its particular context as
valuable as any other note. . .[14]

To be met by the Spirit of God, therefore, is to enter the Eternal
Now. And any sense of mission which springs from that encounter
must reflect that urgency of appeal and action. 'Behold now is the
accepted time. Behold now is the day of salvation.' The Holy Spirit
confronts us both in the beckoning potential and in the immediate
choice. So his name is disclosed both as 'I will be what I will be'
and 'I am what I am.'

This is why the prophets play fast and loose with time to the great
confusion of us who live by clock and calendar. Scholars will argue
till the last trump as to whether a particular oracle refers to the
king who has died or the king who is yet to come. But to the
prophet who has encountered the Spirit and has learned to see the
connection between things and the meaning behind them, past or
present, tomorrow or the end of the world, are all totally Now, because of him in whose sight the thousand years between Thotmes
and Darius are but a day.

This gift of creative bisociation, the source of symbols and parallels, is the source of sacraments also. And it is in these that we most vividly experience the rolling up of time.

> It is only because we are in the Holy Spirit that these occasions constituted by water and bread and wine become for us meeting places with God. . . To the unenlightened eye the career of Jesus of Nazareth is something belonging to the remote past, long, long ago, buried beneath the advancing avalance of events. . . Yet through the power of the Holy Spirit, these almost immeasurably distant events become present and effective for us. The Holy Spirit is the Spirit of the perennially present God. . . But the Holy Spirit does not only look backwards, recalling the events of our redemption so that they are contemporary with us. He also in his activity in the Church looks forward. . .[15]

To one whose knowledge of reality and whose sense of purpose spring from the mysterious experiences of encounter which the Spirit of God creates, the now of those moments and the hereafter of Christian expectation are an indivisible image. The destiny of the universe is known in the I-and-Thou confrontation of the single individual with this overwhelming God: and there is no other ground of assurance about the future of either the man or the cosmos. Professor Hodgson beautifully expressed this insight in his book on the doctrine of the atonement.

> If, as individuals, personally imperfect and sinful men yield up their imperfect and sinful bodies and are given a new life in which is fulfilled God's creative and redemptive purpose for them, why should not his cosmic purpose involve the yielding up for destruction of an imperfect and sinful world by an imperfect and sinful human society?[16]

That confident surrender of the unfulfilled and sinful man or the unfulfilled and sinful world into the hands of a forgiving and perfecting Creator is only possible and only knowable because a perfect human life was once committed through death into those hands. What that means, and how it was linked with the Creator Spirit, must be the subject of the next chapter.

## NOTES

1. Trevor Ling, *Buddha, Marx and God*, Macmillan 1966, p. 178.
2. Ibid., p. 185.
3. Sir Alister Hardy, *The Living Stream*, Collins 1965, pp. 282f.
4. Sir Alister Hardy, *The Divine Flame* (2nd series of Gifford Lectures), Collins 1966, p. 175.
5. Hardy, *The Living Stream*, pp. 284f.
6. Douglas Webster, *Yes to Mission*, SCM Press 1966, p. 48.
7. G. A. Smith, *The Book of Isaiah, I–XXXIX* (The Expositor's Bible), Hodder & Stoughton, 1888, p. 26.
8. H. R. Mackintosh, *The Christian Experience of Forgiveness*, James Nisbet 1927, p. 25.
9. Jürgen Moltmann, *Theology of Hope*, SCM Press 1967, p. 180.
10. Paul Tillich, *The Eternal Now*, SCM Press 1963, pp. 23f.
11. Moltmann, op. cit., pp. 226f.
12. Ibid., p. 223.
13. Herbert Butterfield, *Christianity and History*, G. Bell 1949, pp. 65f.
14. Ibid., p. 67.
15. R. P. C. Hanson, *God: Creator, Saviour, Spirit*, SCM Press 1960, pp. 76f.
16. Leonard Hodgson, *The Doctrine of the Atonement*, James Nisbet 1961, pp. 132–3.

# 5

## BIRTH

*The Spirit in Jesus and the Focus of the Mission*

So far I have said nothing exclusively Christian apart from asserting in the last chapter the new happenedness of the promises in the risen Christ. And it is essential for our doctrine of the Holy Spirit to recognize that so much can be said about him which is universal. Just as he works anonymously through all the processes of creation, so to all men of all beliefs at all times he gives the unexpected opening of eyes, the deep awareness of that 'other' – God or creature – the overwhelming gusts of power, the double vision of what is and what might be, the call to sacrifice, the gifts of prophecy and prayer and healing and ecstasy. The more we learn to recognize his actions the more we shall find him in the life of the world everywhere. Unless we hold on to his universality we cannot rightly interpret the uniqueness of the Christian experience of him; for what Jesus had, and afterwards shared, was not any new quality in the Spirit himself but a new *mode* of relationship with him.

One might say the moon has never been the same since 20 July 1969. That grey dusty expanse stretching to a blue-black sky was indeed a new moon to the millions of televiewers. And yet this was the same chaste and dangerous huntress by whose bright sickle on that very night the tides were hauled up along all the shores of the world and a thousand boys were emboldened to kiss their first girls. None of the ancient magic has gone, but the new mode of knowing is so different that even now it is hard to relate it to the old.

The first Christians found themselves living at what they believed to be the beginning of the new age with most of their questions about it still unanswered. It was, for example, extraordinarily difficult to be sure about their continuity or discontinuity with the past. Jesus himself saw that the new wine must have new bottles, yet he never dissociated himself from Judaism as such. The first Christian community in Jerusalem remained like an adventist sect within Judaism until Stephen's outrageous speech precipitated a deep alienation. Yet even as the new movement fanned out across the Mediterranean world and began to adapt its message to the categories of Greek thought, the main theological issue of the apostolic age continued to be the connection between the old and the new. The final severance of child from parent built up a load of guilt on both sides that has bedevilled the relationship for twenty centuries.

The New Testament writers all insisted on the continuity. Their passion for Old Testament quotations and Old Testament imagery is proof of this. New they might be, yet only as a new Israel, heirs of Abraham, upon whom all the promises were being fulfilled. 'In order to understand the unique character of the Spirit's reality in primitive Christianity, one must go back to the significance of the Spirit of God in the Old Testament.'[1]

Yet in that extraordinary springtime of the Spirit new ideas were continually budding and breaking into flower which seemed to have no root in the old dispensation. The last epistles of Paul and those of John contain notably fewer Old Testament references, while obscure or colourless words become common coinage filled with new meaning to define experiences for which nothing in the old vocabulary was adequate. Marcion in the second century was only carrying this sense of discontinuity and newness to its logical conclusion when he protested that the God and Father of our Lord Jesus Christ must not be identified with the Yahweh of the Old Testament, though the Catholic Church declared him wrong to go so far.

At the heart of this ferment of new life and new meaning was an unheard-of relationship with the Holy Spirit. It could only be described as the outpouring or fulness of the Spirit. It happened as a direct result of the 'glorification' of Jesus Christ – his death, resurrection and ascension – and it brought into being a distinctive and unique society with a common life, love and unity of a completely new sort. The Spirit of the New Testament is essentially the spirit of Sonship, which is the spirit of Jesus himself. When the members of this new fellowship talk about Holy Spirit it is obvious that they are not speaking of moments of sudden possession or exceptional endowment but of a permanent presence; not so much of a power as of a partner who lives in their life; not so much of an individual encounter as of a life in fellowship.

The name most commonly used is 'Holy Spirit' and this itself is almost a new usage. This form is used only seven times in the Old Testament, but eighty-eight times in the New. On the other hand, the terms 'Spirit of God' or 'Spirit of the Lord' which occur sixty-seven times in the Old Testament are used only twenty-five in the New. What is even more remarkable is that the total references to the Spirit from the beginning of the Bible to the end of the third gospel number 126 while from that point onwards there are 196. In other words, it is only in the epistles and the Gospel of John that the Spirit appears in that fulness in which the Christian church has always known him, and it is clear that it is only the church which has ever known him in this unparalleled way. In a disturbing flash of insight the Gospel of John says with reference to the death and resurrection of Jesus: 'the Spirit had not yet been given, because Jesus had not yet been glorified', which R. P. C. Hanson suggests might be better rendered: 'it was not yet Spirit', as one might say, 'it was not yet spring'. That is exactly how it must have appeared to anyone looking back from the end of that prodigious first century. There had never been anything like it before, and it had all stemmed from Jesus.

So the earliest Christian preaching, exemplified in the pentecostal sermon of Acts 2, with a clear reference back to Psalm 68, pictures the victorious Messiah ascending to his Father's side to claim the long-promised gift, which he had now won for mankind, and pouring it out upon his waiting church.[2] And this was associated at the same time with Joel's promise that the Spirit of God should be poured out upon all flesh. The various references to the 'Spirit of promise'[3] refer back to this and other Old Testament passages[4] rather than to the words of Jesus, since the idea of 'the promises' throughout the epistles always has this connotation.

This is why we can only reach our understanding of the Holy Spirit in primitive Christian experience via the Old Testament prophets' understanding of the Spirit of God. The content they had given to that word *ruach* was projected into their promises of the new age, and it was the fulfilment of those promises that the first Christians believed had come to pass. What they had seen in Jesus and now experienced in themselves was not a new Spirit but the same dynamic and creative *ruach*, now available in that unprecedented way that the prophets had foretold. Pannenberg has this to say:

> According to Isa. 11.2, the Messiah not only will be filled and driven by the Spirit but the Spirit will be continually joined with him, will rest upon him. Third Isaiah (Isa. 61.1) also understood the Messiah as the bearer of the Spirit: the Spirit rests upon him. According to Second Isaiah (Isa. 42.1), not only the Messiah but all Israel will share in God's Spirit in a new way at the end of history (cf. also Ezek. 36.27; Isa. 44.3). In his last vision in the night Zechariah saw the Spirit of Yahweh come over all peoples; the wagons of the wind bear *ruach Yahweh* into the four corners of the world (Zech. 6.1–8). Finally, Joel also promises the pouring out of God's Spirit on 'all flesh' for the end time (2.28).[5]

Jesus' continuous and total possession by the Spirit was, together with his resurrection, the ground on which the apostles came to be convinced that he was not only Messiah but Son of God. His unique unity with the Father was, as they saw it, both given and attested by his unique relation with the Spirit. One tradition clearly associated his special endowment by the Spirit with his birth, thereby establishing him as Son of God from the start. 'The Holy Spirit will come upon you, and the power of the Most High will overshadow you; and for that reason the holy child to be born will be called 'Son of God' (Luke 1.34). Another view connected Jesus' special relation with the Spirit with his baptism. 'At the moment when he came up out of the water, he saw the heavens torn open and the Spirit, like a dove, descending upon him. And a voice spoke from heaven: "Thou art my Son, my Beloved".' (Mark 1.10–11.) But the strongest line of teaching was St Paul's who found the Spirit's unique action upon Jesus most particularly in his resurrection. 'On the human level he was born of David's stock, but on the level of the spirit – the Holy Spirit – he was declared Son of God by a mighty act in that he rose from the dead' (Rom. 1, 3, 4). I find no conflict between the three points of emphasis, for quite clearly 'Jesus was what he is before he knew about it', as Althaus has said,[6] and he inwardly knew about it before it was finally vindicated. What I find so significant is that in each of these three lines of teaching Jesus is seen to be uniquely Son of God through his unique union with the Holy Spirit.

It is because Christ's mode of relationship with him must always

The Annunciation    *Franciabigio*

The Baptism of Christ (*detail*)
*Piero della Francesca*

be understood as the characteristic *par excellence* of the new age that we find only a handful of explicit references to the Holy Spirit in the synoptic gospels apart from the birth, and the baptism. At first glance this is most puzzling. Yet it is entirely typical of the great reserve that characterizes all Jesus' teaching about himself and his role in the popular expectations of the messianic age. The sparseness of statements about the Spirit corresponds with the fact that the title *Christos* or *Messiah* occurs only fifty-three times in the four gospels (and never once among the Q sayings), whereas we find it 280 times in the rest of the New Testament.

Incidentally, this contrast, which can be paralleled in respect of other matters of doctrine, lays a considerable mine under the logic of those who argue that the four gospels are such a reflection of the subsequent teachings and polemics of the early church that we must give up the hope of penetrating beyond their didactics to any objective history. According to this theory one should have expected many sayings and many miracle-stories pointing to some aspect of life in the Spirit, such as that late redaction to Luke's version of the Lord's prayer which reads: 'Thy Holy Spirit come upon us and cleanse us'. But the fact that the evangelists themselves did not make such a gloss suggests that in the extraordinary silences of Jesus concerning many of the central doctrines of the apostolic age we are securely in touch with that which preceded the church's thought.

What conclusions can we draw from this comparative silence of Jesus about the Holy Spirit? We might argue that he scarcely, if ever, thought of his communion with God in terms of Holy Spirit. But I hope to show that in fact he knew both the overwhelming impact of the Old Testament *ruach* and that constant permeation by the divine life which is the hall-mark of the new creation. The silence, I think, can be explained in three ways.

Believing that life-in-the-Spirit is the life of the end of the ages, his teaching about the Holy Spirit was bound to be wrapped up in metaphors of apocalyptic vision. 'He was speaking of the Spirit' (John 7.39) is the fourth evangelist's comment on Jesus' picture of the living water: there must have been many other occasions when he spoke of the Spirit in metaphors or synonyms. 'There be some here of them that stand by who shall in no wise taste of death till they see the Kingdom of God come with power' (Mark 9.1) is surely such a statement. So also, probably, is the parable of the fig tree:

'When her branch is now become tender, and putteth forth its leaves, ye know that the summer is nigh' (Mark 13.28). And what of the new wine in the old wine-skins, the fire kindled upon the earth, the lightning spreading from the east to the west, and many of the parables of the Kingdom? The experience these describe is unlike anything except the power of the Spirit in the church.

Secondly, Jesus must have hesitated as much to speak openly of the Spirit, as of the Messiah, because the popular image which the word would conjure up was too far from the truth. If, in fact, Jesus laid any claim to the messianic title it was only in the context of his servanthood and suffering; he would only allow the word inasmuch as it pointed to the cross. It was widely believed that the special endowments by the Spirit of God, particularly the gift of prophecy, were being withheld from the time of the last of the great prophets until Messiah should come. The reappearance of a prophet in the person of John the Baptist had caused enough controversy and misunderstanding to make Jesus hesitate to confide his understanding of Holy Spirit to any but the most intimate circle of friends, and even to them only as he entered upon the glory of his self-offering.

Thirdly – though this can only be speculation – we have to ask how far one who lived totally and uniquely in the Spirit could himself be conscious of that Spirit. His whole attention was focussed unchangeably on the Father. That love was absolute; not like our romantic loves which always leave a bit of the mind free to observe and enjoy our own loving. Even we with all our self-observation can never, as I have said before, directly discern the Spirit himself: we know him only by the fact that we are seeing things we could never have seen without him. It is this aspect of the silence of Jesus, his unconsciousness of the Spirit, which in the end compels us to recognize that here for the first time we see Man in total and unbroken union with the Holy Spirit.

To put it this way almost invites the charge of 'adoptionism' – that is the teaching, early rejected by the church, that the human Jesus so supremely won his spurs that at some point – baptism, transfiguration, resurrection or ascension – he was adopted as the Divine Son and taken into the being of God. For fear of this patently inadequate account the church began from the fourth century to minimize the part the Spirit played in the earthly existence of Jesus and, as we have already seen, to drive a wedge between the almost identical concepts of Spirit and Logos. But in its earlier innocence the primitive church found it natural almost to identify the divine nature in Jesus with the Holy Spirit:

> '*He who was manifested in the body,*
>   *vindicated in the Spirit,*
>     *seen by angels;*
> *who was proclaimed among the nations* (I Tim. 3.16).

In another of their early hymns is found:

> *The first man Adam became a living soul,*
> *The last Adam a life-giving Spirit* (I Cor. 15.45 R V).

Surely it was their recognition of the complete identity of the life of the human Jesus with the life of the Holy Spirit which led the first Christians to identify also their new life 'in the Spirit' with life 'in Christ'. 'God sent forth the Spirit of his Son into our hearts crying, Abba!' (Gal. 4.6: cf. Rom. 8.14, 15). 'He that is joined to the Lord is one Spirit' (I Cor. 6.17). 'If Christ's name is flung in your teeth as an insult, count yourselves happy because then that glorious Spirit which is the Spirit of God is resting upon you' (I Peter 4.14).

Whatever it was that Jesus Christ came to do for us, it is certain that he had to do it as a man not as a *deus ex machina*; whatever impact he made upon his apostles and, through them, upon both the church and the world, he made it through his manhood. I meet that manhood, it is true, not simply in a 'Jesus of history', but in the living Christ, my contemporary. I have never seen God nor shall I, I believe, except in this one Man. To the end of time and in eternity it is in his manhood alone that I know God. Anything less than this – or as some would say, more than this – is a denial of the incarnation. And to me, a man, God could come completely in no other way.

Whenever a baby is born, it is a kind of summing-up, a culmination of everything that has ever happened before. His parents and his grandparents live on in him, and not only they but all the forgotten generations are, as it were, incarnate in the new-born child. The history of the race is in his veins. In every baby this hidden, ceaseless flow of experience and response breaks surface and emerges at one particular point. The child that was born that night in the city of David on the eve of the census was no exception. But subsequent events led a few people to affirm that in this birth something more emerged than the common heredity of humankind. What broke surface then was not simply the sum total of all that had been, but its cause; not the surging processes of creation alone, but creativity itself. We call Mary's child 'Emmanuel' because we see in him the God who has been always with us, always in the midst. There is no need for him to intervene as a stranger from an outside world. He is already here.

*And yet will the wind of heaven wear the shape of a man,*
*Be mortal as breath, before men, for a sign, and stand*
*Between good and evil, the thieves of the left and right hand.*[1]

To think of the birth of Jesus as an emergence rather than as a breaking-in from outside is not a new idea. 'All that came to be was alive with his life, and that life was the light of men . . . he was in the world; but the world, though it owed its being to him, did not recognize him. He entered his own realm, and his own would not receive him' (John 1.4, 10, 11). Or, as the creed simply puts it: He was conceived by the Holy Ghost. What we see in Jesus is the Creator Spirit, the activator of all being, focussed entirely into one human spirit. Or, looking at it the other way round, we see manhood completely surrendered to, and possessed by, the Spirit of God.

This is the new kind of man. This is, if you like, the next unimaginable step forward which man had to take in obedience to the lure of the unfulfilled. But inasmuch as man never could or never would take that step, the God who always works from inside the processes took the step for him, as a man. For all we know, that may have been how every previous 'step' was taken.

If we look into this life in terms of his absolute oneness with the Holy Spirit we see a perfect reflection of all the marks of the Spirit's activity which we have previously noted: the intensity of awareness and communion, the insistent demand for choice, the self-oblation and sacrifice, the double vision of creative insight, and the freedom of the incalculable *ruach*. If we had been able to imagine all the characteristics of the Spirit of God fused and focussed in one human personality we should have pictured a figure like Jesus of Nazareth.

The story opens in a gust of *ruach* power. The setting for his birth was one of those pietistic groups which maintained a silent protest against the compromising formalism of Saducee-Judaism.

They were by no means unrelated to the communities of the Essenes. The messianic expectations of such groups were fired by a passionate nationalism and spirit of revolt, of which the Magnificat hymn may be seen as a supreme expression. Today we would also describe them as 'pentecostal', though they appear to have encountered the Holy Spirit in purely Old Testament terms: coming upon them, overshadowing, and moving one after another of them to inspired utterance.

Again at the start of his public ministry Jesus is found in the setting of a revivalist movement. His baptism may have signified his decision to become publicly associated with the movement, and according to the Ephesus tradition behind the fourth gospel which reflected some memories persisting from the Baptist's circle, Jesus identified himself with them for perhaps a full year.[8]

But far more significant than his association with this type of movement is his own baptism and its sequel. This, as I said in the first chapter, is crucial for our understanding of Christ's mission and our part in it. According to Mark's gospel the opening words of Jesus' own proclamation were: 'The *Kairos*-time has come.' What had brought the messianic kingdom out of the future into the present was his possession by the Holy Spirit. In that moment he had heard the words declaring him to be both God's Son and also God's Suffering Servant. (Ps. 2.7, where 'Thou art my Son' in the Septuagint version might be translated 'Thou art my house-servant', is followed by 'In whom I am well-pleased', quoted from the Servant Song of Isa. 42.1.) Under the compulsion of the Spirit he goes to his combat with the devil and emerges victorious; he has bound the strong man. Now armed with the same Spirit he comes to unbind the prisoners and let the brokens victims go free. 'The decisive change in the ages', writes James Dunn in an important study, 'was effected by the Spirit coming down upon Jesus. It is this unique anointing of this unique person which brings in the End.'[9]

As I have said, I think it would be one-sided to fasten exclusively on the baptism or the birth or the resurrection as *the* moment of the Spirit's action upon Jesus. But I want to stress the visible continuity between the *ruach* of the Old Testament experience and the Spirit in the life of Jesus. We are familiar with the superb restraint of the four canonical gospels contrasted with the legendary extravaganzas of the same period. Yet I wonder whether our taste for common sense may not have blinded us to a strong element of the uncanny in the figure of Jesus as the gospels in fact portray him. In our own time Sholem Asch among novelists and Epstein, Piper and Sutherland among artists have sensed and captured this quality in forms that are highly disturbing and so the more likely to be true. Margaret Field, the anthropologist, points to a parallel between the Spirit driving Jesus into the wilderness after his baptism and the experience of the primitive prophets of Ghana, who almost invariably begin a career of divination by running off in a state of possession into the bush where they remain lost for weeks or even months. Even after the start of his own distinctive ministry Jesus exhibited many strange and incalculable traits. When the crowds surge after him, seeking or threatening, he suddenly cannot be found. He reads men like a book and has an even more disturbing ease of communication with the deranged and the devil-possessed. Though we must think of all the powers exercised by Christ, not as superhuman, but as being inherent in manhood where manhood is whole and complete, yet to recognize this does not silence the exclamation, 'What sort of man is this?', nor does it eliminate that mingled amazement and dread with which his disciples followed him.

The baptism of Jesus and the experiences that followed it in the wilderness have all the appearance of a typical disclosure-encounter or 'annunciation', as I have called it. In that experience the Spirit made him aware in a new way of his own significance vis-à-vis Israel and his unique relation to God as Son and Servant. I think it is possible to detect other annunciation experiences in the gospels which were decisive turning points in his understanding of his own mission. Such was his encounter with the pagan woman of Syro-Phoenicia. When first she accosted him he believed that his vocation was strictly limited to the house of Israel; but in her gay, irrepressible importunity he saw a faith that outshone that of his own people, and his vision was enlarged. And which was the moment when it dawned on him that his disciples whom he had certainly called to share in his final conflict and sacrifice, would not be in it with him at the end?

Jesus, then, knew the flashes of sudden recognition, of seeing the ordinary in an extraordinary way, which the Holy Spirit gives to every man. But, beyond that, he seems to have been able to live every moment in that state of vivid receptivity and communion

towards the 'Thou' of the world around him, which Buber says is
for the rest of us a holy place wherein we are not able to remain.[10]
He saw all commonplace things with an artist's intensity of appre-
hension, and across the communication gap of the centuries he has
made the whole world see with his vision the corn seed falling
among the thistles, the sparrows on the market stall, the speck of
sawdust in an eye, and the patch on an old coat. By the same
alchemy of his supreme awareness he has made us all include an
unknown centurion, a Jericho tax-collector, a madman from Deca-
polis, and a thief on the gallows among our most familiar acquain-
tances. It is in his unquestioning availability to all who cross his
path and in his openness as a man among men that we see what it
means for a person to be possessed and driven by the wind of the
Spirit. I do not think it is simply because the stories had been stream-
lined by use before ever they were written that we feel in all his
recorded encounters with others a current of intense communication. The whole of his being is concentrated on each particular meeting and he never appears to be looking over the shoulder of the one
he is talking to. To a degree which I cannot discern even in the
greatest of his saints, his relationship to God was always that of a
man in his concrete togetherness with all men. What is so astonishing about him is that in all his uniqueness his true self exists in the
gathering together of the two or three. This is perhaps where he
most differs from John the Baptist: he seemed to delight in his share
of the interdependence of all mankind. 'Friend, lend me three
loaves' was for him a most natural request to make at midnight on
someone else's behalf. Poor amongst the poor, and aching with
compassion for the misfits and the sinful, he nevertheless lived life
as a continuous celebration and wanted to be remembered as a
man with a cup in his hand. Though he shrank from the bitterness
we had all put into that cup, he drank it like a toast: 'This is the
cup my Father has given me; shall I not drink it?'

That word of open-eyed but trustful dedication points to the
dominant I-Thou relationship in this Spirit-possessed life, namely his
incomparable awareness of God. More than all the others who
absorbed his whole attention, this was the Other in whom he was
immersed. God was the never-forgotten presence, yet Jesus' relation to God was never dutiful; it was ardent and glad and totally
relaxed. It expressed the absolute acceptance of his creaturehood
and an untroubled dependence, without a shadow of subservience. It

was the fully responsible partnership of one who, in Bonhoeffer's phrase, 'made his whole life a response to the question and call of God'. This astonishing relationship was perfectly expressed in the baby-word '*Abba*', 'Daddy', in which we catch the actual sound of Jesus' most characteristic and intimate utterance. Jeremias has said:

> With the help of my assistants I have examined the prayer literature of ancient Judaism – a large, rich literature, all too little explored. The result of the examination was that in no place in this immense literature is this invocation of God as *abba* to be found. . . No Jew would have dared to address God in this manner. Jesus did it always, in all his prayers which are handed down to us, with one single exception, the cry from the cross: 'My God, my God, why hast thou forsaken me?'[11]

The immediacy of the *abba*-relationship with God is the gift of the Holy Spirit. The very word, in its elemental simplicity, is the voice of the Holy Spirit, the sound, one might say, of the eternal communication between the Father and the Son: *Ben! – Abba!* 'In that cry' says St Paul, 'the Spirit of God joins with our spirit in testifying that we are God's children . . . and Christ's fellow-heirs' (Rom. 8.16, 17). But before Pentecost there were none with whom Jesus could share this *abba*-relationship, this 'right to become children of God' (John 1.12). So the uniqueness of this naive form of address also betrays a profound aloneness. 'No one knows the Son but the Father, and no one knows the Father but the Son' (Matt. 11.27). On that self-revelation from the Q sayings C. H. Dodd makes this sensitive comment:

> He has found no one who really knows or understands him, not even those nearest to him; but there is One who does know him – God, his Father. And in that same intimate, personal way he too knows God. Here, we may legitimately infer, is to be found the driving force and the source of energy for an almost impossible mission; here certainly the source of the inflexible resolution with which he went, knowingly, to death in the service of his mission.[12]

Here also is to be found the confident authority of Jesus which set him apart from the religious teachers to whom men were accustomed. To borrow support for his truth by quoting other authorities would be a denial of the immediacy of his communion with the Father. The Roman centurion recognized this when he approached Jesus on behalf of a member of his household who was gravely ill. No need to come in person, he said, a word from you will cure him. I know, for I am myself under orders, with soldiers under me.

The 'company commander' just because he is loyally obedient to his superiors, can issue orders which have behind them the ultimate authority of the emperor himself. The authority which Jesus is expected to exert is subject to the same condition. It is a remarkable argument. At least it suggests how the personality of Jesus impressed itself on a complete outsider. But still more remarkable is that Jesus appears to have endorsed it.[13]

Then, as now, it was the truth *of* Jesus, and not the truth *about* Jesus, which convinced and converted. 'It is no longer because of what you said that we believe, for we have heard him ourselves and we know that this is in truth the Saviour of the world.' That is the constant testimony of the fourth gospel. Men either found that he compelled belief or they were impervious to him. The common people sensed the authority of his own person and it was not derived from the evidence of scripture like that of the scribes. To those who questioned his authority he had no answer except to point to another example of a self-authenticating man, John the Baptist. 'All who are not deaf to truth', he said to Pilate, 'listen to my voice.' But when Pilate asked him 'Where have you come from?' he gave him no answer. That was his point of vulnerability. No words can add to the Word. For at the end of the day there is no authority which is not self-authenticating. Men are not convinced by teaching but by encounter – 'because it is there'. The doctrine follows, as a way of explaining the impact.

This authority of Jesus found expression in another word which he used as no one else did, the word, 'Amen!', 'Yes!'. 'Whereas', says Jeremias, 'according to idiomatic Jewish usage the word *amen* is used to affirm, endorse as appropriate, the words of another person, in the tradition of the sayings of Jesus it is used *without exception* to introduce and endorse Jesus' own words.'[14] No other writer in the New Testament uses it in this way. But it was such an idiosyncrasy of Jesus that Paul later wrote: 'With him it was, and is, Yes. . . That is why, when we give glory to God it is through Jesus Christ that we say "Amen"' (II Cor. 1.20). Again in the letters to the seven churches the hot-and-cold, yes-and-no church of Laodicea is addressed by 'the Amen'.

On the lips of Jesus, Amen is equivalent to the prophets' constant affirmation: Thus saith the Lord. And in him we see most clearly the special gift of the Spirit who 'spake by the prophets', the double vision that sees two apparently unrelated ideas superimposed in a single image. We have seen how supremely Jesus used this gift in the parables; and in him, as in all the prophets before him, this terrible awareness enabled him to see in juxtaposition what is and what should be. This is the Spirit of discernment at work, the Spirit of judgment, and there is neither creation nor re-creation without him. The light must be separated from the dark before there can be any new worlds. The potential must be held over against the actual before there can be any development. The way forward always leads through a death.

To live in the Spirit is to be agonizingly aware of the contrast between what is and what should be, and it is in the very nature of the prophet or the artist that he must at all costs bring this contrast home. The wrath of God is only another name for the divine dissatisfaction. The unfulfilled, the spoiled, the second-best must be exposed to a clear, unambiguous disapproval. The Spirit, wherever he moves, must 'confute the world and show where wrong and right and judgment lie' (John 16.8). And because the manhood of Jesus was totally possessed by this Spirit and one with him he was bound to carry the placarding of sin to its ultimate conclusion on the cross.

To say 'You are Simon: you shall be called Peter' is the act of creation opening the door to an individual conversion: to say 'Destroy this temple – the old Israel – and in three days I will raise it again' is the same act of creation opening the door to the Kingdom of God. Announcing the Kingdom, the central theme of Jesus' teaching, was essentially the word of a prophet, a word of both judgment and promise. Jesus took his stand with groups like the Qumran community and the Baptist's circle in proclaiming judgment upon Israel, not simply one more visitation of punishment, but the final judgment as far as this nation was concerned. The people of God had reached the end of the road. 'Do not presume to say to yourselves, "We have Abraham for our father". I tell you that God can make children for Abraham out of these stones here. Already the axe is laid to the roots of the trees' (Matt. 3.9, 10).

There is going to be a baptism in the fire of destruction, but also in the wind of the Spirit.[15] Meanwhile there is a baptism of repentance for remission of sins. So make yourselves ready to enter the coming Kingdom. 'In the prophetic interpretation of history', says Dodd, 'Israel dies to rise again. In terms of the existing situation, the present Jewish establishment is doomed; the true people of God will emerge from its ruins.'[16] Jesus takes on at that point. Patching the old coat will only make things worse. The old skins will never do for the new wine. The barren tree may have another year or two but then if there is no fruit it will be cut down. He is saying the same thing as those who declare today that the system itself must go before the new can come. But for him the promise outweighs the judgment, for the promise has already been fulfilled. The true 'system', from out there in the future, is already working upon its components to order and direct. Out of his own overwhelming awareness of the Father he knows that the Kingdom of God, the Israel of the new age, has come. So the call is: Repent, believe, enter. His ministry is both a demonstration of the signs of the messianic age and a recruiting campaign. As he and his fishermen followers draw in the net it is full of the most unlikely fish. This woman imprisoned by Satan for eighteen years, now freed from her bonds, she is a true daughter of Abraham (Luke 13.16). Zacchaeus with his ill-gotten gains – this man too is a son of Abraham (Luke 19.10). Tax-gatherers and prostitutes are entering the Kingdom ahead of the respectable citizens with all their excuses (Matt. 21.28–32; 22.1–10). These are the lost sheep of the house of Israel, Abraham's true children. Yet the little dogs also eat up the crumbs that drop from the children's table (Matt. 15.22–28). The Roman company commander shows more faith than can be found in Israel, for now the outsiders are coming from east and west to feast with Abraham while those who were born to the Kingdom are driven into the dark (Matt. 8.10–12).

It is here in his search for faith that we see in Jesus another unmistakable mark of the Spirit that possessed him, namely the insistence on choice. To say 'You are Simon: you shall be called Peter' is to make a man responsible for the contrast between what is and what should be. To hold a man responsible means both an act of judgment and an act of faith. Today we are trying more than any earlier generation not to believe in responsibility. Our idea of sympathy is to diminish responsibility by laying the blame on parents, glands, environment – anywhere but at the door of this poor victim of circumstance. That is not Jesus' way. The one thing he seems to have condemned utterly was evasion of choice. The man in the parable who was afraid to risk his bag of gold and brought it back uninvested and uncommitted was flung out into the dark. To choose is to commit yourself. To commit yourself is to run the risk of failure, the risk of sin, the risk of betrayal. Jesus can deal with all those, for forgiveness is his metier. The only thing he can do nothing with is the refusal to be committed. Even Judas should do quickly whatever he chooses to do and be responsible.

There could be no other way with men and their problems, for freedom is the very air of the Kingdom, the freedom of those who know themselves to be sons of God. 'The slave is one who has no permanent standing in the household, but the son belongs to it for ever. If then the Son sets you free you will indeed be free' (John 8.35). Such sayings from the fourth gospel, we feel, are the very breath of the man we see and hear in the other gospels, whose style of life so fully matched his teaching. Do not be anxious for your life. Do not be anxious about tomorrow. Do not be anxious how you are to speak. There is a quality of freedom about Jesus which, once met, changes our very ideas of what it means to be fully a person.

What most confused his critics was that he conformed to no pattern. What were they to make of the wandering teacher who typically carried no purse and had nowhere to lay his head and yet appeared to be fond of parties, particularly in disreputable company? How were they to tie him down to a particular breach of the law when his real fault seemed to be a general independence of all the ordinary pressures and claims which both bind and buttress the individual in society? His sense of property was casual and he expected men to lend boat or beast as unhesitatingly as he would have handed over coat and cloak to them. He steadily disobeyed the demands of what we regard as self-interest and self-preservation. He seemed to pass elusive and free as the *ruach* wind through all our interlocking structures of duty and obligation. His whole manner of life and even more the manner of his dying, was a challenge to necessity.

The order of necessity is the order of separation from God . . . Necessity appears when Adam breaks his relation with God.

Then he becomes subject to an order of obligation, the order of
toil, hunger, passions, struggle against nature, etc., from which
there is no appeal. . . And death is then the most total of all
necessities. Necessity is definable as what man does because he
cannot do otherwise. But when God reveals himself, necessity
ceases to be destiny or even inevitability. . . For Christ, even
death ceases to be a necessity. 'I give my life for my sheep; it is
not taken from me. I give it.'[17]

So Jesus defies necessity all along the line. If money has become a
necessity, he said, a man should give it away. If the sin of hand or
eye takes away a man's freedom he is better off without them.
Though he stayed with his mother until well into adult life, yet
several times he startles us by seeming to abjure the ties of kinship.
He refused all the unconditional claims of his society and his
nation. He defied the dominance of tradition and culture and
would not conform with the popular conceptions of goodness. He
laughed out of court the easy notion of the rich and healthy that
men get their deserts in life. Men, he said, did not have to be good
for God to accept them; for God dealt only in gifts not wages. So
Jesus rejected altogether the concept of a rigid code of law, abstract
and uniform; and yet, in free obedience, he discovered infinitely
more exacting meanings in the teachings of the Torah, uncovering
it, as it were, from under a pile of dusty lumber. The best of the
Pharisees were men of principle: that is not how anyone would
describe Jesus. Even to call him 'good' is to miss the point; God
was his reality, not goodness (Mark 10.18). He would never have
said with today's moralists that love means justice.[18] Champions of
right and of rights were familiar to him, but he moved in another
world of uncalculating generosity. 'These late-comers have done only
one hour's work, yet you have put them on a level with us, who have
sweated the whole day in the blazing sun.' 'I never once disobeyed
your orders; and you never gave me so much as a kid . . . But now
that this son of yours turns up, after running through your money
with his women, you kill the fatted calf for him.'
  No rules – only God! No conditional merit – only forgiving
acceptance! The openness of such a stance threatens every religious
system and calls all principles in question. 'What of the law? It was
added to make wrongdoing a legal offence. It was a temporary
measure pending the arrival of the "issue" (the Christ) to whom

the promise was made' (Gal. 3.19). So 'Christ ends the law' (Rom. 10.4). Paul's classic controversy against the whole concept of law was a faithful reflection of Jesus' own style of life.

But the conflict did not cease when the primitive church finally broke out from the regulations of Judaism. The church itself has been the persecutor again and again. For it seems to me that more Christians are driven by the desire to be good than the desire for God, and put their faith in Christ only as a more successful way of enabling them at last to keep the law.

Natural man seems to grow up with a desperate need to be approved of. Whatever may be said to the contrary, he feels 'in his bones' that he has to be a good child to keep his parents' love, and long before he has learned that love is not dependent on his goodness or badness he has created the great shadowy arbiter, his pitiless super-Ego. 'Let me be such', he cries, 'that the ancestors, the great gods, the law, will approve. Let me be such that I need no longer be afraid of being found out. Let me be such that I can bear to live with myself.' So guilt, shame and conscience are built into an iron cage, and we call the bars of it the pillars of the moral universe. Those shadowy but inflexible pillars frame every tragic drama, and the hero is broken on them in the end, often for attempting a new truth, a more dangerous freedom, a more risky love.

But now Christ comes breathing the air of comedy, or rather, the air of that peculiarly Christian form of drama, tragi-comedy, which takes the tragic dimensions seriously but enfolds them in a more embracing redemption. The pillars, he declares, are not the ulti-mate framework of the world. 'Your heavenly Father makes his sun to rise on the good and bad alike and sends the rain on the honest and the dishonest' (Matt. 5.45). What an epitome of the spirit of true comedy that is! 'I choose to pay the last man the same as you; surely I am free to do what I like with my own money. Why be jealous because I am kind?' (Matt. 30.15). 'I do not condemn you either. You may go; do not sin again' (John 8.11). In a world where there is no condemnation but a welcome to anyone who can accept the fact that he *is* accepted, goodness takes on an entirely new meaning. For the first time one can be good gratuitously because it is no longer necessary to be good. One really can 'sin no more' because it has ceased to matter in the old sense. For it was the awful obligation to be good and the awful consequences of failure that made it so impossible. No wonder the teachers of Judaism saw that the pillars of their society were being shaken.

> For the Pharisee every moment of life becomes a situation of conflict in which he has to choose between good and evil. . . These men with the incorruptibly impartial and distrustful vision, cannot confront any man in any other way than by examining him with regard to his decisions in the conflicts of life. And so, even when they come face to face with Jesus, they cannot do otherwise than attempt to force Him, too, into conflicts and decisions in order to see how he will conduct Himself in them. It is this that constitutes their temptation of Jesus.[19]

So the confrontation is staged in a number of great set-pieces. The Messiah has bound the strong tyrant and is setting the captives free; but he does it on the Sabbath. It is a choice between two kinds of priority, the priorities of spontaneous response to particular situations or the unchanging priorities of the iron pillars. For the sake of the law's integrity this *must* be called the work of Beelzebub. To say this is to choose the cage in preference to the freedom, the fixed mind in preference to Spirit-given awareness, *I-It* in preference to *I-Thou*. This is the sin against the Holy Spirit, which, alone of all sins, is unforgivable because it denies forgiveness.

So generation after generation Christ in his saints will be crucified by whatever system is in power. It is the only way in which their protest can be incorporated into his and validated by resurrection. For, by the only terms that law can understand, Jesus must be condemned. Judaism has always seen that necessity, often with regret, and Christians have gravely misjudged the other faith through failing to recognize the regret. So in the preliminary hearing by night in the high priest's house, Jesus was first questioned about the whole tenor of his teaching, if the fourth gospel is to be followed, and only after he refused to give evidence were witnesses called. From the start the charge was blasphemy, and Caiaphas by his intervention finally got it to stick. For, as Pannenberg puts it, 'either Jesus had been a blasphemer or the law of the Jews – and with it Judaism itself as a religion – is done away with'.[20]

So the glorious liberty of a son of God, the gift of the Spirit, brought Jesus to death for blasphemy. He had foreseen this outcome many months before and not only had he refused to swerve from his course, but he had accepted his inevitable execution as an act of redemption for others, taking upon himself the messianic woes that must precede the final breakthrough of the Kingdom. It seems that almost to the end he hoped that his 'founder members' in that Kingdom might carry their crosses with him. But in the event he went forward entirely alone – the only perfectly free man.

What was the Holy Spirit doing at Calvary? First, in a mystery that we cannot plumb, he must have been about his eternal employ between the Father and the Son, holding each in awareness of the other, in an agony and bliss of love that must for ever lie infinitely beyond our understanding. For Jesus this included both the forsakenness and the ultimate trust. This is a theme that stirred the imagination of many artists. But beyond that inwardness of the Trinity, the Spirit of communion spilled out into other awarenesses: his concern for others, surpassing the pain, and their deepening perception of him. The thief's and the centurion's recognition, whatever it means, was the start of a turning of eyes that has been going on ever since. Here in its ultimate intensity is the power of God and the wisdom of God.

I can find no better words to describe what happened next than the familiar opening: 'And the earth was waste and void; and darkness was upon the face of the deep: and the Spirit of God was brooding upon the face of the waters. And God said, Let there be light: and there was light' (Gen. 1.2–4).

It is a strange thing that the church's teaching about the Holy Spirit should have largely lost sight of the role accorded to him in the New Testament epistles as the agent of Christ's resurrection. I have already quoted the opening of Romans where Paul seems to be repeating a primitive two-stage definition of Christ's nature, human and divine. 'On the human level he was born of David's stock, but on the level of the spirit – the Holy Spirit – he was declared Son of God by a mighty act in that he rose from the dead' (Rom. 1.3, 4). In the hymn I have also quoted before from I Timothy 3.16 – 'manifested in the body, vindicated in the Spirit' – the second phrase again refers to the resurrection; and I Peter 3.19 is probably another liturgical verse bearing the same meaning. Once more in Romans the agency of the Holy Spirit in raising the dead to life is clearly indicated: 'If the Spirit of him who raised Jesus from the dead dwells within you, then the God who raised Jesus Christ from the dead will also give new life to your mortal bodies through his indwelling Spirit' (Rom. 8.11).

The Trinity (*detail*)
*Austrian School*

The Trinity    *William Blake*

The risen Christ is not only a universal Messiah to inaugurate a new Israel drawn from the ends of the earth: he was that before his passion. Now he is the second Adam to pioneer a new kind of manhood. The Kingdom of God is a new creation brought into being out of nothingness through the working of the Creator Spirit.

But this is a devastating reversal of the judgment of Caiaphas. Pannenberg has this to say:

> The resurrection reveals that he died as a righteous man, not as a blasphemer. Rather, those who rejected him as a blasphemer and had complicity in his death were the real blasphemers.[21]

But, further, he shows that the Jewish people in their passionate loyalty to the law are representatives of all human institutions and of the universal idolatry of obligation and conformity, and of all that feeds our self-complacency.

> Then the Jewish people actually represent humanity in general in its rejection of Jesus as a blasphemer in the name of the law . . . Jesus died the death all have incurred, the death of the blasphemer. In this sense he died for us, for our sins.[22]

And, one must add – for without it all is still unreconciled – he died forgiving us. We know this, not simply because Luke said so, but because he never learned how to withhold love.

To each one that awful reversal of right and wrong is brought home whenever the Holy Spirit opens our eyes to recognize the living reality of that man of terrible freedom and to hear his words: 'I am Jesus whom you are persecuting.' If that painful moment of truth is necessary for an individual's salvation, how much more needed it is by an anxious guardian church, blindly hostile still towards the protester and the unorthodox.

But then: 'Our former persecutor is preaching the good news of the faith which once he tried to destroy' (Gal. 1.23). To be confronted by the living Christ through the Go-Between Spirit is a discovery that cannot be kept to oneself. We have seen the full range of the mission of the Holy Spirit, and that many of the causes he initiates are being better served by men of other allegiances than by Christians. The Spirit whose going and coming knows no bounds is continually pointing to the man Jesus and claiming for him a unique significance; and many know it who will never enter the church. The *confessio* they might make if they ever wished to become so articulate, which is unlikely, has been written in a little book born out of anger and disappointment over a compromising church.

If I had no other faith to live by, I should yet live and believe with him, and one single beam of his light in our existence seems to me more important than the full sun of any orthodoxy. For . . . what is decisive for all time is not how much we have believed, but that we have believed and followed him, however little we have understood about him.[23]

That is the point at which the mission of the Spirit becomes a gospel.

## NOTES

1. Wolfhart Pannenberg, *Jesus – God and Man*, SCM Press 1968, pp. 169f.

2. Acts 2.33 – an image arising naturally from combining the Hebrew original of Ps. 68.18, 'thou hast received gifts' with the Aramaic Targum (quoted in Eph. 4.8), 'thou has bestowed gifts', both of which could have been read in the synagogues.

3. Eph. 1.13; Luke 24.49; Acts 1.4; 2.39.

4. Isa. 32.15; Ezek. 39.29; Zech. 12.10.

5. Pannenberg, op. cit., p. 170.

6. Paul Althaus, *Die christliche Wahrheit*, C. Bertelsmann, Gütersloh 1962, p. 440.

7. W. S. Merwin, *The Isaiah of Souillac*, from *Poems of Doubt and Belief*, Macmillan, NY 1954.

8. Acts 18.24–5, 19.1–7; John 3.22–4; 4.1–3.

9. James D. G. Dunn, *Baptism in the Holy Spirit*, SCM Press 1970, p. 26.

10. Martin Buber, *I and Thou*, T. & T. Clark, paperback ed. 1966, p. 52.

11. Joachim Jeremias, *The Prayers of Jesus*, SCM Press 1967, pp. 96f.

12. C. H. Dodd, *The Founder of Christianity*, Collins 1971, p. 52.

13. Ibid., p. 50.

14. Jeremias, op. cit., p. 112.

15. Wind and fire may simply parallel the winnowing fork and fire of judgment (Matt. 1.11, 12). It is not certain how central to John the Baptist's message was the promise of Spirit-baptism, as is asserted by James Dunn in *Baptism in the Holy Spirit*. The dozen or so baptized by John, whom Paul met at Ephesus, had not heard of the Holy Spirit.

16. Dodd, op. cit., p. 89.
17. Jacques Ellul, *Violence*, SCM Press 1970, p. 128.
18. E.g., Joseph Fletcher, *Situation Ethics*, SCM Press 1966, pp. 87–102.
19. Dietrich Bonhoeffer, *Ethics*, SCM Press, 1971 ed., pp. 12–13.
20. Pannenberg, op. cit., p. 255. See also Otto Betz, *What do we know about Jesus?*, SCM Press 1968, pp. 83ff.; Ethelbert Stauffer, *Jesus and His Story*, SCM Press 1960, pp. 100ff.; and Dodd, op. cit., pp. 157–59.
21. Pannenberg, op. cit., p. 259.
22. Ibid., p. 263.
23. Ernst Käsemann, *Jesus Means Freedom*, SCM Press 1969, pp. 36–7.

# 6

## BREATH

*The Indwelling Spirit and the Humiliation of the Mission*

A grain of wheat, says Jesus, according to St John, remains a solitary grain unless it falls into the ground and dies, but if it dies it bears a rich harvest. The occasion was that pregnant confrontation with the group of Greeks who were in Jerusalem for the festival – representatives of the great world beyond the tiny province of Judaea and its introverted conflicts. Their search for Jesus came as another temptation to short-cut the way to the world's renewal and have a mission without a cross. But though his soul was thrown into turmoil the bait was refused. The seed died. And then began the proliferation. He who was uniquely Son of God will now bring many sons to glory through his sufferings (Heb. 2.10). In himself alone he had been the new Israel; now more and more are to be grafted into it (John 15.1; Rom. 11.22–24). The new kind of man is to bring forth a new mankind (Rom. 5.14–19). He was the foundation stone; now the whole new temple is going up (Eph. 2.20–22). He was the start of the new creation and now that creation is being brought to light (Rev. 2.14; Eph. 1.9–10). He who was possessed by the Spirit of God in a new and únique way now passes on the gift to those who have faith in him (John 20.21).

Life in the Spirit had been lived uniquely by the new man Jesus Christ through the total identification of his manhood with the Creator Spirit. But it did not end with that perfect life. Because of the solidarity of mankind something entirely new had entered the very nature of manhood itself. That unity of the human Jesus and the Holy Spirit, which from henceforth was so naturally to be known as 'the Spirit of Jesus', had been offered up to God so that it could be offered back to man. The Passion according to St John ends with the deliberately ambiguous words: 'He bowed his head and gave over the Spirit'. It was given to the Father so that it could be received back from the Father and given to men. Poured out in that one death, it was now poured out on all flesh. The love of God which had burnt up the heart of Jesus has been 'shed abroad in our hearts'. In all these ways and many others the New Testament writers assert that the fusion of Holy Spirit with manhood which was unique and new in Jesus Christ has been passed on into the fellowship of the church, so making it his body. In that body a new kind of man is growing up within the fabric of the old. 'The Church', said Bonhoeffer, 'is nothing but a section of humanity in which Christ has really taken form.'[1]

But before following up this thought through the teaching of the apostolic age it is important to recall what we have already seen as the main characteristics of the Spirit, otherwise the needle will slip back into the old grooves.

The one whose presence we are to discern in the life of the new fellowship is the Go-Between who works by opening our inward eyes, making us aware of some 'other' beckoning and calling in its separate identity. Consider, for example, the great number of references to sight in the three accounts of St Paul's conversion in the Acts. This gift of awareness, we have seen, operates dynamically by holding before God's creatures in a single vision both what is and what might be. In this way the Spirit draws the whole created universe, but especially mankind itself, towards greater complexity, sensitiveness and personhood. But since the incarnation, the Spirit does this particularly and supremely by drawing man's attention to Jesus Christ in whom alone the meaning of personhood is fully revealed, and from whom alone true manhood can be imparted to the sons of men. 'No one can say "Jesus is Lord!" except under the influence of the Holy Spirit' (I Cor. 12.3), for he it is who, first and always, turns our eyes upon Jesus and enables us to see what otherwise is strangely veiled. In just the same way, says St Paul, is the true Torah veiled from the minds of them that hear it read in the synagogues. But 'when one turns to the Lord the veil is removed. Now the Lord of whom this passage speaks is the Spirit' (II Cor. 3.17). And the result of that open, unclouded vision of Christ is that we ourselves begin to be changed into his likeness; 'such is the influence of the Lord who is Spirit' (v. 18). Because it is the Spirit who enables the Christian community to see the sovereignty of the risen Christ, Peter can say: 'We are witnesses to all this, and so is the Holy Spirit' (Acts 5.32). And so the ideal prayer for such a community at all times is 'that the God of our Lord Jesus Christ, the all-glorious Father, may give you the Spirit of wisdom and vision by which there comes the knowledge of him' (Eph. 1.17). For the same gift of awareness by which we recognize the authoritative truth of Jesus, enables us to see with his eyes a wide world of mystery and promise. ' "Things beyond our seeing, things beyond our hearing, things beyond our imagining, all prepared by God for those who love him", these it is that God has revealed to us through the Spirit. For the Spirit explores everything, even the depths of God's own nature. . . A man who is unspiritual refuses what belongs to the Spirit of God; it is folly to him; he cannot grasp it, because it needs to be judged in the light of the Spirit. A man gifted with the Spirit can judge the worth of everything' (I Cor. 2.9–16).[2] But again, even as we read that passage, let us beware of reading into it our fixed idea of the kind of thing the Spirit wants us to see differently from 'the man who is unspiritual'. It may not be anything we call 'religious'. It could be the daily paper or the institution one works for or a television play.

Then, again, we have seen that the Spirit acts upon all things by compelling choice. This arises from his quality of absolute freedom as the Spirit of 'otherness'. He who makes the one aware of the other must by his very nature strive to ensure that the 'otherness' or 'separateness' of every entity is as unimpaired as is his own. I shall never truly see any other creature, nor the God who is within and beyond, unless first I deeply recognize that the one I confront is totally free of my seeing. So the Spirit who can no more be bound than the wind, refuses to bind anyone with ties of obligation or convention. He enables men with discernment and holds them responsible for their own choices. And again, since the incarnation this invitation to man's free choice is focussed supremely upon Jesus. The Spirit points to him, especially to his self-oblation on the cross, saying: Choose! It is the unveiled vision which we have just spoken of that gives man this terrible freedom of choice concerning Christ, for 'where the Spirit of the Lord is there is liberty' (II Cor. 3.17). The author of Acts makes it very clear that to live and be moved by the Spirit's guidance is to open oneself to the most unguessable options. But the alternative to a continually open choice is to live by a code of regulations which always in the end leaves a man self-condemned. 'For the written law condemns to death, but the Spirit gives life' (II Cor. 3.6). What Paul playfully calls 'the life-giving law of the Spirit' could not be less like the state of bondage to rule and scruple, custom and canon, praise and blame, from which it sets us free (Rom. 8.2). But of course it exposes the Christian to the same fear and hatred as the freedom of Jesus aroused. 'If the world hates you it hated me first, as you well know. . . They will ban you from the synagogue; indeed the time is coming when anyone who kills you will suppose that he is performing a religious duty' (John 15.18; 16.2).

And, again as we have seen, a third aspect of the Spirit's creative activity is his continuous substitution of the principle of the self-sacrifice on behalf of another for the natural drive of self-interest and dominance. He urges all creatures to live by this principle not as an act of virtue or martyrdom but as the only way to life that is real. This, of course, finds its culmination in Jesus Christ, without whom we could never have suspected the centrality of this principle in the whole scheme of things. Life through dying. Life for others. This is to be the ethos of the new community, the sheep among wolves. And by this the presence of the Spirit will be known. 'If Christ's name is flung in your teeth as an insult, count yourselves happy, because then that glorious Spirit which is the Spirit of God is resting upon you' (I Peter 4.14).

That, then, was the Spirit which had totally possessed the manhood of Jesus, not for a passing moment of insight, nor for the duration of a particular task, as men had experienced the Spirit in the past, but in an indissoluble union. And after the ascension the apostles and other disciples waited as he commanded them, to be possessed by the same Spirit in the same indissoluble union. It was Pentecost that made them Christians and transformed them into a church. According to Luke, Peter had no doubt that that was the moment when they believed in Christ with saving faith and consequently were baptized with Holy Spirit. 'The Holy Spirit came upon them', he reported afterwards of Cornelius and his company, 'just as upon us *at the beginning*. Then I recalled what the Lord had said: "John baptized with water but you will be baptized with Holy Spirit." God gave them no less a gift than he gave us *when we put our trust in the Lord Jesus Christ*' – that is, on the day of Pentecost (Acts 11.15–17).

From that moment the new-born church assumed that the

Spirit would be similarly given as an immediate answer to anyone's repentant faith in Jesus Christ, together with the remission of sins. The culmination of Peter's sermon directly after the decisive event was: 'Repent and be baptized, every one of you, in the name of Jesus the Messiah for the forgiveness of your sins and you will receive the gift of the Holy Spirit' (Acts 2.38). The gift of the Spirit, therefore, is evidence that the washing away of sins has taken place (Acts 15.9: cf. Titus 3.5, 6). So in the epistles the new relationship with the Holy Spirit is the equivalent of justification. In Galatians Paul gives this testimony: 'We too have put our faith in Jesus Christ, in order that we might be justified through this faith, and not through deeds dictated by law' (Gal. 2.16); and a few verses later he applies the same principle to the Galatians, but with an alternative phrase: 'Answer me one question: did you receive the Spirit by keeping the law or by believing the gospel message?' And he goes on in connection with the gift of the Spirit to instance Abraham's faith in the same terms as he employs in the Epistle to the Romans in connection with justification (Gal. 3.5, 6; cf. Rom. 4.2, 3). It is the gift of the Spirit that brings about the new birth of the Christian. 'That which is born of the flesh is flesh, and that which is born of the Spirit is spirit' says the Gospel of John, echoing here (as, indeed, it later clearly restates) St Paul's analogy of the free-born and the slave-born sons: 'As at that time he that was born according to the flesh persecuted him that was born according to the Spirit, so it is now' (John 3.6; 8.33–36; Gal. 4.29 R S V). But the slave-born becomes as the free-born if the true son can impart to him his own Spirit. 'God has sent into our hearts the Spirit of his Son, crying "Abba! Father!" You are therefore no longer a slave but a son' (Gal. 4.6: cf. Rom. 8.15, 16; Eph. 2.18). He who knew himself to be the beloved Son through his unique possession by the Spirit of God, shares with us now his *abba*-relationship with the Father by filling us with the same Spirit.[3]

The new relationship with the Spirit and the new relationship with Jesus are indistinguishable. Life 'in the Spirit' is identical with life 'in Christ'. So it is equally possible to say that the Spirit in us gives us Christ – 'Anyone who does not have the Spirit of Christ does not belong to him' (Rom. 8.9 R S V), or to say that Christ in us shares his own unique possession by the Spirit – 'This is how we can make sure that he dwells within us; we knew it from the Spirit he has given us' (I John 3.24).

The Pentecost experience, therefore, is seen as the model of every Christian's initiation into Christ. This is what Christian baptism is meant to symbolize – the baptism in Holy Spirit which John had foretold (Acts 11.15, 16).[4] Through that baptism the Christian believer is incorporated into the life of Jesus, into his suffering, dying and rising again, into his new manhood and his possession by the Spirit. Baptism in water in the name of Christ is the sacrament of the baptism in Holy Spirit which unites us with the living Christ (I Cor. 12.13). But as in the other great sacrament, the Spirit alone gives life, the flesh is of no avail. So in those earliest days, where baptism in the Spirit had evidently been given, life-giving repentance was assumed, and the sign of water-baptism was added without delay (Acts 11.17, 18). But where water-baptism, even with faith in Christ's name, was not accompanied by the baptism in the Holy Spirit (perhaps because of unworthy motivation or because a deep enmity had first to be publicly reconciled) it was seen to be defective, and had to be made good (Acts 8.14–17). But, apart from such anomalies, I cannot find in an honest weighing of all the relevant New Testament passages any evidence that the fulness of the Holy Spirit depended on either a subsequent rite or a later experience'. Nor, as Professor Lampe has convincingly argued, is there any evidence that New Testament references to 'the anointing' or 'sealing' of believers point to either a supplementary or a preliminary rite; they are metaphors of the gift of the Holy Spirit by which a man is made a Christian, and if they may be applied, by extension, to any external rite, that can only be water-baptism.[5]

By taking permanent hold of the waiting disciples as he had taken hold of Jesus, the Holy Spirit effected a kind of extension of the incarnation, bringing them into everything that could be available to them in Christ. This was their 'Christening' by which they were made to be as Christ in the world, his body filled with his very Spirit. Contrary to many sermons, the Holy Spirit was only incidentally given to empower them for their mission; the direct result of his coming was an outburst of praise to the Lord of whose presence in their midst they had suddenly been made aware. The polyglot crowd, overhearing and miraculously understanding, asked one another: What can this mean? As Bonhoeffer puts it: the Spirit says through the church the one Word which everyone understands. It is a Word which makes men responsible, even though the word is immediately capable of mockery and misrepresentation, and that is the price of the visibility of the church. This is the true sequence of mission: a surpassing awareness of the reality of Christ, corporately shared, expressing itself in thankfulness and wonder, causing the world to ask questions to which an answer must be given in a form that every hearer can understand.

> In one sense . . . Pentecost can never be repeated – for the new age is here and cannot be ushered in again. But in another sense Pentecost, or rather the experience of Pentecost, can and must be repeated in the experience of all who would become Christians. As the day of Pentecost was once the doorway into the new age, so entry into the new age can only be made through that doorway.[6]

As one by one men and women have their eyes opened to see the overmastering reality of Christ and put their faith in him, they are baptized in Holy Spirit and joined to the Spirit-filled society. For the Spirit's power, as well as his mission towards the whole world, operates always in the interactions of community rather than in the recesses of the individual soul. The church, then, because it is possessed by the Spirit of the New Man, Jesus Christ, lives the life of the new mankind in the midst of the old world.

But, alas, one has only to say such things to be thrown into the most painful depression and cynicism. The church as we have known it could scarcely look less like a new kind of man. As often as not it appears to be the greatest deterrent to man's commitment to Christ. We can search in vain among all the churches and sects for anything resembling what is described in the New Testament, let alone what is promised there. Follow the debates of the central synod or council of any denomination through the course of a year, note what took up most time or roused the sharpest attention, and ask if this is either relevant to the bitter needs of men or strikingly different from the ways of the world. Go, as I have done, to those most deeply engaged in the field of race relations in Britain, ask them what a Christian organization might contribute, hear their retort, 'What makes you think that Christians have anything special to offer?', and then remember how deserved that answer is in most of our congregations. Read again, as Albert H. van den Heuvel has suggested, the indictment of the complacent community of Laodicea, or the unloving goats of Matthew 25, or the man who did not forgive though himself forgiven, and recognize 'the merciless photograph of our churches' that is presented to us.[7]

What went wrong, that for so many dark centuries the church could use in the name of her Christ the sword, the stake, and the anathema? What went wrong to cause what Monica Furlong calls 'the baffling one-sidedness which so often marks Christian thinking when the conventions, and in particular the sexual conventions, are challenged'?[8] What went wrong that so many features in the life of what used to be called 'younger' churches must be edited out of the missionary magazines – like the recent murder of a convert from Islam whose request for baptism threatened the peace of the frightened Christian community? What went wrong, that so often throughout history and certainly today, those who show evidence of a transforming power are narrow and stereotyped, while those who are free and compassionate lack a convinced message?

So one's love for the church oscillates between angry disappointment and tolerant extenuation. The weary debate goes on and on in the heart that is compelled to see what is and what might be.

After all, are we not the forgiven community and should we not forgive ourselves? It is of the essence of that healing which we call reconciliation that it always includes both the recognition and the containing of the wrong, and by a strange alchemy this happens both in the one who forgives and the one who is forgiven. Healing comes when one learns to say: 'This person is afraid of me and really hates me, I can understand it now and contain it in a real compassion, without fearing or hating in return.' And more often than not, though not always, this attitude liberates the other person so that he, in his turn, is able to say the much harder thing: 'I know now that I am afraid of this man and hate him for it, but I no longer have to hide or deny these things; because I can acknowledge them, the poison has gone out of them, and I can live with them.' The very things which divided and destroyed are turned into a bond of sympathy and humble understanding which are the seeds of love. To accept forgiveness one must forgive oneself; and to offer forgiveness one must forgive oneself. And this is true of the church also.

In any case, there have always been the saints. Perhaps these 'little Christs' are the fruit which proves that the dry branches are still part of the true Vine. And how miraculously they have reflected his likeness in all their variety! Francis of Assisi and Teresa of

Avila, Nicholas Ferrar and George Fox, Tykhon of Voronezh and the Curé d'Ars, Edward Wilson, explorer of the Antarctic, and Apolo Kivebulaya, apostle to the pygmies, Simone Weil, Dag Hammarskjöld and Martin Luther King – across the centuries and the different traditions they show an astonishing family likeness, recognizable in the same ardent awareness, piercing discernment, defiant nonconformity and total self-abandonment that we have noted in Jesus.

But if hard cases make bad laws, saints make bad history. And in any case a Christian's choice of saints is as highly selective as his choice of texts. If the gospel is only for 'top people', Christ died and rose in vain. We have to ask how this Spirit-filled society, the church, stands as a whole in the life of mankind.

Sierra Leone was conceived as a humanitarian and Christian experiment. There has been an unbroken continuity of Christian witness in that small country for almost 170 years, supported during most of that period by a government that fostered the church's institutions. Yet today all the Christians there amount to only 5% of the population. In the nineteenth century that tiny church was providing most of the Christian missionaries in Ghana and Nigeria, but that stream of evangelistic enthusiasm appeared to dry up fifty years ago. The church which founded the great Fourah Bay College as the nursery of the indigenous ministry throughout West Africa has itself only twenty-five clergy today, most of them elderly. Numerically, however, the Sierra Leone churches are strong compared with Japan where there is only one Christian in every 150 people, or Bangladesh, where the ratio is one in 500.

Far more serious is the extreme weakness of the traditional forms of ministry, which are still the only kind the churches are prepared to recognize. Though the avowed aim of almost every missionary agency has been the creation of self-supporting independent churches, they and the churches are the prisoners of a system which perpetuates dependency upon funds from the western world. Even in those congregations which are not impoverished there is, generally speaking, very little sense of responsibility for the main-tenance of the church's institutions, still less for its extension, and the major preoccupation of the church in most parts of Africa and Asia is how to keep its head above water.

Yet, when all is said, if the weakness of the churches were only structural there might be little cause for dismay. The discovery that there are not many wise, not many mighty, not many noble in the church should not come as a surprise. That is not where we find the contrast between the church we know and the church the New Testament promises. Our true humiliation lies elsewhere. Much talk about the church's lack of relevance is unperceptive, I believe, because it exaggerates her failure to involve Christians in political or social action. In those fields today the leadership of some churches, at least, is beginning to be associated with radicalism, and those churches are losing money because of the stand they take, which is no bad index. For a long time past people's attachment to a church has been akin to their recreational pursuits;[9] but, if it is still limited mainly to their leisure-time, it is at least becoming more like collecting for Oxfam than playing at the tennis club. No, I cannot press the charge of irrelevance too hard in those terms. What I fear is that the church is only changing in marginal ways, switching from passivity to activism, but still failing to connect with men either in their real extremity or in their real excitement. According to Monica Furlong:

> What has disappeared is the old sense of the creativity of religion, liberating, releasing, making men joyful, helping them to grow. Christianity appears as a tired religion, dog-eared around the edges, talking in tired language, shrinking from bold new thought and courageous new ideas.[10]

A good deal of the trouble is that we are trying to make do with a cheap relevance that costs us no more thought than reading the headlines – though, God knows, even that would be an improvement in some congregations! It is no credit to Christians to add their names to the national sign-in for world development or to protest with the rest about a cricket tour or a threat of genocide if, like so many of the rest, they forget all about it as soon as a fresh crisis captures the news. That is not letting the world write the agenda, but letting the mass media write it. Irrelevance and cheap relevance are equally caused by my failure to visualize what it will mean to respond to Jesus Christ in the real world in which I, with others, do a job, enjoy a home, think and interact. The disciples waiting in the upper room in Jerusalem had an uncomfortably clear idea of what it would mean if they started to live the life of Jesus in that city. But somewhere along the road the church stopped being so specific in its appeal to men. Colin Williams has asked:

Has it not become clear now that to call them to conversion, to call them to accept Christ as Saviour without helping them to see the nature of the changed life that is required by Christ as Lord, is in fact one of the grave dangers of the Church today? So, for example, for us to ask men to be disciples of Christ without enabling them to see how Christ is at work in the race revolution ... is to practise an evangelism that can be in fact false witness – a religious escape from Christ's demands.[11]

Monica Furlong makes exactly the same point in respect of the Christian's obligation to think, as well as act, to the limits of his capacity.

It costs a Christian more to read Hochhuth, to read Hannah Arendt, to read Beckett, Mailer, Pinter, to look at Guernica, and *then* to tot up the cost of behaving like Christ in contemporary society, than to make a 'decision' in an emotional whirl and a mental vacuum.[12]

So there are reasons enough for disillusionment. However much we may forgive ourselves, the church of our day does not look as if it is offering man in the power of the Holy Spirit a secret that even angels are on tiptoe to learn (I Peter 1.12).

Yet the Word of the Lord questions us, as it did Jonah: 'Doest thou well to be angry?' If we are disillusioned, had we any right to our illusions in the first place? Life in the Spirit is our foretaste of the new world, not its final fulfilment. His indwelling is the seal with which God stamps us with the mark of his ownership, to ensure that we shall be known as his when finally he enters into his own.[13] Our possession by the Spirit is also called by St Paul the pledge of our coming inheritance.[14] Both are metaphors of a guaranteed future and an unfulfilled present. So the gift of the Spirit, like the resurrection of Jesus, frees us from the past to live in that which is flowing to meet us.

This binds us, with all our sure and certain hope, into solidarity with the patient, painful birth-pangs of the whole creation. To that extent we enter into the Son of God's experience of constriction within the bondage of unredeemed humanity. We who are sons and heirs, wait for God to make us his sons (Rom. 8.16, 23). There are two ways of enduring that paradox. We have to set ourselves to become what we are. But we may also say that by being already what we are going to become, yet maintaining solidarity with the whole of mankind and the whole of creation, we are being in the world what Jesus was – the dough of the consecrated first sheaf which, when kneaded back into the lump, makes all the dough holy (Rom. 11.16). To be the very power of God yet to wait in frustration and hope until the whole be brought to fulfilment, might be called the *kenosis*, or self-emptying, of the Holy Spirit. For him it has been so from the beginning. If now we are caught up into his being, we must share his humiliation as well as his power. 'How long, O Lord, how long?' 'O, faithless and perverse generation! How long shall I be with you? How long must I endure you?'

So we live in the Spirit, suffering with the Spirit, in the long wait between Pentecost and the Parousia, the final arrival. T. S. Eliot felt that our own times in particular call for the posture of patience. For we have reached such a vacuity of meaning that we no longer know what we should hope for and any move will be in the wrong direction. But his well-known words contain the essence of the Christian's situation in every period.

> *I said to my soul, be still, and let the dark come upon you*
> *Which shall be the darkness of God . . .*
> *I said to my soul, be still, and wait without hope*
> *For hope would be hope for the wrong thing; wait without love*
> *For love would be love of the wrong thing; there is yet faith*
> *But the faith and the love and the hope are all in the waiting.*
> *Wait without thought, for you are not ready for thought:*
> *So the darkness shall be light, and the stillness the dancing.*[15]

If this is the attitude our true situation in the light of eternity calls for, then our impatience with the church may be only baying for the moon. We need the reminder that Geoffrey Ainger of the group ministry in Notting Hill gave in his small book, *Jesus our Contemporary*.

Just about the last place we expect our Revolutionary to come from today is the Church. Can anything good come from Nazareth? . . . The problem for the contemporaries of Jesus in Palestine was that he did in fact grow up in Nazareth. He did not suddenly appear among them 'from nowhere'. This is very much our problem too. One of the reasons for the tremendous interest of young people in Bonhoeffer's idea of religionless Christianity is precisely their disenchantment with the 'Nazareth' of the contemporary churches.[16]

The significance of Nazareth in the story the gospels tell, as Charles de Foucauld grasped, consists in the fact that it was the place of the hiddenness of Jesus. And the indwelling of Jesus in the church, or the Spirit-possessed nature of the church and its existence as a new creation, is also something which is hidden. It is, to use St Paul's phrase, a mystery, something given but also something which is 'not yet'. 'Here and now, dear friends, we are God's children; what we shall be has *not yet* been disclosed' (I John 3.2). 'In fact we do *not yet* see all things in subjection to man. But we see Jesus. . .' (Heb. 2.9 mg). 'I have *not yet* reached perfection, but I press on, hoping to take hold of that for which Christ once took hold of me' (Phil. 3.12). So long as we remain in time, non-omnipotence and non-fulfilment are the raw materials with which we have to build up even the church of God. This also is a fact we have to contain and forgive. In the hope and the mutual forgiveness of the fellowship, rather than in its achievement, Jesus can be seen. It is this that makes it possible to look at the church with realism but without despair.

But this does not answer the real problem. One can associate a community, possessed by the Spirit as Jesus was, with weakness, non-attainment and frustration, but not with betrayal or pre-pentecostal panic. We seem to be dealing with something that went wrong from the start, like the Franciscan movement once Brother Elias had seduced it into power. Of course a movement must be embodied in some organized form but, once Christians had begun to think of the church as a structure to be compared with and related to other structures in society, it became one of the very principalities and powers that the gospel was supposed to withstand. So began a long struggle for recognition, privilege and, ultimately, control. The time came when few Christians questioned either the virtual identification of the institutional church with the political order of society or Christendom's role as creator and preserver of European culture. Painfully, this historic institution has had to learn to relinquish more and more of its influence to newer structures of authority and communication, but it has gone on thinking of itself in relation to society in the same old terms. Despite its theology of secularization, the World Council of Churches, in its own *vis-à-vis* with governments and global organizations, perpetuates this concept of 'the church' as a distinct system among other systems. The Christian service of men in their need so quickly embodies itself in church-controlled service institutions, on which the churches come to rely for their status and which compete with similar institutions under other authority. Unable to lose its life in order to save it, the community of the New Man seems willy-nilly to have become very early in its history just one more of the establishments which are innately predisposed to crucify any new man.

Not only have we institutionalized Christ; we have also tried to legislate for the Holy Spirit. The authenticity of the Book of Acts is gloriously apparent in the inconsistency of the various incidents of the Spirit's intervention from the day of Pentecost onwards. Just consider the changeableness of his comings. Not long after that first great beginning the building where Peter and John and their friends were praying was rocked as they were filled with the Holy Spirit a *second* time (Acts 4.31). Shocking theology! He did not come to the Samaritan converts when they were baptized, but only after Peter and John had come from Jerusalem to confirm them like good Catholics (Acts 8.16, 17). Ananias, though not an apostle, laid his hands on Saul in Damascus and after that he was baptized; the purpose of his visit was that Saul might be filled with the Holy Spirit, but the narrative does not specify the precise moment when this happened (Acts 9.17-19). It is, however, quite certain that the Spirit came upon Cornelius and his relatives and friends before they had even asked for baptism, though it is not clear whether they were, to everyone's surprise, included in an outpouring on the whole company, believers and enquirers alike, or given the baptism in the Spirit by themselves – Luke simply says 'the Holy Spirit came upon all who were listening to the message'. At any rate Peter, as we have remarked earlier, assumed their repentant faith and their cleansing from sin and authorized their baptism then and there (Acts 10.44–48). In most other instances Luke mentions either baptism or the gift of the Spirit, but it is obvious that he is not describing the events in full.[17] But in the unusual case of those in Ephesus who had known only the baptism of John he is careful to specify both a fresh baptism and the laying on of hands, followed by the gift of the Spirit (Acts 19.5, 6). To complete this picture of irregularity, Luke makes a point of mentioning some form of speaking in tongues subsequent to the coming of the Spirit, on the day of Pentecost, in the household of Cornelius, and upon the group in Ephesus, but not on the other occasions. Furthermore, the apostles laid their hands on the seven to set them aside for their new ministry, and the congregation laid hands on Paul and Barnabas to commission them for their new work, but in neither case does Luke mention any special gift of the Spirit such as is mentioned in the First Epistle to Timothy. The Holy Spirit does not appear to have read the rubrics! He will not and cannot be bound.

Christians, on the other hand, put on a sorry display of special pleading and dishonest handling of the evidence in their efforts to harness his freedom to their particular family coach. One gasps at the unblinking effrontery of many ecclesiastical assertions. 'In ministering Confirmation the Church doth follow the example of the Apostles of Christ'[18] – not a word to suggest that it is a very open question indeed. 'It is evident unto all men diligently reading Holy Scripture and ancient Authors, that from the Apostles' time there have been these Orders of Ministers in Christ's Church: Bishops, Priests and Deacons'[19] – yet it does not require such exceptionally diligent reading to notice that in the New Testament 'bishop' and 'presbyter' are alternative names for the same officer. But the fantastications of individual scholars are even harder to credit. One finds Dom Gregory Dix contending that the laying on of hands at Samaria was an ordination of prophets,[20] and Darwell Stone, following Calvin himself, alleging that what the Samaritans received through Peter and John was not the Spirit himself but additional special gifts.[21] R. M. Riggs takes the pentecostal view, in defiance of verse 16, that Luke is here recording a *second* gift of the Spirit to the Samaritans,[22] and two others of that persuasion, by the familiar legerdemain of shifting the 'barely possible' through the 'might-be' and the 'probable' till it becomes the 'certain', come up with the conclusion that 'wherever Luke mentions the gift of the Spirit he also mentions the gift of tongues'.[23]

Such tortuous efforts to codify the Spirit in his freedom are not, unfortunately, the private aberrations of theologians. They reflect only too accurately the temper of all established religion, and that very passion for the law which crucified Christ for his noncon- formity. Of course the church must lay down its norms for doctrine and practice, but we should be as ready as the weather forecaster to admit that however reliable our calculations most of the time, we cannot command the wind. And when the Spirit disobeys our canons we should avoid the absurd sin of rigidity. I wish the church of Jesus Christ had had the humility and humour of the scientists to declare publicly that our laws, like theirs 'are not statements of what *must* happen, but of the relative chances of a variety of alternatives'.[24] Then long before now we might have seen Peter's heirs in Rome ceasing to call any Protestant Cornelius common or unclean, and an Anglican Jerusalem desiring to lay no further burden on the Gentile Church of South India. Orthodox and Baptists might have acknowledged that the Spirit in his freedom has more than one way of making a Christian, and Paul of Canterbury might have found a simpler way of ending his sharp contention with the Methodist Barnabas. It is rigidity that divides us, not truth, for truth would set us free. We shall come no nearer the mind of Christ by further talking for, in Bonhoeffer's phrase, 'we shall never know what we do not do'.

But our church is averse to doing. It refuses to choose. That is why the Spirit can do nothing with it. Six years ago Albert H. van den Heuvel wrote this tremendous impeachment of our post-war betrayals:

If somebody has sufficient courage to make a study of cynicism, he should buy the reports of all major ecumenical gatherings, read them, and see what the churches said together. Then he should go to the balcony of his house and look over his city at the churches that are standing there, from which steeples have risen to heaven since the Middle Ages, and see how nothing has happened to them. Lay training centres in Europe were largely domesticated. Built as places where Christians were trained for their lonely experiments of faith in the world, they became instruction houses for the churches' middle class. The house church experiments in many places stopped. Youth work experiments in many places stopped . . . The Bible study circles, which were so numerous in the first years after the war, dwindled because Bible study is difficult. No church in the whole world really practically applied the new partnership of the laity and the clergy . . . When we look back at the period since 1945, we see the renewal movement imprisoned in carefully defined and tentative experiments which were never allowed to become a strategy. . . When the world changed around us, the churches remained the same.[25]

How can we possibly say, then, that we are the community of the Holy Spirit, the Spirit of awareness and creation and judgment and freedom, the Spirit of love that throws its life away? Do we have to understand that the church that is promised in the New Testament is not going to be the new manhood all of the time, though the new manhood is in her, emerging only at those moments when she remembers that she is the forgiven and forgiving community? Within a short time after Pentecost the Jerusalem church was squabbling about property and the distribution of relief. And, not long after, more serious divisions broke the fellowship in the north of Palestine. Yet it was in that Jerusalem church that Saul of Tarsus heard Stephen praying 'Lord, do not hold this sin against them', and from that northern church Ananias was sent to welcome the persecutor into their trust. Between those two moments Christ became alive for Saul.

So perhaps we are meant to discern moments in the existence of the old manhood when the new manhood lives. The fire has been kindled on the earth but as yet it is only flickering, though every time it blazes up our confidence is renewed that the church is in Christ and Christ in her. If any man be in Christ, there is a new creation, but the disciple has to abide in Christ and the Spirit has to abide in him. Assurance we have as his Spirit bears witness with our spirit, but never complacency. For grace is neither cheap nor automatic, and life in the Spirit is reality, not make-believe or dogmatic fiction. The freedom of the children of God must include the freedom to grieve the Holy Spirit and lie to him, to resist and quench him.[26] The Creator Spirit will never diminish our responsibility, individual or corporate, not even to keep us in unity with Christ. There must be faith, someone's faith, every inch of the way.

Is that enough – flowers in the desert, but not yet the whole desert blossoming? Is a spasmodic salvation all that we may expect?

Cast in those terms the question uncovers the flaw in my expectations and the cause of my disappointment. Salvation is knowing that I am accepted because of Christ, not because I have grown perfect. The church will never be a selection of winners but only a company of those who accept one another as Christ has accepted them. So, very frequently, when Paul speaks of the Holy Spirit he speaks in the same breath of the 'flesh', the self-life, and of the unending conflict between them.[27] There is no promise that the conflict will grow less fierce, for selfwill 'cannot be refined and educated into holiness';[28] all it understands is defeat. Yet it must always live to fight another day, for without the raw drives of nature we should be un-men. The opposite of wilfulness is not weak-will but surrendered will. The rugged Luther understood this, and on one of these Pauline texts he commented: 'It may hence be also understood who are the true saints. They are not blocks and stones, as the Sophists and monks dream, who are moved by nothing whatever, or never feel the lust of the flesh.'[29]

So perhaps we are wrong to castigate ourselves as individual Christians, or corporately as the church, for our betrayals. After all, the church is not meant to be that part of the world which has become more righteous but that part of the world which knows how to confess its sin. 'It is a sign of the living presence of Christ', said Bonhoeffer, 'that there are men in whom the knowledge of the apostasy from Jesus Christ is kept awake not merely in the sense that this apostasy is observed in others but in the sense that these men themselves confess themselves guilty of this apostasy. . . By her confession of guilt the Church does not exempt men from their own confession of guilt, but she calls them in into the fellowship of the confession of guilt.'[30]

But no – even that sounds horribly like one more excuse. The occasional saint, the spasmodic Christ-likeness, the hiddenness of the redemption, the righteousness not of ourselves, the confessing and forgiving community – are these not all too morbid, too intro-verted and, basically, too unreal, to impress anyone, least of all ourselves? The simple sense of Nietzsche's challenge: 'His disciples will have to look more saved if I am to believe in their Saviour' fixes us on a pin from which no metaphysical wriggling can release us.

I know, at least, that it has fixed me. Long ago Jesus Christ laid his spell upon me. Incomparable and inescapable, my relationship with him is more real and more consistent than with any other being, and I could worship no one but him and the Father of whom he assures me. The Spirit has made me intensely aware of him and opened my eyes to a good deal else. But this has not, so far as I can see, made me any different from those who do not have this faith, nor overcome any of the human difficulties. Many of my friends would see nothing amiss in this but for me it is an aching disappointment. I know very well how other Christian friends would account for all this, each according to his ideology, but I do not find that any of the explanations fit the facts. This is not written as a confession; but I am tired of Christian evasions and I have found it very hard to match the New Testament account of the Christian life with my experience. What I have seen is that most really believing Christians are more scrupulous, patient and personally caring than others, both among their neighbours and in the church organizations, more unselfish too, perhaps, though that is much harder to weigh. Many are very dedicated people but fewer seem to be deeply joyful. We seem to have a far stronger sense of meaning and purpose in life, and those of us whose convictions are genuine meet death when it comes more peacefully than most. But, taken as a whole, we are no less timid and conventional than everyone else, no less tied-up over sex, though probably not so muddled; there is just as little real communication in a great many Christian homes, just as much greed, apathy and prejudice in our attitudes to society, and probably rather more intolerance and depression. What has become of the new manhood and the new age?

I am no longer persuaded by those who will say it has nothing to do with these subjective and private victories or defeats, that Christians were never meant to be distinguishable from the rest of mankind, and should now shrug off these self-centred distractions and simply serve others where their needs are most felt. No human need is purely sociological or political, and any deep concern for persons will soon uncover their clamant hunger for meaning, for personal liberation from the past, and for a healing of relationships. Any would-be 'helpers' who cannot say they know where *these* needs can be met, even though they say it 'as one beggar telling another where bread is to be found', are blind leaders of the blind. So, once again, do we look like those who are finding meaning, liberation and healing? And if not, how can we be the church?

What I want to say next is best expressed in words that I used seventeen years ago though then I did not understand them as I do now. 'We stand afraid, each of us isolated in his defeat, confronted by the demand of Christ and the crying need of a world without God, and in our moment of truth we whisper to ourselves: *The Word of God tells me I am this and I know I am not. It says the church is all that, and I know we are not.* But why does each of us only say these things to himself? The way forward is the way to someone else.'³¹ So ingrained is our fiction of the Christian success story that one finds it very hard to make such an abject admission to a brother man. Yet when two are at the end of their tether, and say so to each other, something much more than a bond of sympathy is created. Just such a moment occurs at the climax of Tolstoy's play, *The Power of Darkness*. Nikita, the splendid, swaggering, wenching labourer, who settled down with his master's wife after she had poisoned her sickly husband, has now seduced her backward, sixteen-year-old step-daughter and murdered the baby at birth to conceal the fact from the girl's absent fiancé. During the wedding party he comes out into the cottage yard, thinking to make away with himself, and stumbles over the drunken form of old Mitrich, the odd-job man who once served in the Guards. Kneeling face to face in the stinking straw they weep on one another's shoulders. 'I love you', cries the old soldier, 'but you're a fool! You think I'm a warrior? No, I'm not a warrior, I'm the very least of men, a poor lost orphan! Well, then, do you think I'm afraid of you? No fear, I'm afraid of no man! As I don't fear men, I'm easy.' To the cool spectator it is no more than the maudlin self-pity of two broken drunks. On the day of Pentecost also the cool spectators blamed the drink. But to the guilty Nikita it was the hour of vision and rebirth. 'You tell me not to fear men?', he asks, springing to his feet. 'Why fear such muck as they are?' answers Mitrich. 'You look at 'em in the bath house. All made of one paste!' A moment later, as Nikita begins his confession before the wedding guests, his old father cries out in an ecstasy, 'God! God . . . it is here!'³²

It is only a surmise, but I wonder whether something like that encounter did not happen on the day of Pentecost. The elation of the resurrection appearances was over. They were without direction. There was nothing to do but wait. A reaction into fear, doubt or guilt would be likely. Did Peter then turn to John, Andrew to Philip, to share the despair that was in them? That would have been a deeper confrontation than they had allowed to one another before, the truth of the one exposed to the truth of the other, I and Thou. And so he was there – the Spirit – where the 'one' and 'one' was more than 'two'. The Spirit of communion, the unity of the Spirit, possessed them in bonds of peace.

We have still not studied the 'and' (see p. 29). Even now we make the mistake of imagining that God can be one more name on the list of those present. But since he is never one more character alongside or beyond the other characters, one and one will not make three. God the Spirit can never be additional: he can only be addition itself — the addition sign between 1 + 1, the 'and' between Peter and John, the Go-Between. That 'and', like the silence in Anthony Bloom's story of the old lady at prayer, is not just a conjunction; it has density and richness; it is a presence. But we must not look directly at it; for as soon as it is objectified it becomes a fantasy god, an idol. Whatever has to be done now, Peter and John must do it together on their own, not looking over their shoulders for any third party – *etsi Deus non daretur*. This is the paradox of faith. It is in the real absence that we meet the real Presence. 'If I do not go away, the Advocate, the Go-Between, will not come.' '... alone, yet I am not alone.'

Whether in fact they were made one in the self-exposure of despair, as I have guessed, or in a greater ecstasy of wondering joy, does not greatly matter. I am not saying that the occasion for his coming must always be mutual confession, though in a world and a church that has so deeply betrayed that would be most natural. And I am certainly not saying that we can hasten the coming of the Spirit by any exercise or technique. All we are told to do is to wait. But what matters is that the Spirit should be allowed to give the profound openness and communion in which he is present.

On that Pentecost morning their sudden discovery of him in their togetherness came like a gale of wind and a rain of fire. They could see now that that was always the way of it. 'Where two or three are gathered together, I am there.' Had he not sent them out always in pairs, one and one? That was the pattern they stuck to in the coming years. Peter and John go up to the Beautiful Gate, and 'Look at us – at our one-and-one-ness' they say to the lame man. Paul and Barnabas, Paul and Silas, Barnabas and Mark, Titus and the unnamed brother – there was a regularity in the pattern that makes an apostle look odd, literally, if he goes it alone. Like a peal of bells the word *allelōn* – 'one another' – rings through the pages of the New Testament. 'Accept one another – *allelōn*.' 'Serve one another – *allelōn*.' 'Wash one another's feet', 'confess your sins one to another and pray one for another', 'forbearing one another and forgiving each other', 'teaching and admonishing one another', 'comfort one another and build each other up', 'bear one another's burdens', 'love one another as I have loved you'. Those who have the flow of mutuality in their relationship with each other need not be vocal or exuberant in expressing it. What is left unsaid between two reserved men may be a deeper communication than much flaunting of fellowship. But where two or three are given this togetherness in Christ's name, though they are far from perfect or complete as individuals, the New Man is known in their midst. There is still only one who can claim that title. The church is not the new mankind; it only provides the medium through which the one New Man, Jesus the Christ, is present. Peter is not, after all, 'a little Christ', nor John. But in Peter *and* John the new manhood and the new age is present and powerful – and hidden. There is no ground for boasting. The New Man is always 'not I, but Christ'.

Our English translations of the epistles conceal the all-important plurals 'Christ in you – all of you – the hope in glory'. 'Present your bodies (plural) a living sacrifice (singular)' – not a collection of living sacrifices, but one corporate offering of our bodies as a group. So also in I Corinthians 6.19, 20, Paul actually uses the phrase 'your (plural) body (singular)' – not 'your bodies', as though our togetherness makes one body which is the temple of the Holy Spirit. And this is precisely what he says in Ephesians 2.20–22. Of course it would be possible to exaggerate this, and we should not ignore the great individualist texts: Romans 7.7–25; Galatians 2.18–21; Philippians, 3.4–14. But, if we are honest with our actual experience of the new life in Christ, we surely have to admit that it is only while we remain in the love and truth of the two or three gathered together that we know as a fact the deadness to sin and aliveness to God which we are led to expect. That shared life does truly seem to be 'dead' – that is, totally unresponsive and non-conductive – as far as sin is concerned.

Not in our greater goodness, then, but in our openness to one another in Christ's name, the Spirit possesses us. This means that his presence is not confined in an exclusive circle. Wherever the two or three together in Christ's name open themselves to those who cannot yet name that name, the Spirit of God is in the 'and' between them also – in the 'and' between the two apostles and the lame man whose gaze is riveted upon them, in the 'and' between Peter and Cornelius, in the 'and' of every profound and loving dialogue. Klaus Klostermaier, who has described with such delicacy his experiences of deep communion with Hindu devotees, says: 'We rarely, if at all, spoke of God. Strangely, my friends whom I thus met also told me that, if we sat together silently, they often understood more than if we talked.'[33] When the truth of the one was exposed lovingly to the truth of the other the Spirit came upon them. But the Spirit does not give himself where our encounters are glib, masked exchanges of second-hand thoughts. Our defences must be down, broken either by intense joy or by despair. One way or the other we must have come to the end of ourselves. So this shameful humiliation of Christians, not only in our generation but at all times, is better far than their self-congratulation, for it is the pre-requisite of a renewal of the Holy Spirit. It is worth remembering that the root of the words humiliation and humility is humus. To be down in the straw and the dung and the refuse – Paul's words – is to become the soil in which the seed of Christ's manhood falls and dies and brings forth the harvest.

Here is the meeting of the four elements: we the earth, and the Spirit the wind, the water and the fire.

## NOTES

1. Dietrich Bonhoeffer, *Ethics*, SCM Press, 1971 ed., p. 64.

2. See also John 16.8–10.

3. See also James D. G. Dunn, *Baptism in the Holy Spirit*, SCM Press 1970, p. 53 *et passim*, to whom I am indebted for confirmation of many of my own convictions.

4. While agreeing in general with Dunn's thesis, I cannot limit the symbolism of water-baptism in the New Testament to being the expression of the believer's faith.

5. II Cor. 1.21, 22; I John 2.20, 27; Eph. 1.13; 4–30. See also G. W. H. Lampe, *The Seal of the Spirit*, Longmans Green 1951, pp. 4–7, 78–93.

6. Dunn, op. cit., p. 53.

7. Albert H. van den Heuvel, *The Humiliation of the Church*, SCM Press 1966, p. 50.

8. Monica Furlong, *With Love to the Church*, Hodder & Stoughton 1965, p. 24.

9. See William Pickering's article 'Religion – a Leisure-time Pursuit?' in *A Sociological Yearbook of Religion in Britain*, ed. David Martin, SCM Press 1968.

10. Furlong, op. cit., p. 10.

11. Colin Williams, *Faith in a Secular Age*, Collins 1966, pp. 116f.

12. Furlong, op. cit., p. 56.

13. II Cor. 1.22; Eph. 1.13; 4.30; Rev. 7.2, 3; 9.4 See also Lampe, op. cit., pp. 7–18.

14. Eph. 1.14; II Cor. 1.22; 5.5.

15. T. S. Eliot, *East Coker*, lines 112–14, 123–8, from *Four Quartets*, Faber & Faber and Harcourt Brace Jovanovich Inc 1944.

16. Geoffrey Ainger, *Jesus our Contemporary*, SCM Press 1967, p. 85.

17. In the case of the Ethiopian, Lydia, the Philippian gaoler and the Corinthian converts, baptism only is mentioned; in the case of the converts at Antioch, the Spirit only (Acts 8.38; 13.52; 16.15, 33; 18–8).

18. Preface to the Alternative Order of Confirmation of the Church of England, 1928.

19. Preface to the Ordinal of the Church of England, 1662. There are excellent reasons for a threefold ministry without such bland dogmatism.

20. Gregory Dix, *Confirmation or Laying on of Hands*, Theology Occasional Paper V, p. 18.

21. Darwell Stone, *Holy Baptism*, OUP 1899, p. 75.

22. R. M. Riggs, *The Spirit Himself*, 1949, p. 52.

23. Robert Banks and Geoffrey Moon, 'Speaking in Tongues', *The Churchman*, Vol. 8, No. 4, 1966, pp. 280ff.

24. See p. 28.

25. Van den Heuvel, op. cit., pp. 51f.

26. Eph. 4.30; Acts 5.3; 7.51; I Thess. 5.19.

27. Gal. 5.16ff; 6.8; Rom. 8.4—11.

28. H. C. G. Moule, *The Epistle to the Romans* (The Expositor's Bible), Hodder & Stoughton 1893, p. 214.

29. Martin Luther, *Commentary on the Galatians*, 5.17, trs. J. Owen, Seeley Burnside 1845, p. 486.

30. Bonhoeffer, *Ethics*, pp. 90, 95.

31. *Man in the Midst*, Highway Press 1955, p. 69.

32. Leo Tolstoy, *The Power of Darkness*, V.2, trs. L. & A. Maude, Constable 1914, p. 91.

33. Klaus Klostermaier, *Hindu and Christian in Vrindaban*, SCM Press 1969, p. 37.

*Part Two*

# STYLE OF LIFE

# 7

## GROWING

*The Evangelical Spirit and the Structures of Mission*

'The church exists by mission as fire exists by burning.' It is not by chance that Emil Brunner chose that great biblical metaphor of the Spirit and his mission. Jewish teachers had taken the burning bush to be a symbol of the ideal Israel on fire with God's purpose and action in the world, yet unconsumed. The true church also exists by being the inexhaustible fuel of the Holy Spirit's mission in the world, and though this is a change of metaphor from the last sentence of the previous chapter, it really says the same thing. While they burn together the branches and twigs *are* the fire, yet they do not in themselves constitute the fire. The fire, rather, contains them, living around them in the interstices, and if a twig drops to the ground the fire that seemed to be in it soon vanishes. Only in their togetherness can Christians remain alight with the fire of the Spirit. That is the sole purpose of our visible fellowship – to be the fuel upon which the fire is kindled in the earth. The church must be shaped to carry out that purpose or it will be as frustrating as a badly laid fire. The question we have continually to put to the organization and structure of the church is this: does it bring Christian face to face with Christian in that communion which is the sphere of the Holy Spirit's presence?

Our theology would improve if we thought more of the church being given to the Spirit than of the Spirit being given to the church. For if we phrase it in the second way, although it is the New Testament way, we are in danger of perpetuating the irreverence of picturing God's Spirit as a grant of superhuman power or guidance, like a fairy sword or magic mirror to equip us for our adventures. Unless all I have said so far is utterly mistaken, the promised power from on high is not of that kind at all. As I said in the last chapter, the primary effect of the pentecostal experience was to fuse the individuals of that company into a fellowship which in the same moment was caught up into the life of the risen Lord. In a new awareness of him and of one another they burst into praise, and the world came running for an explanation. In other words, the gift of the Holy Spirit in the fellowship of the church first enables Christians to *be*, and only as a consequence of that sends them to do and to speak. It is enormously important to get this straight. Being, doing and speaking cannot in practice be disentangled, but if we put our primary emphasis on preaching or on serving we erect a functional barrier between ourselves and our fellow humans, casting ourselves in a different role from the rest of men. Hence the professional jealousy of Christians, so often disconcerted when other humanitarians undertake the same service and other faiths propound the same truths.

The Holy Spirit is given to enable 'the two or three gathered together' to embody Jesus Christ in the world. And what was his role and his relationship to the world? He came to *be* true Man, the last Adam, living the life of the new age in the midst of the world's life. His deliverance of men from various kinds of bondage, his existence for others, the laying down of his life, were not a task which he undertook but a function of the life of the new Man, just as breathing or eating is a function of physical life. What made his preaching of the Kingdom distinct from John's was that he not only promised but lived the Kingdom life. That is why he said that the least of those in the Kingdom was greater than John. And Kingdom life is not primarily religious but human. His parables make it clear that life in the Kingdom is the normal life that is open to manhood where man is found in his true relation to God as son – the *abba*-relationship. So the thirty years of hidden toil at Nazareth were to him not a mere passing of the time but were the very life of Man he had come to live. There he learned to say 'My Father has never yet ceased his work and I am working too', and by virtue of his absolute, glad obedience-in-co-operation Jesus as Man was able to be the vehicle of God's existence for others, as all men were potentially made to be. 'If it is by the finger of God that I drive out the devils, then be sure that the Kingdom of God has already come upon you' (Luke 11.20).

But the 'you' upon whom the Kingdom has come are not people

in the church but people in the world. To say 'Jesus is Lord' pledges us to find the effects of his cross and resurrection in the world, not just in our inner lives, nor in the church.

As Bonhoeffer said:

> The space of the Church is not there in order to try to deprive the world of a piece of its territory, but precisely in order to prove to the world that it is still the world, the world which is loved by God and reconciled with Him. The Church has neither the wish nor the obligation to extend her space to cover the space of the world. She asks for no more space than she needs for the purpose of serving the world by bearing witness to Jesus Christ and to the reconciliation of the world with God through Him.[1]

The way in which Jesus both declared the Kingdom and lived in the freedom of the Kingdom provides the model of what the church is created to be. The church is not the Kingdom but, through the Spirit indwelling their fellowship, Christians live the Kingdom life as men of the world. Elsewhere Bonhoeffer pointed to the essential difference between the true church and 'a religious fellowship'.

> A 'religious fellowship' is concerned to put the religious above the profane, to divide life into the religious and the profane; it is concerned with an ordering of value and status. . . The Church, as a part of the world and of mankind created afresh by God's Spirit, demands total obedience to the Spirit which creates anew both the religious and the profane. . . The second creation of God by Christ in the Holy Spirit is as little a 'religious matter' as was the first creation.[2]

The mission of the church, therefore, is to live the ordinary life of men in that extraordinary *awareness* of the other and *self-sacrifice* for the other which the Spirit gives. Christian activity will be very largely the same as the world's activity – earning a living, bringing up a family, making friends, having fun, celebrating occasions, farming, manufacturing, trading, building cities, healing sickness, alleviating distress, mourning, studying, exploring, making music, and so on. Christians will try to do these things to the glory of God, which is to say that they will try to perceive what God is up to in each of these manifold activities and will seek to do it with him by bearing responsibility for the selves of other men.

Yet while this life in the Spirit is essentially human and worldly, it is kept alive by the 'one-anotherness' that is given between those who are open to the truth of each other in the name of Christ. Some enthusiasts for a secular Christianity today would dismiss even a minimal gathering together of Christians as a relapse to the sort of religious fellowship Bonhoeffer contrasted with the true church. But this seems to me an exaggeration of his position. In the last but one of his letters to Eberhard Bethge, with whom he had shared all his explorations into 'religionless Christianity', he said: 'It is certain that in all this we are in a fellowship that sustains us.'[3] The fellowship in Christ's name is necessary to sustain the *cantus firmus* beneath the flowing counterpoint of ordinary human life. The ideal shape of the church, therefore, is such as will provide this with the least possible withdrawal of Christians from life in the world. I shall return to this point a little later.

But beyond these two forms of responsibility which we might call natural response and fellowship response, Christians are also called to an evangelical response. By this I mean that Christians cannot avoid trying to make articulate the promise and invitation Jesus made articulate. They are caught up into the desire of the Spirit of God to make men profoundly aware of Jesus Christ, of what he is in himself and of what he makes available for the whole world, so that in him they may be confronted by the question and call of God, and make their free choice. This pointing to Christ can only be done by the Holy Spirit, but he may use both the words by which we tell of him and the style of life we live in him. The church makes Jesus visible by becoming, through the 'supply' of the Spirit of Jesus Christ, the obedient Son and the suffering Servant, as he was.

We have already seen that the most characteristic forms of the action of the Spirit as Creator Redeemer are a constant pressure towards greater personhood, the creation of new occasions for choice, and the principle of self-surrender in responsibility for others. These must be the marks of any evangelism which is truly Christ's evangelism.

It must be deeply personal rather than propositional. We have already seen that the truth which converts is the truth *of* Jesus, not the truth *about* Jesus. How strange it is that people who have met the Truth should imagine that they are called to propound truths! How unlike Jesus himself, who would never violate the freedom or responsibility even of his enemies, are those who would win the world with a loud-hailer in one hand and a book of church statistics in the other. Christ-like evangelism consists in the passionate serving of the personhood of men in protest against all the depersonalizing pressures of the world. It consists also in that quality of faith in people as people, which can on occasion bring them to what is truly repentance more radically than any disparagement. To point to the cross is to point to one for whom people mattered supremely and whose very presence in silent suffering brought a hard-bitten non-commissioned officer to look twice at what seemed commonplace and rise to a more truly human personal response.

Then, secondly, Christ's evangelism always creates the occasion for choice, and then leaves men in their freedom to choose as they will, with no other pressure than the appeal of the person of Christ. This is a development from the respect for personhood. More often than not it will not appear to be a religious choice at all. 'Choose ye this day whom ye will serve' is not a question which must always be formulated in terms of rival gods. The real direction that a soul takes towards heaven or hell is mainly determined by an infinite number of almost infinitesimal choices, any one of which may be of ultimate seriousness. Yet the issues for Christ or against him are usually decided in these quite secular terms, and it is in those moments that evangelism can be decisive. It was not a religious decision that the second murderer took when he dissociated himself from the general storm of abuse directed against the man on the middle cross and, instead, spoke up for him: 'We receive the due reward of our sins: this man has done nothing amiss.' It was a strong man's response to basic, human justice. But it meant that he had already chosen to be with Jesus. He had unwittingly ranged himself with God in his suffering in the world.

This is why, as I said in the last chapter, an appeal for faith in Christ needs to be 'earthed' in some context in which an actual step may have to be taken, or a stand made. The classic example of the soul-question *in vacuo* was the rich young man's 'Good Master, what must I do to win eternal life?' But as soon as he showed himself dissatisfied with the stereotyped *in vacuo* answer, Jesus brought him down to his own particular brass tacks: 'Sell everything you have and give to the poor.' In our appeal to men we shrink from making faith so specific, for fear, so we say, of preaching salvation by works of merit. But this was nothing of the sort. The economic answer was, for that particular man, the way to declare his absolute trust in Jesus as an alternative to trusting his investments: 'Come, follow me.' If he threw away his securities he would have to rely on the Jesus-group to look after him, and they were in no position to promise anything except a share-out of whatever came their way. It was an invitation to change the very foundation on which his life had been built for another one. But 'Come follow me' was also a pledge that if he would only start out in this unthought-of and impossible direction there was a way through; that if only he would begin living without his past a new future would be given; that if only he would 'die' he would be 'raised again', now, in this world. How can secular, normal man in any century understand the forgiveness, liberation and promise which Christ is offering him until he understands the specific challenge which Christ is throwing down to him? Yet it seems a long time since the church was as pointed as John the Baptist, Paul, Francis or Wesley when setting forth the way of salvation for property owners, security police, news-editors, shop stewards or the directors of investment trusts. Heaven forbid the church should moralize instead of bringing good news; but generalities are news for no one.

And, in the third place, an evangelism which is truly Christ's must involve self-emptying sacrifice for the other. This means not only stooping under the other's burden but recognizing it as a common burden. If we speak of reconciliation with God, or with men, it can only be as those who know how much they need this themselves. We invite men to join us in becoming what has been promised for us all. This is not to say that the Christian brings no conviction. He has been equipped by the Spirit and his theme is 'what we have heard and seen with our own eyes and felt with our own hands' (I John 1.1). But because he has not yet attained and sees darkly still, even more because he knows that the same Spirit who conjoins him and God conjoins also him and his neighbour and is the element in which they meet, person to person, he is not calling to the other across a gulf of discontinuity. He can trust that Christ will be discovered as he and another work out the questions together since he himself is always seeking that which he is proclaiming.

Dr Cicely Saunders, the founder and medical superintendent of the St Christopher's Hospice in South London, has told of a patient, a man close to death, to whom she had given a set of photographs of himself at a children's party. Against her protests he badly wanted to pay for them.

> 'I am not a beggar,' he said. 'I know you aren't,' she answered, 'but yet in a sense we all are. We haven't got anything of our own really.' 'We've got to learn to take,' he said. Then, opening his two hands beside hers on the bed cover, he added, 'That is really all it is – four hands together.'[4]

That is a symbol of all true evangelism, in which we minister salvation to each other. For every time Christ is made more real to someone else through my presence or my words, he is made more real to me. And whenever hands are stretched out in my company to receive the grace of the Lord Jesus, what a fool I am if my hands are not stretched out too!

Every preacher, it is said, has only one sermon, and that is as it should be, for in all true evangelism the church is talking to itself, if it did but know. In addressing men she says, as a matter of simple fact, 'We sinners', but with equal conviction, 'We children of God'. Geoffrey Ainger, in the book I have already quoted, refers to *L'Etranger*, the novel by Camus, in which a priest, trying to convince an unbeliever, pulls open a drawer, takes from it a silver crucifix, and brandishes it at him to reinforce his argument, Jesus, comments Ainger, did not call us to wave the cross; he called us to carry it.

Which brings me to consider seriously the view which is argued by many today, that to serve men and to strive for a more humane and just society is the whole mission of the church since this is the mission of God in history. In true revolutionary style, this service-theology is deliberately stated in such a way as to polarize Christian opinion, by setting up a parody of the ideas that are being attacked and by stating its own position as starkly as possible. So labels like 'pietism', 'proselytism', 'reformism', are used as offensive weapons, and unqualified generalizations are stated as axioms – 'the church's vocation is to servanthood and not to salvation', for example. It is not surprising that what, in most cases, is really being said has been misunderstood. Gibson Winter, for instance, argues that the 'healing' of persons in their inwardness, and in their family and neighbourhood, needs to be augmented and largely replaced by the servanthood of the laity in the metropolis – by which he occasionally seems to mean little more than planned urban development. But he sees that servanthood is a prophetic ministry, interpreting the human situation to men in the light of the gospel which 'discloses forgiveness as the foundation of the New Mankind'.[5] Hoekendijk attacks what he calls propaganda and church extension and limits evangelism to 'the establishment of *shalom*' – the social harmony and fulfilment that God has in mind for the world. But he calls to the scattered Christian minority to demonstrate the *shalom* in little, ecumenical groups, each a token of what the Kingdom will be, serving men by reforming the structure of a segment of society.[6] J. G. Davies appears to want to cut out individual conversions from among the aims of the church engaged in mission, though what he objects to is found to be those distortions of evangelism which almost every evangelist condemns. Yet Davies makes it quite clear that he is not advocating a 'service only' view of mission, and he endorses Bonhoeffer's claim that 'a life in genuine worldliness is possible only through the proclamation of Christ crucified; true worldly being is not possible or real . . . in any kind of autonomy of the secular sphere; it is possible and real only "in, with and under" the proclamation of Christ'.[7]

I find this emphasis and approach attractive both because it challenges our many self-preserving, church-exalting activities, and because I welcome resistance to what Hoekendijk has called 'this constant temptation to the church to speak when it should act'. But in some respects it is an oddly pre-Christian theology. Perceiving what God is doing in the movements of history and trying to do it with him; offering a prophetic interpretation of events; and nerving men for action through the power of a future which eschatological hope projects back into the present – all these can be derived from faith in the Creator Spirit who spake by the prophets and promised the Messiah. What seems to be missing is the good news that the promises *have been* fulfilled, the Messiah *has* come, died and risen, and the life of the new age *is already* accessible through the forgiveness of the past and the gift of the Spirit. This, as I understand it, is what Gibson Winter means by 'confessional proclamation' and I do not believe it can be superseded by what he calls 'prophetic proclamation'.[8] If a theology of hope means that we lose our assurance of the already-given-ness of the Kingdom, then it is defective.

But in any case the careful qualifications of writers like Winter, Davies, Hoekendijk, Gregor Smith, Margull and Colin Williams, have been ignored by the school of thought that simply identifies mission with service in the world. Precisely because the recovery of a proper understanding of the service element in mission has been so liberating for Christians in this century, it is important to get it into the proportion of the New Testament. If we hope to build a service-theology on the example of the apostolic church in the Roman world, or on the actual use of words like *diakonos* (servant), *doulos* (slave), *pais* (houseboy, like French *garçon*), *huperetes* (attendant), we shall be disappointed. These words are applied exclusively either to the service of God and his purposes – reconciliation, new covenant, word or testimony – or to the service of one another, especially the poor and sick, within the Christian fellowship.[9] Jesus himself is identified with the Suffering Servant of Isaiah's Servant Songs and, by the happy use of the word *pais* in the septuagint translation, this servanthood was already known to be the same as sonship.[10] We come nearest to the central concept of servant-theology in the great passage that speaks of Christ taking 'the nature of a slave', which seems to refer more to his relationship to the whole world than to his relationship to the Father.[11] And certainly we cannot limit to the Christian circle his own declaration: 'Even the Son of Man did not come to be served but to serve and to give up his life as a ransom for many' (Mark 10.45).

That reference suggests that Jesus' own existence for others involved far more than simple service: it was to be nothing less than an act of deliverance. This is clear also in the treatment of his healings and the feeding of the multitude: they are all seen as victorious rescues of the victims of demonic powers, and so they declare the arrival of the messianic age. His service of men, therefore, was always *kerugmatic*, part of the announcement. This is the link back to the prophets' promise of justice and deliverance from oppression, summed up in the Magnificat, and the link forward to that final judgment upon social indifference by Jesus' self-identification with its victims, prefigured in the parable of the sheep and the goats. On the evidence of the New Testament it is impossible to be 'for others' in the world except by seeing and responding to the human situation in terms of an all-round deliverance by a Messiah who has already come and 'bound the strong man'.[12] The context in which a Christian serves the world is Christ's victory over the power of evil.

Provided one sticks to those terms, it seems to me both legitimate and necessary to argue that in our own day, and probably at

all times, the 'powers' from which men need deliverance are embodied in many forms, including especially the massive economic,
political and cultural structures in which we find ourselves imprisoned. In one of four lectures which Professor C. F. D. Moule
gave on the subject of 'Biblical insights into human nature and
destiny', he described the despotic grip of these structures:

> We all know what it is like to find ourselves part of a vast, im-
> personal system which seems to move with the inexorable in-
> evitability of a machine to the brink of disaster. The economic
> and political network which drags peoples into war or persons
> into unemployment as if for nobody's fault in particular, is as
> if some demonic force beyond our control were moving people
> about the world like pawns in its evil games. . . It is the familiar
> climax of a nightmare when one must scream but has no
> voice.[13]

The same impulse that sends Christians into the healing ministries
or the relief of the poor must send them today into the human
struggle against the titans that Professor Moule describes. It is no
deviation for us to move into a more direct role in inducing social
change and the break-down of historic systems. But the Christian's
solidarity with mankind and his involvement in the human struggle
has to be *kerugmatic*; which means that he affirms that Jesus has
already defied and mastered the 'powers' with which we are contending, and has broken their *necessity* for us.

The New Manhood is here in our midst and will meet us at the
end of time; it will not be *more* here in the next chapter, nor in the
penultimate. It is laughable to identify it with the new metropolis
or any revolutionary utopia; yet the next chapter is specially our
concern, for in it also we must declare that Jesus is Lord. We are not
called to work for a new humanity. We work for a juster, more
humane order of society because we *are* the new humanity, inasmuch as the Go-Between Spirit makes us one with Christ.

If we could only hold on to that insight we might be less prone to
the crusader mentality which Bonhoeffer deplored in his *Ethics*,
where he wrote:

> One of the characteristic features of church life in the Anglo-
> Saxon countries , . . is the organized struggle of the Church
> against some particularly worldly evil, the 'campaign', or, taking
> up again the crusading idea of the Middle Ages, the 'crusade.'[14]

Bonhoeffer found all such campaigns self-defeating because they intensified the very evils they tried to combat. So he concluded that 'it is necessary to free oneself from the way of thinking which sets out from human problems and which asks for solutions on this basis'. The gospel compels us, of course, to do all we can to liberate people and society from what are called their 'problems'; but even more it demands that we liberate them from the very assumptions that underlie our use of the words 'problems' and 'solutions'.

I am disturbed by the influence of technology upon theology. We live in an age when it is assumed that everything that is bad or imperfect constitutes a 'problem' which may be mechanical or biological, psychological or sociological or spiritual. We may disagree as to what *kind* of problem confronts us at any time, but doctors, engineers, social workers, economists and clergy, all accept without question this idea that life is a confrontation with problems and that every problem has a solution if only we can find it. If a man or a movement does not solve the problem then there has been a failure. And in such a world the church seems to labour under an impossible demand to justify its existence by being the superstar of the problem-solvers, the answerer of the ultimate questions.

How have we got into this way of thinking? I believe that a number of different causes bring it about.

The first is a quite basic fact of man's psychology. The human infant's extreme helplessness makes it imperative for him to believe in his omnipotence. Every time this illusion of omnipotence is threatened by his mother's absence, trust and contentment give place to fear and rage. But the onset of fear can be held off for longer and longer periods provided he has what Winnicott calls 'good enough mothering'. That word 'enough' is crucial to the Christian view of man. Good enough mothering enables the infant to relinquish the illusion of omnipotence in favour of a 'good enough competence' of his own, in the form of reaching out, calling, moving towards, and so on. Unfortunately, if the mother fails to offer good enough mothering for any reason, or if at a later stage the family group fails to prove trustworthy enough to enable the child to explode his omnipotent fantasies, then the tendency to revert to them will persist even in the adult.

Then it is easy for him to focus all these feelings outside himself in the image of a 'problem', and to give rein to his infantile fantasy of omnipotence by convincing himself that there is a solution to this problem waiting to be discovered. Meanwhile discontent looks for a scapegoat: 'Why don't *they* do something?' is a constant question in this fantasy world.

The second characteristic of our nature which contributes to the fantasy is closely allied to the first. It is our childish inability to contain the contraries of our existence. Growing up towards maturity means learning to hold together the good and the bad feelings, the love and the hate, the frustration and the self-assertion, the creation and the destruction, in one's self and in other people. All of us fail to do this at certain times and to a greater or lesser degree, and then we try to reconstruct our world in the old, over-simple black and white. 'If only . . .' we say, and stake all our en-thusiasm on a single panacea that either disappoints or does more damage than it repairs. Which, of course, is what the problem-solver thrives on!

We would do better to look for the kind of help that fortifies us to come to terms with the realities of good and bad, love and hate, in ourselves and our world, and to live triumphantly *with* and *through* those evils that may by grace and skill be alleviated but will not be eliminated 'till he comes'.

A third cause of our problem-mindedness is, I believe, the devel-opment during the last 400 years of what we vaguely call 'the scientific approach'. Basically, this consists of isolating the pheno-menon that has to be studied – a series of earth tremors, for ex-ample, or a diseased tissue, or a section of a city – analysing all the data, then finding and testing an interpretation of the data in order to obtain control and impose one's will.

The pursuit of this kind of control demands a total objectification or, putting it the other way, the observer must achieve a complete detachment from the object he is studying. Hence the ideal of the so-called 'objective consciousness' which can think of a chicken as an egg-laying machine or of a monkey as an experiment or of a man as a naked monkey.

Now it is perfectly true that when the surgeon is actually bent over my inert body I do not want his concentration distracted by any feelings of dislike or admiration. But if, on approaching my bed a few days after, he refers to me as 'the gall-bladder', I feel alienated. I am glad to be his object, his problem, on the operating-table – but I am not simply 'a problem' or 'an object' once I come round. But this is the price we pay for the technological approach. Man advances his power over nature, including his own nature, by defining the data as a problem, isolating them, and then seeking a solution. In truth, reality cannot be chopped up in this way, the facts cannot be 'isolated'. Yet in the interests of a technique the facts are distorted and squeezed into the predetermined shape of the problem as the expert poses it. Only those questions that are capable of reduction to a computer code can be answered, so any other questions are ruled out of court and presumed to be not real questions at all! The devastation of our environment is one result of the ruthlessness of technology; the devastation of the realm of ideas may be just as serious.

Of course I welcome the discovery of a new grain of wheat or rice that will double the yield of grain in a land of starvation. Of course I rejoice over the new drugs that may eliminate leprosy, tuberculosis and every other scourge, ancient or modern. Of course I look hopefully to the new insights of economic and social planning to free us from the old determinism of want and waste, over-crowding and over-cropping.

But what I am pleading for is that we be guided by realities rather than fantasies, by the kind of realities that confront me almost every time I read a batch of letters or study the weeklies.

For example, a school system designed to produce for new African nations the vital elite of technical and administrative leaders who can replace expatriates cannot at the same time be the right system to equip the mass of rural workers with the modern skills, the mental attitudes and the strong cultural continuity which they need for happiness and fulfilment in the only life that is open to them. That is a situation that offers wide opportunities for experiment. But insist on seeing it as a problem to be solved and you condemn yourself to frustration.

Or consider the dilemma of the social worker in India who sees quite clearly that by raising the expectation of life of the child population and of the elderly he is certainly condemning a greater number of people to death by starvation. That, surely, is enough to confound those who express their concern for human happiness in terms of problems to be solved once and for all.

Already, since the welfare state was accepted as the answer to many social evils, our older generation has become used to a much more regimented world. It is our children who rebel, not knowing the problems from which we found deliverance but detesting the solutions by which we did so.

Problem-mindedness seduces us into putting too much faith in the expert. But one's own competence is preferable to an enslavement to the expert even though it may be good enough only to alleviate the difficulty without solving it. Young nations as well as young persons prefer to live with their problems of poverty, inefficiency, weakness and corruption so long as they can keep their independence and resist patronage. And there is no patronage so bad as that of the expert.

The strongest objection to the problem-solving attitude to man and his world is that man needs problems more than he needs solutions. This is because he is a being with immortal longings and an indelible ideal and he suffers his greatest harm whenever, for a while, success sends him out believing that his ideal has been reached and his longing satisfied. The Bible pictures man stretched in unending tension between his idealism and the intractable problems of existence, or – using biblical words – between the image of God and the fallenness of nature and sinfulness of man.

Job never found an answer to the problem of unmerited suffering. The problem remained insoluble, but in it he met God. That is where man always meets God. That is where man most frequently meets his fellows. For he is so constituted that he needs problems more than solutions. His soul thrives on questions but grows sickly on answers – especially answers served up by others and, most of all, answers laid down by authority. That is what caused the young American protest-leader priest, Daniel Berrigan, to write these words from prison:

> Lover, child, in the immense dignity
> of birth or death refuse an answer
> There is no answer
> The genius of the gospel is in the name of man
> to refuse an answer.[15]

Does not this suggest something more modest for the church's role? Once again let me make my position clear. I do not say the church should set its face against those who organize themselves to solve the problems of society, but it should not compete with them. For it has a different task. In its corporate aspect as a gathering of Christians or as one of the organized structures in society, the church is not called to solve human problems, but to make people more sensitive to the reality of other people. It is not the political speeches of public figures in the church nor the scoldings of the social gospel that send Christians into the fight, but the quickening of compassion and the kindling of awareness by the Spirit of Jesus through the scriptures, worship and fellowship of the church.

But I have just spoken of the church as 'one of the organized structures in society', and maybe that is the source of our frustration and shame. Certainly that is the concept of the church which journalists have in mind when they ask 'What is the church doing about it? or 'How will the church react?' And that is the concept most Christians endorse when they try to justify the church by replying 'It is not doing too badly.'

But I want to suggest that if the Christian contribution is not being given in the arena of race conflict or housing or Third World development, we may blame Christians for not doing it, we may blame 'the church' for not teaching them to do it, but we should not blame 'the church' for not doing it. We are talking about a denomination or coalition of denominations, with its systems of authority and management and its top decision-makers and spokesmen. This, it seems to me, is not a bad way of organizing Christians in order to get certain things done, but as a theological entity it does not exist. The New Testament uses the word 'church' with a number of meanings, but this is not one of them. When we speak of the church as an institution among the other institutions we turn it into one of the power structures, one of the principalities and powers, in fact; and it is from these that the gospel would set us free. The church can no more be an organized structure over against other structures than God can be an entity over against other entities. Perhaps this is what lies behind the divine disapproval of King David's attempt to count the people of God: their strength, indeed their very existence, was not of a kind to compare with other nations. What matters is not what the church does as the church but what Christians do as human beings.

When Bonhoeffer said 'the Church is nothing but a section of humanity in which Christ has really taken form,'[16] he would have been more accurate to speak of 'nothing but the innumerable little sections of humanity. . .' For the church is essentially scattered, like seed in the earth, salt in the stew, yeast in the dough. The Christian's milieu is the world because that is the milieu of the Holy

Spirit. Yet the units of the scattered church are not Christian individuals, but twos and threes gathered together to provide the 'one-another-ness' in which the Holy Spirit possesses them. And even in such tiny cells the corporateness is not an end in itself, but God's means of thrusting out into the life-stream of the world those who are 'in Christ in Ephesus'. I said earlier that the ideal shape of the church is such as will provide this 'one-another-ness' with the least possible withdrawal of Christians from their corporateness with their fellow men in the world. That means that the essential unit in which the church exists must be small enough to enable all its members to find one another in mutual awareness, yet large enough for them to be an embodiment of the life of the Kingdom, which is a life of restored human-ness in action. That does not suggest anything very large. 'I doubt', says Professor Moule in the lecture I have already quoted, 'whether, when once "human" size is passed it makes much odds whether it is passed by ten or by a billion.' So much has been said in the last twenty years about Christian cells and house-churches, yet their establishment as the normal unit of Christian community is still so patchy and experimental that it is easy to despair. The marvel is that the 'little congregations' are already coming to be regarded as normative in so many places. The process is bound to go on as the mobility and fragmentation of human societies increases.

We must expect the 'little congregations' to take different forms and fulfil different functions precisely because they are meant to match the different circles and circumstances in which human life and need presents itself. Some will be cross-section groups comprising Christians from all walks of life in a small neighbourhood. Others will be more homogenous, consisting entirely of students, housewives, workers in one factory, or members of one profession. Others again may represent no common sphere of life but consist of friends who have covenanted to come together from many places, several times a year and, in the interim, to hold to one another through the invisible bonds of fellowship and some simple rule. Often a group will just happen through the accidental convergence of Christians, never to be repeated. All will be to some extent ephemeral, as the membership of a group changes, or its function is no longer needed, and this is a strength rather than a weakness since it matches the kaleidoscopic quality of human life.

These small units of Christian presence are emphatically not a half-way house through which the uncommitted will eventually be drawn back into our parish churches. Nor are they an interim structure which ought to grow into new parish churches in due course. In some instances this may be a right development; but all too often it happens for the wrong reasons. It happens because too many people in the church insist upon regarding any other form than the conventional parish congregation as sub-normal and peripheral. They will not believe that such groups may have the fulness of Christ and should be allowed to possess all the resources and all the responsibilities of a local church.

I believe that the parish structure will continue to minister to certain of the various areas of life – family, education, youth, perhaps, in so far as these can be served in neighbourly care. Furthermore, the parish church may have an important function as a cathedral gathering-place of the varied smaller units lest they become in-grown. But it is the 'little congregations' which must become normative if the church is to respond to the Spirit's movements in the life of the world.

To treat these smaller units of Christian presence as being truly the local church in all its fulness and responsibility means that we should expect their activities to include as completely as possible four different aspects of Christian life and witness, namely reflection, service, worship and evangelism.

The first of these group activities is better described as reflection than discussion. Christians ought everywhere to be reflecting together on the meaning of what is happening in the world around them, confident that they will be guided by the Holy Spirit to see what God is doing in their situation, and to understand their calling and responsibility as his people in the world. I believe that far too much Christian discussion, especially where it is led by those of us who are clergy, is pitched at too theoretical a level so that, from the start, those taking part are talking about ideas rather than about facts as they know them. This applies particularly to group Bible study. If we want the Bible to be the living word of God we must read it always with reference to those situations for which we are responsible in our contemporary life. We must not pass like Alice through a scriptural looking-glass either into the historical geography of the Holy Land, or into a realm of theological concepts. The living word always speaks to our own condition in our own world.

Unless the discussions and studies of a group, and its enjoyment of Christian fellowship, are related to its active responsibility towards the situation or sphere of interest which its members have in common, it is likely to become either intellectually dilettante, as do many student groups, or spiritually pietistic, like many revival fellowships. In either case the life of such a group grows introverted, self-indulgent and uncommitted. The only way out is to insist that every Christian group or cell should look for some way in which it can meet a genuine human need in the situation in which it is placed. If, as I have suggested, all group-study and reflection should swing between the two poles of the Bible and the immediate environment or sphere of responsibility, it is bound to point to a particular line of action which the group is being called to take up in service to the world. Failure to go into action at that point is the first step to sterility.

If the aim of all this gathering of the 'two or three' is to enable members to live in that current of mutual awareness and communion which is the gift of the Holy Spirit and the element in which he moves in our midst, then a simple sharing of the loaf and the cup should be the natural summing up of the group experience. In many of the 'little congregations' today this has become a regular and essential element. Someone brings bread and wine to a coffee table, all stand round while one or another reads the scriptures and offers the prayers, and then the authorized celebrant, wearing his ordinary clothes, leads them in the great thanksgiving and the consecration prayer; plate and cup are passed from hand to hand and the denominational question seems irrelevant in such a context. This is what must come – not twenty years hence, but now – as the normal way in which the majority of Christians make the Holy Communion central to their lives. This, I would guess, is what the cottage prayer-meetings, so much a part of the tradition of the Church of South India, need now if they are to have continuing value and greater completeness. This is what I would like to see as the proper culmination of the weekly house-meetings of those tiny groups of Christians in the more remote villages of Iran, the glow of whose simple love, once tasted, can never be forgotten. We must, surely, press forward with those changes in our concept of the ordained celebrant that are necessary to make this possible.

The old denominational barriers are being widely ignored in the small group-celebrations, and this openness is increasingly endorsed *post facto* by the churches' authorities. More and more the necessity of the celebrant being an ordained minister is being questioned, and this is not irresponsible carelessness, for those who ask the question with greatest seriousness are deeply averse to any clandestine disobedience. But something is on the move in the life of the church which may not be held back much longer by technicalities. We need a new look at the meaning of orders and authorization, and in the meantime there is a place for what Hoekendijk has called 'a loyal opposition'.[17]

If the small local units are the true growing edge of the church they must never be 'for Christians only'. They are the points of dialogue with the world. They are the places in which we should expect to find the unbeliever entering into the argument over a Bible passage, the communist comrade sharing the battle for decent low-rent housing, the Hindu or Muslim friend joining in the prayer or even partaking, if only he will, of the loaf and the cup. This does not mean an uncommitted group, but a Christian group in which the uncommitted are made to feel at home. For the ground of all our evangelism is the fact that the Holy Spirit, the Go-Between, not only stands between one believer and another, but between the Christian and every other being with whom he is given the communion of a mutual awareness. If it were not so the border of the church would be an abyss, whereas we know it is a place of meeting where new life is generated.

Of course there are dangers of fragmentation if the church allows itself to be structured in this way. But that is the old problem of the one and the many, the tension between the local and the universal, the contemporary and the timeless, the indigenous idiosyncrasies and the great constants. That tension must not be resolved by denying the autonomy of the small group, for as Victor de Waal has put it 'the local church is not a *part* of the church, but *is* the church in that particular place'.[18] The dangers can be overcome by allowing full scope to the mobility and the openness of the Christian fellowship. Through the apostolate of a continual interchange of persons the separate groups are linked and mutually responsible, and being open to the life of the world they find in their mission their meeting place with one another. It was a Marxist philosopher in Czechoslovakia who recognized and gave the best expression of this principle that I know. Speaking of the apparent conflict between Christ's two words: 'You are the light of the world' and 'Go not to the Gentiles but to the gone-astray sheep of the house of Israel', he said:

> There is a deep creative tension in the hardest task which is always a task in the situation which I know, where people know me and where anything new and any really responsible activity is perhaps hardest, because there it cannot be abstract. There is a deep tension but also a profound relation between this insight and the world-wide relevancy of Christ's message for the whole cosmos, for the whole of mankind, without any exception, without any narrowing.[19]

## NOTES

1. Dietrich Bonhoeffer, *Ethics*, SCM Press, 1971 ed., p. 174.

2. Dietrich Bonhoeffer, *The Way to Freedom*, Letters, Lectures and Notes, 1935–1939, Collins 1966, pp. 47–8.

3. Dietrich Bonhoeffer, *Letters and Papers from Prison*, The Enlarged Edition, SCM Press 1971, p. 391.

4. Recounted in *CMS News-letter* No. 360, May 1972.

5. Gibson Winter, *The New Creation as Metropolis*, Macmillan, NY 1963, p. 81.

6. J. C. Hoekendijk, *The Church Inside Out*, SCM Press 1967, pp. 23–9.

7. J. G. Davies, *Worship and Mission*, SCM Press 1966, ch. 3, quoting Bonhoeffer, *Ethics*, p. 263.

8. Winter, op. cit., pp. 77ff.

9. Acts 6.4, 20.24; Rom. 1.1; I Cor. 4.1; II Cor. 3.6, 5.18; Eph. 6.6; I Tim 1.12 and again Acts 12.25; I Cor. 12.28, 16.15; II Cor. 4.5; Gal. 5.13.

10. Acts 3.13, 26; 4.27, 30.

11. Phil. 2.7. This is the only time the word 'slave' is used of Christ.

12. Matt. 12.28, 29.

13. C. F. D. Moule, the Purdy Lectures (unpublished), delivered at Hartford Seminary Foundation, 1970.

14. Bonhoeffer, *Ethics*, p. 320.

15. Daniel Berrigan, section 11 lines 1–4 of his Foreword to *Quotations from Chairman Jesus*, compiled by David Kirk, Templegate Publishers, Illinois 1969.

16. Bonhoeffer, *Ethics*, p. 64.

17. Hoekendijk, op. cit., p. 92.

18. Victor de Waal, *What is the Church?* SCM Press 1969, p. 76.

19. Dr Julius Tomin, 'A Czech Atheist Considers the Gospel', *Frontier*, Vol. 12, No. 1, February 1969.

# 8

## EXPLORING

*The Freedom of the Spirit and the Search for a New Ethic*

In the life and growth of every young church, it seems, there is one perennial disappointment which more than any other grieves and bewilders both the missionary and the student of church history. Before the first generation of converts has passed away gospel is turned into law. The first fine careless rapture of a new discovery deteriorates into a sorry story of rules of conduct, backsliding, and church discipline. And in the eyes of the non-Christian neighbours the church comes to be known not as a community with a new quality of life but a sect with a lot of unreasonable prohibitions. The appearance of spiritual regression is, of course, exaggerated by the over-optimistic view which almost always prevails in the first generation church. The converts to a new faith are under the overwhelming impact of a very few great simplicities. They have discovered, for example, that God is personal and accessible, or the name of Christ means simply that they are accepted into fellowship in a way they have never known elsewhere, or the person of Jesus himself has won their devoted though largely uncomprehending allegiance. They would rather die than deny or throw away these new-found realities. Their very single-mindedness gives a strong cohesion to their little company. Of Christian teaching they know almost nothing. When it is given they actually hear a reiteration of the simplicities they have already known. I have told elsewhere of the early mission in Buganda where every missionary concentrated his preaching on the atoning death of Christ and the power of the Holy Spirit to purify and ennoble the quality of the Christians; and yet after fourteen years of this when the same preaching was given some of the leading Christians exclaimed

'Why have you been here so long and never told us this glad news before?' The second generation hears far more of the gospel, and understands even more of its implications and demands. At the same time the relation between the Christian community and the wider society becomes more problematical. It was comparatively easy for the first generation to make the great break; and in many parts of the world it was made easier still by the creation of separate Christian villages or townships into which the convert might cross over. But the second generation has to find a workable relationship between the new village and the old. What does the convert do about the funeral ceremonies when his father dies? How does his wife behave when she goes back there to trade? What does he teach his children about their relatives and the obligations they owe them? What does he say when a young man from the old village comes wooing his daughter?

We can see the same process at work in the first Christian community at Corinth. It was all very well for Paul to determine to know nothing amongst them save Christ and him crucified. In the light of that gospel it was fine to wave aside the scribe and the disputer of this world, and basically this must always be the Christian emphasis, most of all in the realm of ethics. But this did not prevent the Corinthian convert from getting into a muddle over the meat in the butcher's shop which might or might not have been offered to the pagan gods. It did not offer obvious guidance to the widow who wanted to marry again or to the two Christians who tried to settle their dispute at law. The gospel itself was a sufficient reason for the Christians to gather on the Lord's day to offer their thanks, but was not a sufficient guide as to how they should behave when they get there. As long as they had a Paul to write to them, they could resolve each of these difficulties by reference to the new life in the Spirit which was theirs. But the spate of new problems did not diminish, and when they no longer had access to a religious genius or worse still, if their sense of immediate communion with Jesus Christ grew less vivid, what other recourse did their leaders have but to set down specific rules and guide-lines to deal with as many contingencies as they could foresee.

In a fascinating series of lectures,[1] Professor Greenslade has analysed the inevitable build-up of the structures of legalism in the early centuries of church history and compared their problems with those of the so-called younger churches of the present day.

Discrimination and an element of legalism, he argues, appear of necessity at the point of entry into the Christian church even before they become necessary in the fellowship of the believers. Has there been repentance, and if so, what are the signs of it? Is there genuine faith and if so, in what form of words is it to be expressed? From these basic questions, it is only a short step to a more detailed enquiry. Is the man a slave? Then he must understand that baptism does not absolve him from his obligations to his master. Is he married? Then the couple must accept the Christian view of marriage from the start. A man with a concubine must give her up or marry her legally, while a slave-girl can be accepted without changing her status, provided she is faithful to her master and has brought up her children well. The enquirer who is a temple priest or astrologer or brothel-keeper or prostitute or gladiator must give up such a profession before being admitted to the church. The ordinary soldier may continue in his provided he refuses to kill; the schoolmaster, if he stops paying the usual homage to the god Hermes; but the highly placed government official is so inextricably bound to offer oblations to the gods and organize gladiatorial shows that he can only be accepted if he will resign the post. It is easy to see how relevant are many of these tests to the situation in which the church finds itself today in a polygamous society or amid a flourishing non-Christian religion. When I attended a mass baptism in a village of South India, the final catechizing of the candidates concentrated mainly upon such questions as: 'What will you do when next the village celebrates a festival?' 'Where will you look for a husband for your daughter?'

If a considerable list of requirements confronted the person who sought entry into the church, this is nothing compared with the system of ecclesiastical discipline which held the church member in the strait and narrow way from the moment he entered the Christian community. To some of the first Christians, says Professor Greenslade, grave sin was an inconceivable paradox. The writer of the Epistle to the Hebrews and Peter in his Second Epistle both suggest that there can be no second repentance if a convert has really fallen away (Heb. 6.4–6; 10.26–31; II Peter 2.20, 28). Hermas, the Christian prophet who wrote the treatise called *The Shepherd* around A D 100, agreed that after the repentance which accompanies baptism no further act of repentance is possible. Ignatius wrote that 'the spiritual man cannot do what is fleshly', and Origen knew people who taught that 'a man believes, he does not sin; if he sins, that proves he does not believe'.

The church as a whole did not follow this extreme severity and absolute and final excommunication was at first limited to such grave sins as idolatry, adultery, murder and apostasy; and by the fourth century even those who were guilty of these offences might be restored at the moment of death. Christians who had committed other serious sins were required to make public confession, after which they entered the order of penitents and offered works of satisfaction for a defined period before being publicly restored to communion. This exacting penitential system was in force until recent years in the mission areas of the Universities Mission to Central Africa, but it had to come to an end when urbanization brought African and European congregations into close proximity and it was no longer possible to impose on the former a system to which the latter could not be expected to submit.

By the sixth century the pastoral needs of the individual Christian had begun to outweigh consideration for the church's purity. Private confession, penance and absolution, already the rule in the monasteries, began to replace public discipline in both the eastern and western churches. Degrees of seriousness as between one offence and another were carefully catalogued. The circumstances of an offence as well as the offence itself were examined with more discrimination. Undoubtedly the church's insight into human motives and states of mind grew deeper through long experience of counselling, and even the deviousness of casuistry arose originally out of a genuinely pastoral concern. Yet, when all is said, this careful weighing of sins and measuring of merit was a far cry from the gospel of grace and the Spirit of liberty. The wheel had come full circle and the church had decided, in effect, that her Lord was wrong after all, and the legalism against which he rebelled was right.

For this, you will remember, was the essence of Judaism. The Torah had been given, it was said, as the greatest revelation of God himself. It was sweeter than honey to the obedient spirit. It spoke not of bondage but of liberation. It offered the gracious counsels of God concerning the true *shalom* or well-being of his beloved people. But his choice of them to be his people must be proved by the evident contrast between their way of living and that of all other nations.

The purity was all important. So the Torah as the divine prescription for moral and social health had to be applied to the totally different circumstances of each new generation. How could they be sure they were keeping it correctly? How could the regulations of a pastoral life be fitted to town dwellers? The meticulous application of the law to contemporary life – the prohibition against mixing meat and milk products, for example – is, after all, simply an expression of that search for relevance which is such a preoccupation of us Christians today. So the traditions, the commentaries, the careful anticipation of every contingency, became as necessary to the obedient Jew as the Torah itself. Even today he feels that the diatribes of Jesus Christ against the traditions of the elders were not, like those of the old prophets, recalling men to the original spirit of the Torah, but were an outright attack upon the heart of Judaism itself.

Islam is wrestling with precisely the same problems in its ceaseless longing for a true theocracy. Kenneth Cragg has this to say:

> Law, then, as the secret of *Falāh* (true welfare) comes in revelation from God. But it still requires definition in the manifold of human activity . . . The Qur'ān, as the first and ruling source of law, is the definitive court of appeal as to the meaning of the good. But Tradition interpreted and enlarged the meanings of the Qur'ān and so became the second element in the structure of Muslim ideology.

But the passionate search for relevance in Islam could not stop short at tradition, any more than in Judaism it could be content with the Targums and the Midrashim. Islamic law needed to be expounded and applied through two other types of directive, the Qiyās and the Ijmā'.

This, then, is the structure of Islam – the Qur'ān, Tradition, *Qiyās*, and *Ijmā'*, shaping the Holy Law that makes the conduct and measures the responsibilities of true Islam. That law was totalitarian in the sense that it pervaded all life and had authority over all realms. Admittedly there were many areas of behaviour where it was indifferent and left many options, not reprehending or commending possible lines of action. It did not seek to be inquisitorial or burdensome. It recognised the natural desires and frailties of men. In some realms it spoke absolutely; in others permissively. But nothing was exempt from it that it saw fit to include.[2]

Is there, therefore, something inherent in human nature or in the nature of religion itself, which impels us towards legalism even when our starting point is a liberation from the law? Must we at least accept as a historical necessity the fact that the road to ultimate freedom of the spirit has to pass through the dreary valleys of legalism?

Walter Freytag often insisted that the legalism of the second generation church was a necessary prelude to the revival of the third generation church. There is an important truth in this. For legalism of a certain kind is a symptom of a more mature conscience. It expresses a new awareness of moral demands and a more penetrating recognition of sin. It may even be necessary for a Christian community to experience the bankruptcy of ethical self-effort and striving before it can re-discover the springs of unmerited grace, just as John Wesley had to come to the end of the moralism of the Holy Club before his heart could be 'strangely warmed' with the assurance of forgiveness. To this extent the missionary who is disenchanted by the rigidity and censoriousness of the church in which he is serving may take hope from a sense of history.

But all too often legalism is a symptom not of growth but of the stultification of growth. It arises not from a quickening of a people's conscience but from the imposition upon them of someone else's conscience. Legalism is bound to appear wherever there is a wide difference between the morality which is preached in the pulpit and the morality which is felt in the community.

If the elders of a Christian congregation in an African village say, as I have heard them say in conversation in their huts, that to call a man a liar does not cause any offence, and that Mama So-and-so, who brews for the communal beer drinks and partakes freely herself, is the best example of good living in the village, then to continue to proclaim in the little church 'we know the laws – don't drink beer, don't tell lies' is not only puzzling to the hearers but positively prevents the growth of any genuine conscience with regard to drunkenness or lying. It also turns attention away from the sins which the community is genuinely aware of but cannot break free from – bitter feuds between families, ruthless exclusion of strangers, both leading to the practice, or at least the dread, of witchcraft. I am suggesting not merely that the Sunday diatribe should be aimed at a different target, but that the pulpit is not the place from which the law can be laid down. Decisions of conscience are best born out of freedom, the freedom that Christ himself brings to minds that are still running along the old lines. For spiritual growth does not come from hearing and submitting to an extraneous regulation, but from following the accepted pattern of behaviour until a disconcerted conscience begins to doubt whether it is really right, that is the moment of truth. Where Christians are still thinking in the traditional ways, they may, of course, grow less and less distinctively Christian, but at least the option is open for an authentic spiritual stride forward. This is more likely to happen if the church trusts the Holy Spirit rather than an imposed discipline. For the Christian ethic emerges at the point where non-Christian lines of thinking are brought up against Christ. This is the true pattern of a church's growth in responsibility: it is at the point of deviation from convention that decision is made.

How refreshing it was, therefore, and how typical of a first-generation church, when I wandered round a small village in northern Nigeria one morning and came upon the Christians with whom I had shared the eucharist the night before, now mixed up with their animistic neighbours in all the daily chores of their community. A girl who had knelt near me the previous evening was helping her mother to brew a great vat of beer. 'Would the headquarters church approve of this?' I asked the young African evangelist. 'Be quiet!' he begged me. 'It hasn't even occurred to them that anyone might disapprove. If the Holy Spirit disapproves, I want them to be able to hear his voice for themselves. But don't put the idea into their heads.' Long ago Mabel Shaw taught us the same lesson from Mbereshi. It cannot have been easy for her year after year to see Christian girls on the threshold of maturity leaving that Christian community to spend some weeks in the traditional initiation school, and returning with their awakening souls darkened and traumatized. Yet she had the wisdom to know that to interfere would be to stand between those young people and Christ and that to impose her own veto might have inhibited them from ever hearing the inner voice which eventually spoke to them and brought them, of their own volition, to defy custom.

The church's strict attention to behaviour was always meant to demonstrate the contrast between the new life in the Holy Spirit and the old, unredeemed life of the world; the irony is that it ended by turning Christianity into one more religious system that was essentially the same in its approach as any of the others.

For there is only one thing which makes the life of the Christian community unique, and it is the same thing as made the life of Jesus Christ unique, namely the perfect freedom and reality of his responses to God and to men. In all his sinless obedience one never gets the impression that he is guided by a moral code. He lived in the world like a prince in his Father's house – 'therefore the sons are free'. Moving in perfect unison with the Spirit of God he has the incalculable quality of the *ruach*. 'The wind blows where it wills; you hear the sound of it, but you do not know where it comes from, or where it is going. So with everyone who is born from Spirit.' Not the conventions of men, nor the necessity imposed by the past, nor the remote control of the principalities and powers, can hold him. And he, on his part, never makes out that he is the victim of circumstances; he is always freely responsible. 'Did ye never read what David did, when he had need? The Son of Man is Lord even of the Sabbath.' 'They sought again to take him: and he went off out of their hands.' 'I told you that I am he: if therefore ye seek me, let these go their way.'

Jesus' whole life was a spontaneous response to the challenge and call of God as it came to him out of every unforeseeable, concrete moment. In every new situation he makes the I and Thou response of a son to his Father. A passage which I have already quoted from Dietrich Bonhoeffer's *Ethics* continues in a beautiful description of the contrast between Jesus' way of obedience and that of the devout Pharisee.

> Jesus often seems not to understand at all what men are asking Him. He seems to be answering quite a different question from that which has been put to Him. He seems to be missing the point of the question, not answering the question but addressing Himself directly to the questioner. He speaks with a complete freedom which is not bound by the law of logical alternatives. In this freedom Jesus leaves all laws beneath Him; and to the Pharisees this freedom necessarily appears as the negation of all order, all piety and all belief.[3]

This is where the true contrast between the church and the world ought to be found. Their thoughts run on different wave-lengths, just as Jesus and the Pharisees spoke to each other on different wave-lengths. It is this spontaneous obedience of the Spirit-possessed life which Jesus wishes to impart to the fellowship of the church.

'I call you servants no longer; a servant does not know what his master is about. I have called you friends, because I have disclosed to you everything that I heard from my Father.' 'Christ set us free, to be free men. Stand firm, then, and refuse to be tied to the yoke of slavery again.' 'Where the Spirit of the Lord is, there is liberty.' 'In Christ Jesus the life-giving law of the Spirit has set you free from the law of sin and death.' 'The man who looks closely into the perfect law, the law that makes us free, and who lives in its company, does not forget what he hears, but acts upon it.' 'Live as free men; not however as though your freedom were there to provide a screen for wrongdoing, but as slaves in God's service.'

Wherever the Christian community is found, whether it be marked by heroic holiness or human sinfulness, it must maintain *this* difference from the way of the world around it or it might as well cease to exist. And let no one be so gullible as to believe that the secularized world is emancipated from the old idea of the law. Moralism and self-justification are as much the bane of our contemporary western value-system as they have ever been in earlier, more sacralized, cultures. A decision-maker in the world of commerce today has only to act as though 'growth' were not the unquestioned aim of every transaction to find himself suspect and isolated. Our magazine articles would have us believe that we live in a thoroughly free-thinking society as far as personal sexual behaviour is concerned; but the evening papers show the ruthlessness of the hue and cry that is raised when a public figure is found to have a mistress, while in 'permissive' circles a boy who prefers not to sleep with the girls that attract him can be brought to the verge of breakdown by the pressure to fall into line. Salvation by observance and conformity is the invariable doctrine of human society, and the counter-culture is no exception. The church itself is never more worldly than when its appeal for humanitarian or political action is based on moralism or guilt.

Furthermore, if we see that life in the Spirit means defiant freedom from the legalism of the world in the realm of personal ethics, we must, if we are to be consistent, insist on the same defiant freedom from the determinism of the world in the realm of corporate ethics. We have already seen how Jesus defied necessity all

along the line: we cannot claim to be possessed by the Spirit as he
was if, for our part, we accept sociological necessity as having the
last word. To say that the individual is so much a captive of the
structures of society that the only way of salvation is by destroying
the old structures and building new is a counsel of despair; for who
is there to bring about the change if all are really being determined
by the structures? The system in that case will stamp its mark even
upon the revolution which seeks to overthrow it. Structures can
only be changed by those who are already freed to stand back from
them and inwardly transcend them. Even sociological change,
therefore, must be activated by personal revolt and response. The
responsible freedom which the Spirit lays upon those who are alive
in Christ makes them agents of liberation through their disobedience
to sociological necessity. They will not fit the theory. They will be
saved in order to save. According to Jürgen Moltmann,

> Only where they appear in society as a group which is not wholly
> adaptable and in the case of which the modern integration of
> everything with everything else fails to succeed, do they enter into
> a conflict-laden, but fruitful partnership with this society. Only
> where their resistance shows them to be a group that is incapable
> of being assimilated or of 'making the grade', can they commu-
> nicate their own hope to this society.[4]

This is where some of the advocates of a new morality are so
wide of the mark. They commend what have come to be called
'situation ethics' on the grounds that these coincide with the
pragmatic secularized attitudes of our day. Harvey Cox, for
example, made much of the assertion that rules of conduct are no
more than relative valuations arising from a particular history.[5]
True enough, though I cannot believe ours is the first generation to
have suspected this. Anyone who supposes that situation ethics
come more naturally to modern men is not only blind to the peculiar
legalism of secularized thought but misses the main point of true
situation ethics, which is that *all* rules, whether outmoded or contemporary, rigorist or mild, are equally set aside in favour of what
Bonhoeffer called 'responsible action in faith and in exclusive
allegiance to God'.[6]

The church which is truly for others must learn to live in the
freedom and truth of the Spirit in order to be the sign of that
newness of life which the Lord has opened up for all men. So the

distinctiveness of those who are set free does not consist in their facing different problems from their fellow men, nor does it mean that some actions are bad, or good, for Christians which are less bad, or good, for an 'ordinary' man. The difference lies only in the motivation. It is important we should get this right. I am always dismayed by Christian moralists who resolve a thorny problem by saying all too blandly that some demands are laid upon Christians, in marriage, for example, or in situations of conflict, which cannot, or need not, be applied to people outside the church. The Kingdom and the way of its peace are for all men. Yet those who live by the freedom and truth of Jesus will be as feared and hated today as in any period of history.

This is the context in which the church must press towards the mark of the high calling of God, that is to say, in which it must believe in its calling to be a new mankind in the midst of the old. This does not primarily mean a higher moral or ethical standard, though we may expect to find the harvest of love, joy, peace – yes, and also goodness and self-control, those less modish fruits of the Spirit. Being the new mankind means living towards one another without rules in the same gloriously responsible freedom and truth as we see in Jesus himself. However often the church seems to make a mess of it, as various congregations in the New Testament obviously did, and however risky and open to misunderstanding such a way of life may be in a missionary situation, the Christian community must persevere in this freedom of the Spirit, learning through its mistakes and drawing endlessly upon the forgiveness of God.

Christians everywhere, therefore, and not only in the western nations, are called to help one another to learn the real meaning of situation ethics properly understood. A classic statement of that true meaning is found in Bonhoeffer's great, though uncompleted, *Ethics*.

> The will of God is not a system of rules which is established from the outset; it is something new and different in each different situation in life, and for this reason a man must ever anew examine what the will of God may be.[7]

This is what Martin Buber means when he says that 'situation upon situation is enabled and empowered by the personal speech of God to demand of the human person that he take his stand and

make his decision'.[8] Another definition which is very like that
was offered by Walter Eichrodt in his interpretation of the Old
Testament concept of divine will as an unconditional demand, laid
upon every man not merely by the situation in itself but by his
personal encounter with God *in* the situation, a demand to which
he must make his individual response moment by moment.

> Time becomes the unrecurring reality which is given by God and
> which . . . inexorably calls for a decision here and now and
> permits no rest in some secure position which is valid once for all.[9]

Joseph Fletcher, who has been one of the best-known exponents
of situation ethics in the past fifteen years, sees that all truly
Christian behaviour must be pragmatic.

> The situation ethic, unlike some other kinds, is an ethic of
> *decision* – of *making* decisions rather than 'looking them up' in
> a manual of prefab rules. . . It does not ask *what* is good but *how*
> to do good to *whom*; not what *is* love but how to *do* the most
> loving thing possible in the situation.[10]

While admitting that principles and general rules are necessary
as 'illuminators' he refuses to accept them as 'directors'.

I have found that many totally committed and experienced
Christians accept this because they know that in fact this is how
they have always obeyed God and made their decisions since they
reached maturity. They still feel, however, that it is irresponsible
and unrealistic to expect children and young adults to find their
way without rules or at least, 'directors'. When a sixteen-year-old
and her boy friend at a party are caught unexpectedly by the
longing and the opportunity to go to bed together, it is cruelly
absurd to suggest that they can start calculating whether that would
or would not be 'the most loving thing possible in the situation'.
When a Bantu schoolboy in South Africa meets a recruiting officer
from the freedom fighters in Mozambique, he certainly knows no
manual of prefab rules: has he anything else but the pressure of
other people's emotions and conventions?

The problem focusses on the question of formation. The decisions
of a mature man or woman may be spontaneous and *ad hoc*, yet
they reflect the person that he or she has become, as well as the
demands of the particular situation. This 'becoming' is never an
entirely intrinsic development; it is never free from outside influ-

ences; it is to a considerable extent formed by example and education. It *may* be better (though it may also be a pretentious blackmail) to say to a child, 'We say sorry to each other after losing our tempers', and to do that in practice, than to command: 'Go and tell Mary you're sorry!' What in fact we never can do is to leave the child to work it out for himself; directly or indirectly, he is being formed into a person with a particular style. Conventional ethics takes it for granted that a person's character is best formed by inculcating rules and prohibitions. The real problem of situation ethics is not that we substitute *ad hoc* responses for a system of regulations but that we lack a sound method of formation that will enable a developing person – and are we not developing all through life? – to find a moral identity that is both consistent and free. In the example I gave in Chapter 3, of the married man and the unmarried girl, the corruption of their relationship grew from his failure to hold on to the truth of what he was and of what she was within the whole truth of their particular situation. It is even more important to be able to say, in defiance of every convention or every new trend, 'No, that would not be me', or 'Yes, that is my true response', than to say 'This is what the situation calls for.' The new kind of formation, therefore, must have in view not a rule of life but a style of life, an authentic personhood which is consistent because it is under God, and free because it is under the forgiveness of God. To know deeply the truth of oneself – both what one is and what one might be – and to be true to that self without turning it into an idol or a tyrant, because one lets the love of God wash over one's own good and bad, this is a morality of freedom which is in keeping with the gospel.

The gospel, however, is not about forgiveness only, but also about enabling. And this is needed because being true to oneself is so extraordinarily difficult. 'The good which I want to do I fail to do.' Situation ethics call for no less willpower than the conventional kind, and that is where we are so pitifully weak. The boy and the girl at the party may both say 'This is not me', yet find themselves in bed together in spite of it. It is at this point that the Holy Spirit may enable a break-through – not, as has so often been taught, by a gift of superhuman moral power but by a gift of awareness, as is always his way. He opens one's eyes to see the situation differently, as one which is demanding a 'Yes' instead of a 'No'. It is almost always easier, because it comes more naturally, to say 'Yes' to life than to say 'No' to an illusion of life. It will not be easy for our boy and girl to go home to their separate beds, but they are more likely to manage it if instead of striving to say 'No' they try saying 'Yes', first to their thankfulness for the joy of life, and then to the integrity and value and truth of one another.

I have earlier drawn attention to Jesus' unique use of the word 'Yes, Amen'. With him it is always 'Yes'. Possessed by the Spirit of life he saw every eventuality in its positive aspect. He met every temptation by saying 'Yes' to a more vivid alternative. In the wilderness his 'No' to the devil's three false salvations was in fact a resounding 'Yes' to the true salvation. 'Yes' to man's wholeness – 'not bread alone'; 'Yes' to man's freedom – no mind-blowing arrival from the skies; 'Yes' to man's sonship towards God – 'him only shalt thou serve'. Even the agony in the garden was less a 'No' to his own will than a triumphant 'Yes' to the cup his Father had given him to drink. 'Abba' and 'Amen' were the characteristic words of the second Adam. The first Adam, by contrast, thought he was saying 'Yes' to selfhood, and found he had in fact said 'No'. He had been deceived concerning both the situation and the true nature of God. The Holy Spirit, on the other hand, opens our eyes to the truth of the situation and the truth of the God who is within and beyond it. When that happens it becomes possible to dispense with the book of rules.

Bonhoeffer, in fact, says much the same thing.

> Principles are only tools in God's hand, soon to be thrown away as unserviceable. To look in freedom at God and at reality, which rests solely upon him, this is to combine simplicity with wisdom.[11]

Unfortunately not every advocate of situation ethics in our time has seen as honestly or as deeply as Bonhoeffer. A shoddy counterfeit of this great biblical concept is being hawked around in a good deal of shallow writing and preaching. It is no new thing that the freedom of the Spirit should be misrepresented as licence or confusion. But because the recovery of the true principle of liberty is so vitally important for the church all over the world, I believe we should try to identify most carefully the elements of falsehood in the fake.

1. In the first place, the counterfeit situation ethic is far more concerned with the justification of a man's action than with its forgiveness. The false reasoning is advanced that if an act can be shown to be justifiable in unusual circumstances then it cannot be

called intrinsically bad. A great deal is made of problem cases. There is the youth, inhibited by dread of impotence, who through the sexual welcome of an understanding woman, becomes capable of making satisfactory and mature relationships with girls. There is the mother, left behind in a communist state, who can join her husband and children in 'the free world' only if she first agrees to sleep with the local head of police. There is the doctor in charge of a child who is physically and mentally smashed beyond repair, yet can be kept indefinitely 'alive' in a respirator. These are actual and painful cases, which underline the inadequacy of 'prefab rules'. Yet the use to which such stories are put reminds one unpleasantly of the Saducees' yarn about the woman taken as wife by seven brothers in succession. All such discussion gives the nasty impression that the self-justification of an individual in a tight spot matters more than the recognition of any inalienable good and evil. Every ethical question then tends to be posed in the form: 'What is justifiable?' or 'What is permissible?' But these questions and the shallow moralism that underlies them draw attention to what we do, never to what we are. Those who ask them seem oblivious of the truth that being evil is so much worse than doing evil, or that, as Bonhoeffer puts it, 'a falling away is of infinitely greater weight than a falling down'.[12] The failure to recognize this is the source of all the legalism against which Jesus protested.

From rightly insisting that truly human response to each situation cannot be prescribed by invariable principles or rules of conduct, it is a false logic to proceed to repudiate the idea of any absolute good and evil. Again and again the only choice open to us lies between two evils. We may be justified in choosing the lesser of two evils and calling it 'right in the circumstances'; we are never justified in calling the lesser evil good. Murder is different from manslaughter, and justifiable homicide from so-called 'judicial killing'. But it is invariably an evil thing to end another human life before its time; it is invariably an evil thing to have to resort to violence even to achieve justice; and it is, surely, infinitely more important that mankind should remain conscious of the truth of that evil than that some unfortunate person should be allowed to believe that the killing he committed when circumstances justified it, 'didn't matter'. 'A bad conscience', says Bonhoeffer, 'may be healthier and stronger than a conscience which is deceived.'[13]

That is the reason why we need to retain the distinction between 'right' and 'wrong' which are relative to the circumstances, and 'good' and 'evil' which are absolute, and this in spite of the fact that the Christian should have learned to look beyond good and evil to God himself. To look beyond something is not the same as dispensing with it. The road to freedom lies through forgiveness and there is no short cut.

Guilt, shame and conscience are the three facets of a single consciousness towards good and evil. Guilt is what we feel towards God or towards life, and consists mainly of a sense of offence. Shame is what we feel towards other people and towards a corporate group, and consists mainly of a sense of lacking something. This is the most potent of the three in our competitive civilization. A psychiatrist has told of the many pathetic people in our mental hospitals who are far more worried about their IQ than by the question whether they are sane or mad. The third of the triad, conscience, is concerned with man's relation to himself, and is anxious mainly about self-justification. To anaesthetize guilt, shame and conscience by denying the absolutes of good and evil is to cancel the gift of awareness by which the Spirit of God brings us to freedom.

> Shame is overcome only in the enduring of an act of final shaming, namely, the becoming manifest of knowledge before God . . . Shame is overcome only in the shaming through the forgiveness of sin, that is to say, through the restoration of fellowship with God and men. This is accomplished in confession before God and before other men.[14]

2. The denial of the absolutes leads to a habit of rationalizing human conduct which in the end blunts our sensitivity and reduces personhood. John D. Davies has pointed out how, in the story of Adam's fall, as soon as man begins treating God's authority as relative he has to start disowning his other relationships as well.

> Previously, there has been reference to 'wife' and 'husband'. But these words do not apply now. Adam finds himself unable to say 'It's all my wife's fault'. He is trying to undo the relationship. He refers to her as 'the woman whom you gave me', not as 'this wife of mine'. The elder son in Jesus' parable does the same; he cannot bring himself to call his junior 'this brother of mine'; he refers to him as 'this son of yours'; and by so doing he disowns his relationship not only with his brother but also with his father.[15]

We see this denial of relationship very terribly in technological man's abuse of the animal kingdom. In face of the problem of food supply for our vastly expanding population it may be necessary to rear birds and beasts by the new intensive methods, until more humane and radical solutions have been found. But if the necessity of the practice means that we do these things without a qualm of unease, which is what a shallow situation ethic would encourage, then something precious is dropping away from our hard-won humanity. In his famous essay, 'The Politics of Experience', the psychiatrist R. D. Laing has written:

> If an animal is debased to a manufactured piece of produce, a sort of biochemical complex – so that its flesh and organs are simply material that has certain texture in the mouth (soft, tender, tough), a taste, perhaps a smell, then to describe the animal positively in those terms is to debase oneself by debasing being itself.[19]

The scientific objectivity, so-called, of our responses is all too often only another name for our alienation from the reality of things. In one way Adam and the elder brother were right: they saw the other person in his or her own self-hood in relation to God and not merely in relation to themselves. Has not the Jew who oblates the blood of the beast he slaughters, or the aborigine who begs pardon of the tree he is about to fell, a more civilized reverence for life and a more honest perception of what he is doing than the pragmatist who sees only so many yards of timber or pounds of beef? One faces the truth *of* the ox or the oak, the other only knows the truth *about* them. However many times a doctor must accept the necessity to kill a human foetus, I believe he will remain a more complete man, and so a more trustworthy doctor, if he continues to feel, every time it happens, that he has something to confess. We know guilt repressed can cause great havoc and so we have come to regard guilt itself as a condition to be avoided at all costs. But would it not be safer to learn what to do with the guilt which is inherent in life itself than to go deeper into this insanity of alienation which could one day rationalize the annihilation of our race? For that is what lies at the end of the road of 'objectivity' – the elimination, perhaps, of all that makes man human in order to secure the survival of the species. Already one of the most distinguished behaviourists is advocating such a course with equanimity.

What is being abolished is autonomous man – the inner man, the homunculus, the possessing demon, the man defended by the literature of freedom and dignity. His abolition has long been overdue. . . Science does not dehumanize man, it de-homunculizes him, and it must do so if it is to prevent the abolition of the human species. To man *qua* man we readily say good riddance. Only by dispossessing him can we turn to the real cause of human behaviour. Only then can we turn from the inferred to the observed, from the inaccessible to the manipulable.[17]

3. The third characteristic of the fake situation-ethic is that it has no regard for the irony and tragedy in human existence. The setting of tragedy is always some great inexorable – the gods, fate, a moral universe, ultimate meaninglessness, according to man's view; the subject of tragedy is always the helplessness and transcendent greatness of man. In contrast to this, the setting of a pseudo-situation ethic is never wider than a particular circumstance, and the subject is the self-satisfied creature of the day. St Paul's cry: 'When I want to do the right, only the wrong is within my reach', is brushed aside with the facile suggestion that in any concrete situation a man needs only to be guided by genuine love to act rightly and with a clear conscience.

'The meaning of all genuine tragedies', says Bonhoeffer, 'is not that one man is right and the other wrong, but that both incur guilt towards life itself.'[18] It is not simply that man frequently has nothing but a choice between two evils; the event so often shows that what he chose was the worse of the two, either because life seems to play that kind of trick or because he deceived himself. This tragic helplessness falsifies communal choices as well as personal ones, as we have seen in Rhodesia, South Africa, Ulster, Vietnam and every other arena of national tragedy. M. F. Thelen believes that 'man always deceives himself into believing that evil is good before he is able to choose it. This self-deception is partly unconscious as Freud and Marx discerned but it is also partly deliberate as is proved by the fact that in his regret or remorse after the deed man confesses that he was not fully deceived.'[19]

Yet what is most strange is the alchemy whereby the tragic account of man, in affirming his helplessness and absurdity, affirms his grandeur and transcendence more surely than any song of praise. The moment of truth when a man sees that, in the clash of the great

opposites, inadequate and perplexed he has been his own execu-
tioner, raises him to greatness and restores his human-ness. Hamlet
does not go down whining that in the concrete situation he had
acted for the best out of concern for others nor does Oedipus protest that he had the courage to choose. Had they done so their stories
would not have been worth the telling. But, like gladiators, their last
act of defiance was to give the sign that acknowledged defeat and in
so doing they ratified not only the mighty absolutes of good and
evil but the immortal worth of man himself. As their tragedy
achieves its end 'we feel that we are greater than we know'.

> It is a central paradox of the tragic experience that this contem-
> plative awe, built out of the elegiac mood, can be the final solvent
> of all anxiety. Like the Church's great hymn, the *Dies Irae*, it
> works by alternations of hope and dread, yet the swan-elegy ends
> with a sense of exaltation, conquest, a blend of pride and
> humility, a sense of the vastness of the forces of the universe, of
> man's helplessness and intrinsic splendour. . . The great tragic
> endings are, in the last analysis, the supreme assertions of a unity,
> a resolution of conflict, that can be terminated in no other way.[20]

That sense of a resolution is real even in those tragedies in which
existence remains pitiless, blind or vacuous to the end. Perhaps it is
because the archetypal sacrifice has been re-enacted, for it is not for
nothing that the performance of a tragedy grew out of the ritual of
an offering to Dionysus. Oedipus prepares himself for death like a
sacrificial victim:

> *Then sitting down undid his squalid dress,*
> *and calling for his daughters bade them fetch*
> *water to wash with from a spring*
> *and some to pour in ritual for the dead.*[21]

Cleopatra makes herself ready with the same ceremonial:

> *Give me my robe, put on my crown; I have*
> *Immortal longings in me.*[22]

And Lear states it straight:

> *Upon such sacrifices, my Cordelia,*
> *The gods themselves throw incense.*[23]

It is Lear who also introduces the theme of reconciliation beyond the tragic expiation.

> *When thou dost ask me blessing, I'll kneel down*
> *And ask of thee forgiveness.*[24]

In that benediction of the 'very foolish, fond old man', are we not back at the nadir-point with Nikita and the old soldier Mitrich on their knees in the filthy straw? Their brokenness becomes the opening of a new kind of coda which Shakespeare attempted in his last plays – an image of resurrection in *The Winter's Tale* and, in *The Tempest*, a new creation called into being by forgiveness.

> *How many goodly creatures are there here!*
> *How beauteous mankind is! O brave new world*
> *That has such people in't.*[25]

The happy ending of tragi-comedy does not work well as an art form because it fits too easily into our wishful fancies. None but the greatest writers can handle it at a deep enough level, the level that lies beyond tragedy. Yet Shakespeare's attempt is at least a pointer towards the 'beyondness' of true Christian freedom. Responsible living is to be found neither in legalism nor in this facile 'play-it-as-it-comes' we have been examining. The freedom of the Spirit by which Jesus lived is not achieved by shrugging off guilt, shame and conscience, but by going beyond them into the realm of forgiveness. It is not achieved by pragmatic objectivity, but by going beyond the truth *about* things to the truth *of* things. It is not achieved by repudiating good and evil, but by going beyond them to the Father. It is worth looking at each of these three in turn.

*Freedom is grounded in forgiveness.* As a recapitulation of what has been said already in Chapter 6, let me speak in the language of personal testimony. The whole doctrine of justification by faith hinges, for me, upon my painfully reluctant realization that my Father is not going to be any more pleased with me when I am good than he is now when I am bad. He accepts me and delights in me as I am. It is ridiculous of him, but that is how it is between us. In consequence I want to show my love for him fully and continuously, and I can do that best by insisting on my freedom to push into his presence, grubby and outrageous, without having first to wash my hands and comb my hair. Once we have grasped this overwhelming reversal of all religious protocol, that God loves us for ourselves as we are and has accepted us because of Jesus and not because we have become good, two things are bound to follow. First, we begin to trust the warmth and spontaneity of love and to welcome the gift of love in all the varied forms and experiences in which it comes to us, with none of the cautious definitions and reservations that reflect our fear of love's demands, temptations and responsibilities. Discipline, certainly, is needed to keep our loving straight, but not fear; for discipline is an expression of deeper love, it is a going-further, but fear is a drawing back. And the second change that God's acceptance of us brings about is to turn us into basically *accepting* people – accepting others just as they are, which does not mean flabby acquiescence or lack of ambition for their spiritual fulness; accepting life as it comes without querulousness; accepting the pain which must inevitably invade anyone who is really open to joy and beauty. This is an attitude of great vulnerability. Such a Christian will be fooled and hurt again and again and will also be sorely tempted and will fall and make big mistakes. But the sanctity which the Holy Spirit promises does not, I believe, come by playing for safety but by letting love for the Lord and love for people demand everything we have.

'Just as the enemy of faith', says John Davies, 'is not doubt but the repression of doubt, so the enemy of grace is not guilt but the repression of guilt.'[26] Forgiveness sets us free from the repression of guilt, free to be guilty if in fact we *are* guilty, free to be guilty if it is necessary to become guilty. This can only be true if forgiveness is continuous, not a past transaction but a ceaseless flow of loving acceptance. Breathing that atmosphere, not only can one forgive, but one can also dare to take the blame just as Jesus did.

> The disciple-community of Christ has again to face the question of which Adam it is representing, the first or the second – the blame-passer or the blame-bearer. The first Adam dissociates himself from the situation of guilt and disorder; when he sees a person in whom disorder is particularly conspicuous, the best that he can say is, 'There, but for the grace of God, go I'. For the second Adam, the grace of God does not distinguish him from the person of disorder; on the contrary, it draws him closer, so that his word is, 'There, by the grace of God, *am* I'.[27]

Nothing less than that freedom through forgiveness can release a man to take responsible decisions in a world in which any decision may be tragic. 'If any man tries to escape guilt in responsibility', says Bonhoeffer, 'he detaches himself from the ultimate reality of human existence. . . He sets his own personal innocence above his responsibility for men.' But he goes on:

> When a man takes guilt upon himself in responsibility, and no responsible man can avoid this, he imputes this guilt to himself and to no one else; he answers for it; he accepts responsibility for it. . . He does it in the knowledge that this liberty is forced upon him and that in this liberty he is dependent on grace. Before other men the man of free responsibility is justified by necessity; before himself he is acquitted by his conscience; but before God he hopes only for mercy.[28]

*Freedom is grounded in truth.* 'If you dwell within the revelation I have brought, you are indeed my disciples; you shall know the truth, and the truth will set you free' (John 8.31, 32). Why should it be *truth* that gives this freedom? Why not deliverance and power, as both pietists and revolutionaries would say?

The person who is not free is the one who is always having to refer to some other source of authority and always having to look for someone else's approval. This means that he or she is always looking away from the business in hand to an external point of reference, like a child in a school play who cannot keep her eyes off the mistress-producer, or a Bantu walking the pavements of Pretoria ever watchful of the white pedestrians, or a tourist visiting a picture gallery with his nose in the guidebook. The child is anxious over what I have called 'the truth *about*' the play – what words come next and when she should cross the stage – and so she will be dependent on the producer until the truth *of* the play takes over and she feels at home in it and is caught up by it. The Bantu is compelled to live with the truth *about* himself and the people around him – that he is black and some of them are white. If he were able to meet their intrinsic reality, person exposed to person, he would still have problems but he would be free to tackle them as a man. And if the tourist lifted his eyes and found them held by a picture that spoke directly to him he might pocket his little book of words and think his own thoughts and make his own response. When the play takes over or the inner reality of persons, white and black, takes over, or the power of a picture takes over, these have their own authority to dictate how one is to respond to them. Then the response will be independent of external authority and may even be in defiance of it. Intrinsic truth will have set them free.

This, moreover, is the only kind of authority which can demand obedience without diminishing the autonomy of the one who obeys. This is because the truth of another being addresses itself to the truth of oneself, and draws it out, compelling one to discover one's own truth more deeply and live it out more freely. Indeed, as I have said before, it is by the other's insistence upon our giving more of ourselves, and in greater truth, to the relationship that we can identify what can be safely loved, and by the absence of such an insistence recognize the impostor that is sentimentalizing and exploiting our response. That is the way in which the 'Thou' authenticates itself, whether it be a work of art, a creature of nature, a person, an institution, a cause, a spiritual being or an image of God. My response is totally subjective, if you like, and consequently totally free.

To be made alert towards that self-validating truth of 'the other' is an annunciation of the Holy Spirit. That is how he shows 'where wrong and right and judgment lie' (John 16.8). At the end of the day we have no other authority to guide our conduct. Commandments and conventions, high principles and the examples of the good, the Bible and even Christ himself, possess no authority until their intrinsic truth authenticates itself to us in this immediate personal impact. Truth can be trusted to carry conviction, and if it does not it cannot be proved.

We ought to have understood that the Bible has no use so long as it is just treated as 'the Holy Bible'. We have to go beyond that and teach people to concentrate on it, not listen to it because it is a 'holy book', but just to listen to it. Similarly we need to tell people just to look at and reflect on the record of Jesus. . . We are, I believe, nearly at the stage when it will be possible to let the Bible speak for itself again because it no longer looks as if we are trying to bludgeon men over the head with it. If a man can attend to the Gospels in an unprejudiced manner, not supposing them to be holy books to be treated with caution and care, then it may well strike him how extraordinary Jesus truly is. But there must be unprejudiced openness to what is really there.[29]

*Freedom is grounded in direct access to God.* That is why it lies a long way beyond the acknowledgment of absolute good and evil. Bonhoeffer's greatest though unfinished work, *Ethics*, relates the true situation ethic, in contrast to the phoney version, entirely to the reality of God. We might have saved many wasted miles and many lost lives if we had taken the trouble to find out what he was really saying.

The concept of reality which underlies the positivistic ethic is the meretricious concept of the empirically verifiable, which implies denial of the origin of this reality in the ultimate reality, in God. Reality, understood in this inadequate sense, cannot be the source of good, because all it demands is complete surrender to the contingent, the casual, the adventitious and the momentarily. expedient, because it fails to recognize the ultimate reality and because in this way it destroys and abandons the unity of good.[30]

The supreme and primary gift of the Go-Between Spirit is the *abba*-relationship whereby a man knows God as 'Thou, Father' and feels that he is known as 'Thou, Son'. When man is true to himself his response is simply and purely a God-ward response. Being free, his response may be yes or no, but it is yes or no to one thing only, the being of God. The God to whom we make our ethical responses cannot be reduced to any other terms, nor in fact would other terms bring him any closer to human comprehension. 'The Christian', says Joseph Fletcher, 'does not understand God in terms of love; he understands love in terms of God as seen in Christ.'[31] Only by knowing God as Jesus knew him, or only by knowing Jesus and finding God in him, can a man learn in each particular situation what he should do.

Because the simple man knows God, because God is his, he clings to the commandments, the judgements and the mercies *which come from God's mouth every day afresh.* Not fettered by principles, but bound by love for God, he has been set free from the problems and conflicts of ethical decision. They no longer oppress him. He belongs simply and solely to God and to the will of God. It is precisely because he looks only to God, without any sidelong glance at the world, that he is able to look at the reality of the world freely and without prejudice.[32]

Anxiety about good and evil implies a totally different orientation. To see one's choices in reference to those great absolutes is to
see oneself no longer simply in one's relation to God but in one's
possibility of doing *either* good *or* evil, and that in itself implies
knowing oneself apart from God, outside God. It was an important
part of Bonhoeffer's argument that this self-reference is the nub of
Adam's falling away, and in complete contrast with the attitude of
Jesus. For the freedom which the Holy Spirit imparted in his consciousness is the freedom of perfect sonship. Every response and
act of his was no more than another repetition of the cry Abba!
Father! And what God was to Jesus, Jesus allows himself to be to
his disciples. It is the function of the Holy Spirit to bring Jesus
ceaselessly to our remembrance in order that we may live and
make all our choices in reference to him. The Spirit-filled life is
the Christ-centred life. 'That I may know him' replaces the knowledge of good and evil.

Again Bonhoeffer says it best of all:

Knowing of Jesus a man can no longer know of his own goodness, and knowing of his own goodness a man can no longer
know of Jesus. . . When Jesus sits in judgement His own will
not know that they have given Him food and drink and clothing
and comfort. They will not know their own goodness; Jesus
will disclose it to them.[33]

Life in the Spirit is then to be a ceaseless personal response to the
call and claim of Jesus in each new situation by the individual
disciple from within the Christ-centred fellowship. So the problem
of ethics is the problem of how to abide in Christ. It is the problem
of faith, and of prayer, and of the practice of the presence in the
midst of a secular outlook. This does not mean that all depends on
a recovery of pietism. 'Abide in me and I in you' is spoken to disciples in the plural. It will be by a deeper discovery of the resources
of group discipleship that we shall be drawn nearer to a Christ-
centred life in the modern world. Nor need we wait for that
deeper experience before we can hope to know the touch and demand of the living Christ in each concrete moment of one day. He
calls us to engagement now. He sends us to Galilee with the promise that we shall meet him there. Like Abraham we have to start
obeying long before we know much of him we obey. At the end of

the day it is not our following of him that gives us any value but his hold on us.


# NOTES

1. S. L. Greenslade, *Shepherding the Flock*, SCM Press 1967.
2. Kenneth Cragg, *The Call of the Minaret*, OUP 1956, pp. 144, 149.
3. Dietrich Bonhoeffer, *Ethics*, SCM Press 1971 ed., p. 14.
4. Jürgen Moltmann, *Theology of Hope*, SCM Press 1967, p. 324.
5. Harvey E. Cox, *The Secular City*, SCM Press 1965, pp. 30–35.
6. Dietrich Bonhoeffer, *Letters and Papers from Prison*, The Enlarged Edition, SCM Press 1971, p. 5.
7. Bonhoeffer, *Ethics*, p. 22.
8. Martin Buber, *I and Thou*, T. & T. Clark, paperback ed. 1966, pp. 136f.
9. Walter Eichrodt, *Man in the Old Testament*, SCM Press 1951, p. 27.
10. Joseph Fletcher, *Situation Ethics*, SCM Press 1966, p. 52.
11. Bonhoeffer, *Ethics*, p. 5.
12. Ibid., p. 47.
13. Ibid., p. 48.
14. Ibid., pp. 8f.
15. John D. Davies, *Beginning Now*, Collins 1971, pp. 219–20.
16. R. D. Laing, *The Politics of Experience and the Bird of Paradise*, Penguin Books 1967, pp. 51f.
17. B. F. Skinner, *Beyond Freedom and Dignity*, Jonathan Cape 1972, pp. 200f.
18. Bonhoeffer, *Ethics*, p. 201.
19. M. F. Thelen, *Man as Sinner*, New York 1946, p. 95.
20. T. R. Henn, *The Harvest of Tragedy*, Methuen 1936, pp. 267–8.
21. *Oedipus at Colonus*, 5th Episode.
22. *Anthony and Cleopatra*, V. ii. 282.
23. *King Lear*, V. ii. 20.
24. Ibid., V. ii. 10.
25. *The Tempest*, V. i. 182.
26. Davies, op. cit., p. 212.
27. Ibid., p. 224.
28. Bonhoeffer, *Ethics*, pp. 210, 216.
29. David E. Jenkins, *Living with Questions*, SCM Press 1969, p. 188.
30. Bonhoeffer, *Ethics*, p. 166.
31. Fletcher, op. cit., p. 49.
32. Bonhoeffer, *Ethics*, p. 50 (my italics).
33. Ibid., pp. 20f.

# 9

## MEETING

*The Universal Spirit and the Meetings of Faiths*

To think deeply about the Holy Spirit is a bewildering, tearing exercise, for whatever he touches he turns it inside out. He gives himself in our most interior and private experiences and then shows that what we thought was our monopoly belongs to everybody. It is his favourite joke to whisper an especial secret behind closed doors and then shout it from the housetops. He goes to great lengths to teach a particular tribe that it is God's chosen people, only to reveal to them that other nations have known the same salvation-history: 'Are not you Israelites like Cushites to me? says the Lord. Did I not bring Israel up from Egypt, the Philistines from Caphtor, the Aramaeans from Kir?' (Amos 9.7). All the rest had had their own exodus and seemed to lack only an Amos to tell them so. Again the Spirit comes upon the disciples of Jesus in such a way as compelled them to say that until then he had not been given, and yet established his continuity with the past. His fire appeared to fall on them alone, yet fulfilled the promise of a gift poured out upon all flesh.

In his vocabulary the words unique and universal have the same meaning. But for us they stand for two distinct modes of experience, neither of which can be submerged in the other. What is given to us alone lays upon us a responsibility and commitment we can never feel for what is common; and the discovery of what we share brings out a strength of fellow-feeling and openness we can never find in our separate identities. Both the particular and the general are necessary for us and the contrast between them will last as long as time and space. But for the Spirit what is here is everywhere, yet would be nowhere were it not first here.

Any theology of the Spirit, therefore, is bound to be somewhat schizophrenic. It may help to recall the more familiar mystery of the pre-incarnate Christ. He exists before everything and all things are held together in him, yet when he came unto his own his arrival was unprecedented. The Lamb was slain before the foundation of the world, and from the beginning the universe was held in existence by the death of its Redeemer. So, had Jesus of Nazareth come down from the cross, creation would have been instantly unmade and time itself unborn. The creeds of the church have not sufficiently recognized that the death and resurrection of Jesus brought a radical change to the Hebrew doctrine of creation. For the patterns of the gospel experience are the patterns of the very fabric of life. The free obedience of Jesus, his dying for us all and his rising again, are both history and universal reality. They happened and they are the way things always happen. And man is saved not by relating only to that historical life, death and resurrection in which the pattern was made plain once for all, but by relating also to that true pattern wherever it emerges in the tissue of contemporary experience. We could never have learned this true pattern of reality if Jesus had not lived and died and risen. But since he gave us that clue we see the pattern everywhere. He is the same not only in the 'today' of the crucifixion and the 'today' of personal conversion, but in all our yesterdays back to the first morning, and on, tomorrow and tomorrow and tomorrow. All men, in their common sinfulness, continue to exist on the earth because they, with all creation, are held in the arms of one who chose at the start of the enterprise to take upon himself the responsibility for whatever went awry. We are citizens of a forgiven universe. Being-in-Christ is a more primary and essential condition of a man's existence than is his ignorance of Christ. It follows that any and every movement of his mind and spirit which can be called an act of faith is truly faith in Christ, even though Christ is still the unknown magnetic pole which draws him. Evangelism, therefore, is inviting a man to become what he is, helping him to accept the fact that he is *already* accepted in the beloved. And, for the same reason, the corollary is true, that the man who is saved is also *not yet* saved because he awaits the awakening of the whole creation to its freedom which has already been won.

In much the same way the Holy Spirit is *universally* present through the whole fabric of the world, and yet *uniquely* present in

Christ and, by extension, in the fellowship of his disciples. But even that unique presence is not enclosed, either in Christ or in his church, but exists between Christ and the other, between the Christians and those who meet them. The centre is always on the circumference, yet it proves to be the circumference of *that* centre and not another. This interplay of the unique and the universal is clearly seen in the witness which the Holy Spirit bears to Jesus Christ. In the first instance, it is the power of the Spirit in the person of Jesus – the works that this man does and the authority with which he speaks – which testify most convincingly, and this is extended in the witness to Christ which the Spirit enables the church to give by its life and its testimony. But that same Spirit also speaks in the hearts of all men, for God has nowhere left himself without a witness that always, to a greater or lesser degree, points to Christ.

The Spirit's witness to the lordship and love of Jesus Christ is, therefore, in itself a kind of dialogue. In the person of Jesus, and in his body, the church, the Spirit calls all men to respond. And like a fifth column in the heart of every man the Spirit himself moves in response. This is what Jesus appealed to when he showed such extraordinary faith in sinful men and women. And if, as I have suggested, the man on the cross was saying Choose! to every individual that watched him there, there was that in the heart of each one of them which turned indifference into attention, reduced mockery to silence, and urged them one way or the other to make a response. It is this which gives us grounds for believing that in any dialogue between the church and the world, or between Christians and men of other faiths, the Holy Spirit is speaking in both participants.

But the awareness of one another in the Spirit involves awareness of the faith by which each lives. For, as Kenneth Cragg says, 'Christianity cannot address men and ignore their gods: it may not act in the present and disown the past or wisely hold forth salvation and withhold salutation. In seeking men for Christ's sake, it is committed to the significance of all they are in their birth and their tradition, both for good or ill.'[1] That is well said because it emphasizes the dynamically personal quality of any faith that men live by. Debates about inter-faith dialogue usually betray too static an idea of what a religion is. It suggests that what shapes men is the truth *about* God whereas in fact it is the truth *of* God.

Consequently a religion is thought to be primarily a body of propositions and regulations, standing over against people who either
believe or do not believe, asking for their allegiance and offering a
way of fulfilment. This static view underlies most of the studies that
go by the name of comparative religion.

But I believe it is truer to think of a religion as a people's tradition of response to the reality the Holy Spirit has set before their
eyes. I am deliberately not saying that any religion is the truth which
the Spirit disclosed, nor even that it contains that truth. All we can
say without presumption is that this is how men have responded and
taught others to respond to what the Spirit made them aware of. It
is the history of a particular answer, or series of answers, to the call
and claim of him who lies beyond all religions. A Jesuit theologian
in India, Piet Fransen, explained it some years back along lines
suggested by Charles Davis, which come very near to what I have
already suggested is the Holy Spirit's characteristic way of working.

> The intimate, divine attraction towards the truth, which is at the
> same time a spiritual and inward light . . . gives a sense and a
> taste for the truth. . . This deep and existential religious ex-
> perience of being attracted by the Spirit towards the living truth
> leads to a personal creed. . . This reflection upon one's experience
> remains, of course, under the influence of the Spirit, but . . . in
> its final formulation may contain false opinions and errors in-
> duced by the social and psychological influences of heredity,
> education and culture, religious environment and national or
> social traditions and ways of thought.[2]

Each particular tradition of response both implies and creates a
certain understanding of reality, a world-view. But while this view
of reality retains its own characteristic identity and ethos, it is
always dynamic and developing, since it is essentially a culture
rather than a theology. For the world-view of a people is sustained
not only by the traditional certainties of their religion but also by
the movement of ideas in their society. Which is a way of saying
that the Holy Spirit speaks to the man-in-the-street as well as to the
man-in-the-pew. This is how it came about that during the post-
war years a whole generation of younger people in Europe, most
of whom have never heard of either Christian or philosophical existentialism, began in fact to view life in an existentialist way,
insisting that it must be lived by *ad hoc* responses to each new

situation with neither guidance from the past nor designs upon the future. This is why the great protests and affirmations of the reformation did not arise purely from the wrestling of the theologians or the outcries of the church reformers, but was an expression of that revolution in the spirit of man which we call the Renaissance. This is why the appearance of Jesus Christ himself and the emergence of the Christian movement within Judaism at that particular moment of history has to be understood, as we have recently learned, in the context of a wider ferment of ideas and expectations, both in the Essene sects and in rabbinic orthodoxy.

Religion, therefore, is a tradition of response; and both these words are equally important. It is traditional in that it maintains a continuity of convictions and attitudes, and this makes it inevitably a conservative force in society; it is responsive in that it reflects even while it transmutes whatever movement of ideas is in the air. The test of any religion's vitality at a particular time is to ask not only how strongly its traditional convictions and patterns of life are still maintained, but also how positively it is responding, with a clear yes or no, to the changing influences and tensions which are affecting the society with which it is involved. To respond does not mean to acquiesce in the effects of every new development but to answer the call of God which comes through the new situation; and, naturally, the call of God will be interpreted in the light of that tradition of response and that understanding of reality which has been inherited from the past. In every religion, therefore, we can find the same tension between conservatism and development, and it must be so if past obedience and present response are both to be seen as an answer to the call of him who is beyond all religion.

So a religion is not the fabrication of priests and theologians but the tradition of a people's response, shaped, albeit, by the peculiar sensitiveness and courage of prophets and reformers and saints. Hitherto, therefore, each religion has grown up inseparably intertwined with a particular culture and history and view of reality. Each has been a unity in itself. Each has its own story of change and growth, in the course of which it may have received influences and insights from other religious systems with which it has been in contact. But it has remained self-consistent and autonomous. Each religion until now has been, in Kraemer's word, 'totalitarian'. It was able to take in ideas and behaviour-patterns from other religious systems and even be transformed by them, but it could not itself grow into becoming another religion. When we salute a different faith from our own we are faced with what Kenneth Cragg calls 'an otherness which cannot be reduced, abated, merged, or interchanged'.[3] So the religions of men could not with any truth be arranged in stages of development and fitted into a simple theory of evolution, as was attempted by Friedrich Max Müller, Professor Monier-Williams and other students of comparative religion at the end of the nineteenth century. And the idea that the other great faiths of men would find their fulfilment by growing into a form of Christianity, or into some even higher universal religion, was naive because it failed to take account of the rootedness of every religion in its own particular culture, and consequently its absoluteness within its own frame of reference. For the most intractable disagreement between the faiths of mankind are philosophical rather than religious. One culture has been built on a different view of existence from another. Here people are satisfied by one kind of explanation, there they need a different kind because the terms which seem to them to be ultimate and incapable of further analysis are different. It is not that one people's explanation contains more truth than that of another, but that a different *kind* of truth is demanded in different cultures and at different times.

We may well ask whether what we call 'scientific' truth is as much at home in an Indian or Japanese world-view as it is in the setting of European philosophy, or whether it is peculiarly the *kind* of explanation that satisfies the western tradition. Will the western 'mind' and the Confucianist 'mind' and the Hindu 'mind' adapt themselves to technology and absorb it in exactly the same way? Or may it be hoped that while western philosophy has given birth to a more successful technology of physics and chemistry than of the human sciences, the heirs of Confucius and Mencius may more naturally develop a technology of social relations, and India a technology of man's unrealized extra-sensory and 'spiritual' capacities?

And if the universal validity of scientific truth needs thus to be incorporated into different systems of explanation before its full potential can be realized, what of that totally universal truth which is Christ? That way of putting the question throws some light on the meaning of dialogue between people of different faiths, on the nature of their agreements and disagreements, and on the processes by which, if at all, Christ is to make himself at home in other households of thought as once he made himself at home in the Graeco-Roman world.

The human agents through whom this at-homeness of Christ was made actual in that seemingly alien world of ideas were those who had first allowed themselves to become men of two worlds. Having learned to move freely to and fro across the frontier between the mind of the Jewish law and the mind of the Greek *stoa*, they could see the miraculous relevance of their Messiah both to the shining ideals and the dark failures of the Gentiles.

But – and I think this point is too often ignored – their understanding of the two worlds and interpretation of one to the other was not a simple interchange of cultures. Paul and Apollos and John were not merely members of the Jewish dispersion engaged in a Hebrew-Greek dialogue. In their experience of the living Christ they were freed from cultural bondage, either to the Jewish or to the Gentile world-view. Christian faith did not offer them a *third* culture, since Christendom was unborn by three centuries or more. But it afforded a detached viewpoint from which to see both the heritage from which they had emerged, and the heritage to which they spoke. And what they saw was that both were being judged and fulfilled by the Lord of all worlds.

The same theological dimension should be a factor in the Christian's participation in inter-faith dialogue today. Though the terms of the encounter must be an equal commitment and an equal openness, the Christian cannot deny the strange detachment from all the religious systems and vocabularies, including his own, which his faltering attachment to the Lord imparts to him. For this Lord insists that his disciples be free, culturally and intellectually, as well as morally. And it is precisely this detachment which releases the Christian to become 'all things to all men' and discover common ground with men of other faiths and ideologies in those experiences of awakening and disclosure which the Spirit gives to all men without discrimination.

There is one living, dying, quality about all mankind. Male and female, old and young, bound in the generations, set in families, hoping, fearing, yearning, striving, toiling, gaining, losing, having, getting, hating, loving – all these are one mortality through all times, faiths and places. In this kinship men talk different languages, but they spell everywhere one humanity.[4]

As the dialogue progresses, love recognizes unities of spiritual experience as well.

The Bible and the Qur'ān are full of the splendour and the mystery of the universe, the fidelities of nature, the strange entrustments of pregnancy and harvest. . . The mercies of God in the different fields of prophet and Messiah, of revelation and Scriptures . . . still have mutual features we must be careful not to miss. The rule of God, the instrumentality of men, the moral of history, the care of time, the reckoning with death, are among them. The diagnosis of sin, despite the different law, has elements in common.[5]

Men of all faiths stand shoulder to shoulder today in defence of the ultimate meanings and in common resistance against materialism. We respect in each other the seriousness with which convictions are held and prayer is offered.

For us there can be no abatement of Christian obligation to meet men in their faiths on the ground that technological civilization has sounded the death-knell of them all. 'Bruised', they are, painfully, and the Church with them, by contemporary changes and much chastened or bludgeoned by modern developments. Yet, for the perceptive Christian, a music remains: the reed may still speak.[6]

But dialogue must probe beyond the glad discovery of similarities to the more painful recognition of differences that are mutually exclusive.

The deeper the appreciation of the other faith the greater the knowledge of what these disagreements really are. Our disagreement with the position of Islam differs from our disagreement with a Hindu, and so on. Let no one belittle those disagreements. I vividly remember one evening when I was staying at a Christian ashram in north India in which a group of missionaries were living at the poverty level of Indian village life and providing a place of intimate meeting with Hindu intellectuals. On this occasion, the head of the community had been reading aloud some of the Bhakti classics of Hindu devotion. I was deeply moved by the ardour and adoration with which these poems expressed love for the ever-present God, and afterwards I exclaimed; 'Surely, the missionary task is simply to name him who has for so long been loved but nameless.' But my friend answered: 'It's not as simple as that. The agony of this fellowship with the Hindu brother is that at the very moment when he and I seem to be saying the same thing in closest unity of experience, I am most aware of the absolute gulf that separates us.'

I have already described how I came to spend a day at the fourteenth-century Zen monastery of Myoshinji on the western side of Kyoto, where some of the monks and members of the college staff had several hours' discussion with me. I remember we talked about the peace movement and also the difference between European and Oriental atheism today. At one point one of the monks who had studied in Germany picked up a phrase of mine about the purposes of God, saying: 'There you put your finger on the greatest difference between us. You Christians make much of the Will of God, and consequently human choices also are of ultimate significance in your scheme of things. But for us the idea is almost meaningless. For if some part of existence is within the Will of God while other things are outside it, such a God is less than the Whole – and to us that means he is not God.' At that moment I also felt the pain of an 'absolute gulf'.

But to stop at the disagreements is to lose faith in the Spirit's gift of communion and communication. To move on from the stage of disagreement to that of a more profound mutual understanding is the most important step in a dialogue and the most important act in evangelism.

But how can that ever happen if indeed the gulf is so deep? Let me say at once that whenever it happens, nothing less than a miracle has occurred. It is the Lord's doing and marvellous in our eyes. Yet there are some things that we in our weakness and blindness can do to prepare for the miracle, and I want to share what I myself have learned from such experiences as I have been given.

First, I would say, pay attention to the real conviction that underlies the precise point at which disagreement appears and then try to turn mere confrontation of opposites into a real and possible choice. This happened, I believe, on an occasion when I was invited to take part in a conversation with members of a Jewish Society. I had spoken of Jesus as standing in the line of all the prophets and calling Israel back to a far more penetrating obedience to the Torah so that purged and reformed she could live in a new freedom of response to the call of God and of the neighbours. But one young

Jew replied saying that Jesus went beyond reform and attacked the very roots of Judaism; while purporting to support the Torah he rejected the Midrashim, which are as essential to the life of Judaism as the Torah itself. At that moment I realized that this gulf which divides Christians from Jews is one which has always run through the body of the church itself – the continual choice between free response and submission to a traditional code. I tried to put this point into words and everyone agreed that this was not only the real issue concerning Jesus Christ but a living option concerning ourselves. In that way we reached a much deeper understanding of each other's convictions. The gulf still yawned before us, but it was no longer between us. We had turned it 'end on' so that it presented each of us with a real and possible choice.

Kenneth Cragg has said that the contradictions between Muslim and Christian fidelity can be seen to arise, in large part, from the different ways in which the Messiah and the Prophet responded to the same situation when it confronted them. Each was sure of his call to show men a new way, preaching, gathering the crowds, training his disciples; and then each was faced with the opposition of religious leaders, rejection and the disaffection of his followers. What did he do? Jesus chose to go on in the same way, in the same spirit. He bowed his head to what was coming; he accepted rejection, failure, and death, entrusting the outcome to God. In the case of Mohammed it looked for a moment as if he too would take the way of suffering; but then he decided to fight back on behalf of the truth. He raised his army and marched on Mecca: and that was the turning point in his career and the birth of Islam. From those two choices one can derive the fundamental difference between the Christian and the Muslim ideas of God's nature. But what a strong case Mohammed has! He takes the theology of power seriously. And more often than not, when confronted by the same choice, the church has taken the Prophet's way rather than the Messiah's. Looked at in this way the basic difference between Islam and Christianity becomes an open option, for the Christian no less than for the Muslim – a choice on which we are still making up our minds. The gulf between is seen, as it were, in cross section. Both I and the Muslim may go forward either on the one side or the other. I said 'cross section'; for it is nothing less than the cross which is now demanding our decision. Once more we see that the evangelism of the Holy Spirit consists in creating the occasions for choice. The servant of the gospel can do no less, and perhaps need do no more.

The second truth that I am learning about the way to deal with the radical difference between myself and the men of a different faith is that I must be patient enough to listen and learn until I begin to see his world through his eyes. At first his view of reality is totally unknown to me. As I begin to catch a glimpse of it, it seems strange; it makes no sense; it may even revolt me. At that point I am sorely tempted to impatience. I want to tell him about my saviour, about the way in which Christ has been the answer to my very English questions, has set me free from my western temptations and fears, has proved himself Lord of our kind of family, and our kind of culture. If I persist and dominate, I may – once in a blue moon – get this other man to adopt *my* Lord, to repent of *my* sins, to pay lip service to *my* ideas of right and wrong. But his own real world, at the place where he feels deeply and reacts instinctively, will remain untouched.

But if I persevere in listening openness I shall begin to see more of that other man's real world. I shall see past what to me are distasteful rituals, alien symbols and concepts that carry no conviction to the insights they are trying to express. I shall come to appreciate his understanding of what a man is, how he is related to his family, to the dead, to the whole of existence, and to the ultimate reality. And, as a final bestowal, I shall be given access to the dark places of that stranger's world – the things that really make him ashamed or anxious or despairing. And then, at last, I shall see the Saviour and Lord of *that* world, my Lord Jesus, and yet not as I have known him. I shall understand how perfectly he matches all the needs and all the aspirations and all the insights of that other world – He who is the unique Lord and Saviour of all possible worlds. And I shall worship with a new-found wonder and falteringly start proclaiming him in the new terms which I am just beginning to comprehend.

So, precisely because of our adoring conviction that Jesus is both universal and unique, we cannot reduce our faith in him to one traditional philosophical or sociological form. 'Christian stripping should be complete', says Raymond Panikkar. 'Christian faith must strip itself of the "Christian religion" as it actually exists and free itself for a fecundation that will affect all religions both ancient and modern. . . What we call Christianity is only one form among other possible ones of living and realizing the Christian faith.'[7]

Christians with a true enthusiasm for the gospel should be the first to welcome the lesson of the Epiphany story of the magi. Those mysterious representatives of the other faiths of mankind found their own way to the child and laid their own particular gifts before him. They didn't really need King Herod's bible-reading, for their own star was a reliable guide to the very end of the journey. Yet it was not in their great learning or their store of experience but in their question, Where is he? that they were most truly wise.

I believe that the search for Christ's relevance is a truer and less static way of describing the aim of dialogue than is the older talk about the one word and light which has inspired other religious systems. For it is not in the propositions, regulations, rituals or traditions of a religious system that his universal presence is to be found, but always independent of these phenomena in the uncontainable unattained to which they point, in the questions men ask about them, and the protests men make against them. It is as judge and saviour of the religious tradition itself that Christ's relevance to each religion will be found. It is not so much that he is the culmination or crown of every religion – that is not how I would express it – but that in him each religion will be brought to fulfilment in terms true to itself, through crisis and conversion.

We need not go all the way with Karl Barth in defining all religion as unbelief. But it is impossible to deny the innate ambiguity of all religions, for in every household of faith it is plain that man uses religion as a way of escaping from God. This is as true of Christianity as of any other religious system. Particularly at this moment in history all religions are caught in the most severe crisis they have ever had to face. As Spencer Trimingham puts it:

Since God transcends so immeasurably human comprehension and experience we look, in other religions as well as Christianity, for a re-awakening to the revelatory experience which is within them. The new demands made upon us by modern life mean that we each seek to discover the ignored or unexploited resources within our religion. . . Men have to submit their systems to judgement, to be prepared to discard, to allow each religion to open itself to its own potential and its adherents enter more fully into their own heritage.[8]

The eternal Spirit has been at work in all ages and all cultures making men aware and evoking their response, and always the one to whom he was pointing and bearing witness was the Logos, the Lamb slain before the foundation of the world. Every religion has been a tradition of response to him, however darkly it groped towards him, however anxiously it shied away from him. When he appears on the scene, entering the consciousness of any particular culture and religion, all the habitual responses, and the total world-view they have built up, are seen in a startling new light. The next story in the Epiphany series tells of the boy who astonished the pundits by listening to them and asking them questions. This is the first independent action recorded of the Messiah and it sums up a mission which was bound to bring him to the cross. For no one has ever listened so penetratingly or asked such devastating questions about every man's religion. His total abandonment to the Spirit sets him free, culturally, intellectually and morally, to stand back and judge the truth of each religious tradition with detachment. 'Except in Christ', asks Trimingham, 'where do you find such condemnation? Christianity differs from other religions more especially in that they have no such built-in system of self-criticism and judgement.'⁹

So his fulfilment of any religion is bound to be no less disturbing than was his fulfilment of Judaism. There his insistence on the freedom to respond to each fresh situation was a protest against the concept of divinely prescribed legislation which had become the very foundation stone of that religion. He was put to death as a blasphemer and an outlaw, and however much Jewry may regret that sentence it has seen no reason to reverse the verdict. Nothing less than the resurrection could show him to be right and all the religious presuppositions of his people to be wrong. Only in that way will he fulfil Hinduism and Islam and Buddhism, and all the secular hopes of man as well. And, in so far as Christianity also has grown into a religious ideology, only through crisis and conversion can Christ bring it to fulfilment. For it is perfectly clear from the biblical record and the history of the church that the divine act and gift of salvation, both for the individual and for his society and culture, comes by revolution, not evolution. The slow formation of a man's personal being may be through a history of Hinduism and in the terms of Hinduism, or through a Christian culture and in Christian terms; or it may be according to the best values of scientific humanism. Salvation also may come to him in any of those terms, but it can only come as an irruption, a revolution, a new creation. That is its nature.

The fulfilment of Judaism will come with the emancipation from slavery to a man-made Law and to racialism; in other words, when the spiritual limitations that man has imposed on the spirit within are transcended; but in whatever way it comes, this does not mean 'when the Jews become Christians'. The response and transformation can only come from within the Jewish community.[10]

As the Holy Spirit turns Muslim or Hindu or Marxist eyes towards the living Christ, the half-truths in their traditions of response will be completed, error will be shown up, disobedience condemned, all evasion of God brought to a halt, and his Son crucified afresh. And out of all that a new Jesus-centred Hinduism, a new Messiah-centred Islam, a new Christ-directed Communism, will be raised up. According to Pannikar,

Christianity in India should not be an imported, fully-fledged and highly developed religion, but Hinduism itself *converted* – or Islam, or Buddhism, whatever it may be. . . The process of conversion implies a death and resurrection, but, just as the risen Christ or the baptized person is the same as previously and yet is a new being, likewise converted Hinduism is the true risen Hinduism, the same and yet renewed, transformed. In one word, the Church brings every true and authentic religion to its *fulfilment* through a process of death and resurrection which is the true meaning of conversion.[11]

Is this anything more than a pious hope? Is there the slightest evidence that things are moving in such a direction? I believe there is, and I would suggest that we should look for it at two levels.

The first is the level of individual response to the magnetism of Jesus Christ. Whatever we may say to the contrary, even though we agree that individual conversions from one culture to another should not be encouraged, this will continue to happen, and it will usually be enormously costly, and there will be many casualties. A missionary asked me in South India some years ago how I would have advised a Hindu woman who came to her confessing that she worshipped only Jesus and daily read the New Testament which she had secreted in the house. 'But', she asked, 'must I be baptized? If I tell my husband even that I have such a desire he will turn me out. Our marriage will be broken, my children bereft of a mother, our family destroyed. Must I do that to them?' My every instinct demanded that I should say 'No! This is not required.' Yet I knew that if, when that point had been reached, I had answered so, I should be saying something different from my Lord's clear demand. 'Oh Lord,' cried the great Saint Theresa once, 'no wonder you have so few friends when you treat them so hard!' The marvel is that in spite of all that he exacts, Christ still compels the allegiance of men from other households of faith. A most sensitive, lonely man from Pakistan spoke at the New Delhi Assembly of the World Council of Churches about his conversion from Islam. All his longing was still for his own people, their language, their ancient culture; and in the factious and generally defeated church of that land he finds little consolation or fellowship. 'I am a Christian', he confessed, 'for one reason only – because of the absolute worship-ability of Jesus Christ. By that word I mean that I have found no other being in the universe who compels my adoration as he has done. And if ever some pundit or theologian should prove me wrong and show that, after all, the High God is not of the character which I see in Jesus, I, for one, would have to blaspheme and turn my back on any such god. I had rather kneel down and worship the next little child that offered me its stick of candy out of love.'

But I have no doubt at all that the Spirit has often opened a man's eyes to the compelling glory of Christ without the mediation of any church, and it has happened within the household of another faith. The first to be permitted to teach the gospel in northern Nigeria found themselves greeted by a handful of people who professed to being already the followers of Jesus Christ. They told the story of Malam Ibrahim, a teacher of the Holy Qur'ān whose studies had slowly convinced him that in its pages a unique office is conferred on the figure of Isa Masih, Jesus the Messiah, as the mediator through whom the prayers of the faithful are offered up to the All-Merciful. So he gathered round him a band of devotees who made their regular prayer in the name of Isa Masih. When the religious authorities found out he was charged with heresy, refused to recant, and was crucified in Kano market-place thirty years before a Christian preacher arrived in the country.

But I have spoken of a second dimension, a second direction in which we should look for the signs of response to Christ within the terms of the other faiths of mankind. Like the submerged mass of the iceberg, the area in which this second kind of response is to be looked for is largely out of sight. It is not a result that can be planned but is, rather, an incidental by-product. That, at least, is what one would have to call it in human terms, were it not that it looks very much like the strategy of God himself. I refer to something that is beginning to happen within the very life of these other faiths themselves, a ferment, a subtle change, brought about by the influence of Jesus Christ upon them, far beyond any conscious impact that Christians are making.

The new vitality of Hinduism in India seems in several respects to stem from a kind of blood-transfusion received from Christianity. Not only is this seen in the philosophical reinterpretation of men such as Radhakrishnan or the social ethics of Vinoba Bhave, but even the cultic expression at the local level is full of borrowings from Christian worship; far more congregational prayer and praise in the temples, with popular hymns sung to sentimental tunes and long pietistic sermons. But it goes much further than this.

Gandhi's devotion to the New Testament is widely known. I was in East Africa at the time of his death and I saw in the store or workshop of every Indian trader and artisan the highly-coloured posters which quickly appeared, portraying Gandhi as a sort of saint, seated in the typical posture of a sadhu. But in almost all of these pictures there appeared, behind and above him, the figure of Christ on the cross. These glossy pictures were not designed for Christians; they were put out by Hindu publishing firms for ordinary Indians all over the world. Yet this was Hinduism's ultimate word about the great leader. Call it, if you like, typically Hindu syncretism; say that this means no more than the acceptance of Jesus as one of a thousand manifestations of God. That is all true. But why only this one manifestation in so many of the pictures? Why of all the gods choose this adopted foreigner and show him at the moment of his humiliation and death?

It is a a characteristic of the Hinduism of South India that at different periods particular manifestations of God become especially popular. It would not be going too far to say that in the country south of Hyderabad and in the vast plain between the Krishna and the Godavari rivers one of the most popular gods of the moment is

Yesu Swami – Lord Jesus. Village people are naming their baby boys Servant of Jesus, their little girls Pearl of Jesus. This is particularly noticeable among folk who have migrated from one part of the country to another and are inclined to look for a hero-protector in a strange environment. The new allegiance often follows a dream or a prayer for healing, desperately offered at a Christian church, which has been answered. In many villages a group of ten or twenty Brahmins meet once or twice a week to read the New Testament together and to make their prayers to Jesus; and when they hear of sick people in the village they go as a group to lay their hands on the sufferer and pray for healing in Jesus' name. Yet for the most part they have no inclination to come out of Hinduism and be baptized.

This somewhat naive popular response in the rural areas is matched by the profoundly philosophical response of Hindu thinkers to the fact of Jesus Christ which has contributed in no small degree to a renaissance of Hinduism itself. In men of a former generation such as Rammohan Roy, founder of the Brahma Samaj, and Keshab Chandra Sen, and also in the critical philosophers like Sri Ramakrishna, Swami Vivekananda and Dr Radhakrishnan, one sees how the massive tradition of response which is Hinduism is wrestling with the self-authenticating truth of a Christ it can neither absorb into its system nor ignore.

A debate is in progress the like of which has not been known since schoolmen of Greece and Rome vied with Christian apologists in their interpretation of Jesus the Messiah. As one would expect, it is in India that the most striking instances of this second dimension of response to Christ are to be found. But in the spiritual vacuum of Japan, though the quasi-Buddhist new religions are attracting the most phenomenal numbers, the person of Christ exercises a most powerful attraction, as the popular excitement over Shusaku Endo's novels in the 1960s has shown. And even in Islam with its intractable fidelities and disavowals, something is stirring, the leaven of recognition is at work. I have told elsewhere of the devout Baluchi tribesman who went on pressing a drug-addicted English hippy to 'pray to Jesus Messiah' until he had brought him to conversion and deliverance. 'For an ordinary man in normal circumstances,' the old Muslim explained afterwards to a Christian friend, 'it is enough that he believe faithfully in God. But when anyone is beset by such evil power as this nothing can save him but Jesus Christ: this I firmly believe.' At a more intellectual level, one of the

Muslim brothers attending the inter-faith consultation at Ajaltoun, to which I have already referred, wrote afterwards: 'A great moment of convergence of feeling and warmth arose (perhaps it was the work of God) when it was pointed out by a Muslim that Islam, having started in history with all triumph and glory, needed, in order to grapple with the fact of the reversal of its historical fortunes, the Christian concept of suffering, a full sense of the tragic to transcend the limiting identity of faith and history. The response from a Christian, pointing how the Christian needed the Muslim, referred to the total sovereignty of God in Islam which could be of great inspiration to the Christian.'

One of the Christians, facing the same issue from the opposite side, found that it led to more deeply challenging questions about his championship of that divine Sonship which he attributes to his Master. 'Am I right to embrace with reverent joy the categorical reality of divine sovereignty in Islam, and yet yearn to find in it, for that very sovereignty's sake, the ultimacy of a love that suffers as my Christian faith bids me? . . . And, if I so contend, am I caring about recognition for the Sonship which the New Testament tells me consists in *not* caring for itself, but in being emptied for love's sake?'

What are we to make of these things? Frankly, I am not by any means sure, though I have tried to show how I see them fitting into a vastly wider and more Spirit-centred theology of mission. I am sure it would be a mistake to read too much into them, but it would be even more wrong not to watch these developments with serious-ness and wonder and humility. Any proprietory pride and gratifica-tion would be grossly out of place. For Christ is not the property of us Christians and if we rejoice when the Holy Spirit opens men's eyes to his glory, we must at that moment remember how often the church has blinded them, and pray that we be not once more a stumbling block.

But of one thing we can be certain: there would be no such ferment, no response at all, within the body and fabric of these other great faiths, if those who, one by one, through the past century and a half, have been touched by the magnetism of Christ, had not paid the costly price of public confession and baptism with all that that entailed. For this peculiar faith to which we are committed has no power and no appeal whatever except the power and the appeal of the cross. In the confrontation of many faiths, all our dialogue, all our witness, all our loving service of men's need must point to that. But in order to point another effectually, we may often have to be on the cross ourselves. Whatever else the strategy of the Spirit may include, that part of it has not been taken from us.

# NOTES

1. Kenneth Cragg, *Christianity in World Perspective*, Lutterworth Press 1968, p. 65.

2. Piet Fransen, SJ, article in *Christian Revelation and World Religions*, ed. Joseph Neuner, SJ, Burns & Oates 1967, pp. 92–3.

3 Kenneth Cragg, *Alive to God*, OUP 1970, p. 4.

4. Ibid., p. 11.

5. Ibid., p. 39.

6. Cragg, *Christianity in World Perspective*, pp. 188f.

7. Raymond Panikkar, *The Trinity and World Religions*, Christian Literature Society, Madras 1970, p. 3.

8. J. Spencer Trimingham, *Two Worlds are Ours*, Librairie du Liben, Beirut 1971, p. 145.

9. Ibid., p. 144.

10. Ibid., pp. 142–3.

11. Raymond Panikkar, article in *Christian Revelation and World Religions*, p. 169.

# PLAYING

*Pentecostalism and the Supernatural Dimension in a Secular Age*

No one can seriously watch and pray for the world-wide impact of Jesus Christ upon mankind without paying attention to the pentecostal movement. Its phenomenal growth in Latin America is a byword, a great part of the spread of independent churches in Africa is pentecostal in character, and the teaching and experience of Pentecostalism is now penetrating churches of both Catholic and Protestant traditions. So much, in fact, has been happening inside the traditional churches since about 1960 that a distinction must be drawn between pentecostal churches and the whole pentecostal movement. The membership of the pentecostal churches, which have stemmed mainly from the Topeka and Los Angeles revival in the USA at the beginning of this century, still vastly outnumbers those in the traditional churches which are being touched by the pentecostal movement. Even so, the latter now include, in the USA, about 10,000 Roman Catholics and, counting ordained people alone, about 1,000 Presbyterians and ten per cent of Anglican priests.

For historical and psychological reasons Pentecostalism has more often than not appeared in conjunction with revivalism, fundamentalism, adventism and sectarianism. Revivalist it is bound to be, since its appeal is to those who feel that their lives as human beings and, if they are Christians, as members of the historic churches, lack some forgotten factor which they are no longer content to do without. But it becomes revivalist in a narrower sense when enthusiasm for the discovery of that missing factor leads to high-pressure proselytism.

Fundamentalism often goes with Pentecostalism since those who have been looking for the lost secret are more prone to identify it with a return to 'childlike faith' in the actual words of scripture, especially if it is the Bible that led them to a deeper experience of the Holy Spirit. Systematic adventism often follows from this literal approach to poetical and visionary texts. And any group that believes it has found a secret to which the main body of believers is blind is liable to sectarianism.

At this point it is worth noting a sociologist's definition of a sect.

The sect is a clearly defined community; it is of a size which permits only a minimal range of diversity of conduct; it seeks itself to rigidify a pattern of behaviour and to make coherent its structure of values; it contends actively against every other organization of values and ideals, and against every other social context possible for its adherents, offering itself as an all-embracing, divinely prescribed society. The sect is not only an ideological unit, it is to a greater or lesser degree, a social unit, seeking to enforce behaviour on those who accept belief, and seeking every occasion to draw the faithful apart from the rest of society and into the company of each other.[1]

But none of these features need necesarily accompany that conscious enjoyment of the fulness of the Spirit to which the pentecostal movement testifies and which is the birthright of every Christian. How generally the historic churches are failing to possess themselves of their birthright was brought home by Bishop Lesslie Newbigin some years ago:

The apostle asked the converts of Apollos one question: 'Did ye receive the Holy Spirit when ye believed?' and got a plain answer. His modern successors are more inclined to ask either 'Did you believe exactly what we teach?' or 'Were the hands that were laid on you our hands?' and – if the answer is satisfactory – to assure the converts that they have received the Holy Spirit even if they don't know it. There is a world of difference between these two attitudes.[2]

The whole weight of New Testament evidence endorses the central affirmation of the Pentecostalists that the gift of the Holy Spirit transforms and intensifies the quality of human life, and that this is a fact of experience in the lives of Christians. The longing of thousands of Christians to recover what they feel instinctively their faith promises them is what underlies the whole movement.

Students of the New Testament differ in their exegesis; but so far my own reading of it convinces me that the Pentecostalist is right when he calls the bestowal of this gift 'Baptism in the Holy Spirit'. But I think he is distorting the evidence when he teaches that this is something subsequent to, and distinct from, becoming a Christian. In the last analysis it is the transforming gift of the Spirit that makes a man a Christian. For anyone who is in Christ there is no further gift to be sought, though he may need to 'stir into flame again' the gift that he has already received (II Tim. 1.6). And classical pentecostal doctrine is certainly straining the evidence when it insists that 'speaking with tongues' is the necessary or normal sign of 'baptism in the Spirit'.

The writings of most of the Pentecostalists and other revivalists that I have read seem to me to look upon the Holy Spirit too much as a supply of superhuman power and wisdom and so to miss the fact that he works primarily by generating awareness and communion, and that whatever power and wisdom he gives derive from that. Again, the Pentecostalist's teaching, though not, as I understood it, his experience, invites the individual believer to receive the indwelling almost as a private possession; whereas the New Testament speaks not so much of the Spirit in the one as of the Spirit in the midst of the two or three. And, partly because of this misplaced emphasis on the singular instead of on the plural, the Pentecostalists have fallen as much as the Catholics and Protestants for the temptation to systematize the movement of God's free Spirit, specifying the conditions of his coming and the signs that prove it. Yet this they can do only by flying in the face of the biblical evidence.

Dr Walter Hollenweger, having himself served in the ministry of a pentecostal church for ten years, has put us all in his debt with his monumental study called *The Pentecostals*.[3] Unlike any previous work on the subject it embraces the pentecostal churches throughout the world, the independent churches of Africa, Indonesia and elsewhere which combine pentecostal and indigenous elements, and the charismatic movement in the traditional western churches. Critical of the dogma – or, as he would say, the lack of theology – in the classical pentecostal movement, he remains pentecostal in practice and believes it to be vital for a truly ecumenical Christianity to 'understand Pentecostalism as an expression of New Testament forms of religious belief and practice which might be following a very independent line, but could not be ruled out on *a priori* theological grounds'.

I want to say categorically that I believe the time has arrived when we must take into account all that is positive in the witness of the pentecostal movement if we hope to press further forward along any of the various roads of liturgical renewal, inter-faith dialogue, the indigenization of Christianity, experiments in Christian community and group experience, the ministry of healing, especially towards psychotics and addicts, and new approaches to church union.

The Pentecostal experience is clearly a factor of special importance in St Luke's understanding of the Christian way. In the third gospel he is at pains to make the point that the great reward of prayer is the gift of the Spirit; and throughout the Acts he lays special emphasis upon the direct communications which the apostles received from the Holy Spirit, and on the gifts of healing, exorcism, prophecy and speaking with tongues. In the epistles as a whole this balance is redressed, and although they contain plenty of references to gifts of prophecy, healing and so on, life in the Holy Spirit is associated mainly with a new relation to God, expressed in the words 'sonship' and 'liberty', and a new degree of love, of life-for-others, which the authors expressed in the phrases 'the fellowship of the Spirit' (II Cor. 13.14; Phil. 2.1), and 'the servanthood of the Spirit (II Cor. 3.8; Gal. 3.5). But, as in the life of Jesus, so now in the life of the church, the 'wild-wind' quality of the Holy Spirit is manifested in the release of a peculiar freedom and a certain strangeness and incalculability.

But St Paul was at pains to emphasize that the more unusual *charismata*, or grace-gifts, of the Holy Spirit are not themselves of the essence of the Spirit-filled life. They are marked by a certain transience; it is inherent in their nature to 'pass away'. This does not mean that they are going to disappear from the experience of the church after the apostolic age, but that we are not to expect of them the same permanence as belongs to the faith, hope and love of the Spirit-filled life. The fulness of the Spirit is known primarily in a new degree of communal awareness of the reality of God and the reality of Jesus Christ, and in a new communal sensitiveness towards other people. When these are present there can be no sense of anything lacking. Life in the Spirit is totally unself-regarding, and any anxiety over the possession or loss of special powers or privileges is quite foreign to it. That impressive exponent of the charismatic movement in the Roman Catholic Church, Father Simon Tugwell, insists that there can be no question of seeking something *extra* beyond the basic gift of the salvation that is offered to us all in Christ. (For those especially concerned with this subject, I would commend his recently published book *Did you receive the Spirit?* Darton, Longman & Todd 1972.) The new relationship to God in Christ is all-sufficient and all-satisfying. To speak of a 'second blessing' is a misnomer.

But, as I have already said, we may be in great need of a rediscovery. For every Christian is meant to possess his possessions, and many never do. The freedom of a son of God should be not merely a legal title but a fact of experience, and essentially a shared experience. It is better to call it incorrectly a second blessing and lay hold of the reality of new life in Christ than to let the soundness of our doctrine rob us of its substance.

What we must *not* do is to think and speak of the Holy Spirit as a magical power which God gives us to make us 'successful' Christians. This was the error of Simon Magus, and it continues to be the error of some revivalist and pentecostalist preaching. We must hold on to the fact that the Spirit works by putting us in touch, making us see. It is surely significant that, when Paul lists the gifts and the forms of ministry with which the Holy Spirit endowed the church of his day, he lumps together speaking in tongues and administration, exorcism and teaching, in complete indifference to the distinction we now draw between natural and supernatural. The powers of the new age which Jesus demonstrated were powers that should be natural to any man as God intended him to be. To say that the pentecostal movement represents 'a recovery of the supernatural dimension' is true only if we mean a rediscovery of the truth that every particle and process of material existence is alive with the activity of God.

All the Spirit's gifts are wonderful; all are marked by a certain spontaneity; but none is meant to be weird. They are incalculable, not incomprehensible. And, what is more important, they are corporate.

I propose to deal in turn with three of these more unusual gifts, examining their place and significance in New Testament times and in the history of the church up to the present day. Then, but not until then, I shall try to suggest how we should reconcile these phenomena in general with the rest of our understanding of God and of man. And in the light of this I shall invite you to consider what the church as a whole needs to learn, or to recover, from the pentecostal movement for the sake of its mission to all the world.

*Healing and Exorcism*   There can be no doubt that the power of Jesus over sickness was regarded as a sign both of his Messiahship and of his possession by the Spirit of God. 'The Spirit of the Lord is upon me because he has anointed me; he has sent me to announce good news to the poor. To proclaim release for prisoners and recovery of sight for the blind, to let the broken victims go free' (Luke 4.18). 'He cured all who were ill; and he gave strict injunctions that they were not to make him known. This was in fulfilment of Isaiah's prophecy: "Here is my servant whom I have chosen, my beloved, on whom my favour rests; I will put my Spirit upon him" ' (Matt. 12.15–18).

To see this connection between Christ's healing power and his unique possession by the Holy Spirit is not to say that his acts of healing themselves were unparalleled. There were healers a-plenty in that Levantine world where eastern and western cultures met. Wandering Magi such as Simon, Jewish healers and exorcists like those at Ephesus ('If I by Beelzebub cast out demons by whom do your sons cast them out?'), besides the doctors and priestly physicians of the Graeco–Roman culture. On several occasions Jesus is shown to have used therapeutic methods that were in common practice. His cures were accepted as miraculous, certainly, but so was almost all healing in that pre-scientific world. This does not mean that there was no exact knowledge of anatomy or of drugs or surgery based on empirical observation. In some directions medicine, as we understand it, had reached a remarkable level of competence. But it was still essentially sacralized knowledge and all healing was an activity in which spiritual powers were engaged.

It is quite natural, therefore, that when the synoptic evangelists write about Jesus' treatment of the sick they prefer, more often than not, to say quite simply that he cured people. The words most frequently used meant simply to give therapy or care, and have no theological overtones. What is more remarkable is the fact that another word altogether which normally bears a distinct theological meaning, is also applied to these bodily cures. This is the word 'to save'. In the Old and New Testaments alike salvation means victorious deliverance. The saviours of Israel were those who overcome her oppressors of old. And it was in this sense that God himself was designated as their Saviour because of his liberating and protective arm. In applying this Pauline word of powerful liberation to the healing ministry of Jesus the evangelists are saying that the cure of disease is one aspect of his victory over everything that binds and spoils God's creation: 'Here is this woman, a daughter of Abraham, who has been kept prisoner by Satan for eighteen long years: was it wrong for her to be freed from her bonds on the Sabbath?' In the thought of the New Testament writers Jesus' victorious struggle was waged against the demonic powers which mastered every aspect of man's life in this world, whether with the burden of disease, or the curse of occult power, or the bondage of sin and guilt. So one might say that every disease cured was an act of exorcism. Our modern distinction between the salvation of the soul and salvation from illness was absent from their thought. The reality of which the miracles of Jesus were 'signs' was his serene authority both to heal *and* to forgive. It was the combination of these two authorities in a total assault on evil, rather than the miracle of healing itself which caused the onlookers to exclaim: 'We never saw it on this fashion!'

This is what made the cures which Jesus performed different from those of other healers of those days. His response towards disease was no more than a part of something enormously wider, part of a total victory over evil in all its forms. That victory reached its culmination in his death and resurrection.

It followed naturally that the community of those who were themselves incorporated into the victorious manhood of Jesus and enjoyed his Spirit-possessed life should receive as one of the gifts of the Spirit the same power of healing. And, again, the difference between this community's *charisma* of healing and the cures performed by the other practitioners of that ancient world lay not in the cures themselves but solely in the fact that the Christians related everything they might accomplish to the struggle in which Jesus had already engaged against the power of evil and they saw the healing of disease as a reflection of the victory Jesus had already won.

When we turn to the epistles, the actual references to healing and exorcism are few. In I Corinthians 12, in each of his three recitations of the *charismata* of the Spirit,[4] Paul distinguished two related gifts – the gift of healings and the exercise of powers – and the second of these probably refers to the authority of exorcism. In the second part of II Corinthians he speaks of the signs, marvels and powers he had wrought as a guarantee of his apostleship (II Cor. 12.12); and in the Epistle to the Romans he uses the same three words to describe the *charismata* which had attended his preaching of the gospel to the Gentiles (Rom. 15.19). The Epistle to the Hebrews also speaks of the signs, marvels and manifold powers by which God was witnessing to the truth of the word that was preached (Heb. 2.4) and this echoes the brief summary of the apostolic commission at the close of the late ending of the Gospel of Mark: 'They went forth and preached everywhere, the Lord working with them and confirming the word by the signs that followed.' But signs, as Jesus knew, are always ambiguous, and as early as the Second Epistle to the Thessalonians Paul was warning his converts against the 'lawless one' whose presence was accompanied by 'all power and signs and deceptive marvels' (II Thess. 2.9). This ambiguity may partly explain the comparative paucity of reference in the epistles as a whole to the gift of healing or, indeed, to any of such *charismata*.

There is less of this diffidence in the Acts of the Apostles, though even there we do not find the healing ministry presented as the constant accompaniment of the preaching of the Word the gospels might have led us to expect. There are four 'umbrella' passages, each describing a period of widespread healing, which somewhat resemble similar comprehensive texts in the gospels. These refer respectively to the ministry of the apostles, especially Peter, in Jerusalem (Acts 5.12–16), the mission of Philip in Samaria (Acts 8.6–8), the mission of Paul and Barnabas in Iconium (Acts 14.3) and Paul's two-year sojourn in Ephesus (Acts 19.10–12). Apart from these, the Acts mentions the healing of the lame man in the Temple, of Aeneas and Tabitha at Joppa, of the cripple at Lystra, the exorcism of the girl at Philippi, the restoration of Eutychus at Troas and the healing of Publius' father and others on Malta – seven occasions in all.

The gospels reveal an unquestioning tradition that Christ's commission to the church included not simply the command to preach but also the command to heal and, even more definitely, to cast out demons. Mark's account of the calling of the twelve specifies a threefold purpose: 'that they might be with him, and that he might send them forth to preach, and to have authority to cast out devils'

(Mark 3.14). Though neither Matthew nor Luke incorporated this passage, all three evangelists include a reference both to exorcism and to healing in their accounts of the first mission of the twelve. Mark tells us that on this mission the apostles healed the sick by anointing them with oil, to which the only other reference in the New Testament is in the Epistle of James, though it was a common therapeutic method among pre-Christian Jews. This would suggest that these disciples very naturally first sought to obey their Lord's terrifying injunction by following one of the more traditional forms of treatment, and only later acquired enough confidence in their inner endowment to heal, like Jesus himself, by laying on hands or by simple word of command.

Before tracing the continuance of healing and exorcism in the history of the church it is worth pausing to notice three peculiarly Christian emphases in the exercise of these gifts in the church of the first generation.

First, as we have already seen, healing is always a demonstration of that total victory which Jesus had won over evil itself. 'Our conception of healing', says Michael Wilson, 'must be wide enough to include sickness, sin, famine in the Congo, and *apartheid* between races.'[5] Secondly, therefore, Christian healing is frequently linked with the forgiveness of sin and set in the context of a forgiven and forgiving community. We may take the passage in the Epistle of James as descriptive of a typical treatment. 'Is one of you ill? He should send for the elders of the congregation to pray over him and anoint him with oil in the name of the Lord. The prayer offered in faith will save the sick man, the Lord will raise him from his bed, and any sins he may have committed will be forgiven. Therefore confess your sins to one another, and pray for one another, and then you will be healed' (James 5.14–16). And thirdly, as appears strongly in this passage, Christian healing is essentially the gift not of particularly endowed individuals but of the Spirit-filled community. This emphasis was specially necessary in an age when the mystery cults and various forms of gnosticism were claiming to endow the individual aspirant, through a long process of initiation and refinement with superior powers such as are promised today by certain schools of yoga. These esoteric sects were ruled by the conviction that there are two classes of men – the natural or fleshly man and the spiritual or illuminated man. The latter through ascetic discipline hoped to win power over nature and over the destinies of other men, including the gifts of healing and prediction. Against this cult of the superior personality the Christian community insisted that the gifts of the Spirit were given primarily to the fellowship as a whole, even though they might be severally distributed among the different members of the one Body (I Cor. 12.4–12).

Michael Wilson has drawn attention to the special significance of the laying on of hands as an act representative of the whole community.

> The minister's hands are the hands of the whole Church. When a minister at the Lord's Table takes bread and breaks it, at that moment all the hands of the whole congregation are with his hands in the breaking. . . In and through his Body, the Church, Christ himself, once again, takes and breaks. In the same way when the minister lays his hands upon the head of a sick person, it is as if the hands of all the congregation are with his hands, focusing their love and prayers for the one in need. It is a corporate act of the Church as the Christ-indwelt community.[6]

Such an act, he explains, is symbolic of the communal acceptance of responsibility for the one in need, offering him the love of a caring group, and this alone may often be sufficient to set a patient free from all anxiety and liberate the processes of healing within his own organism. So Wilson continues:

> The laying on of hands is, therefore, an act through which the Holy Spirit within a community expresses his love. If introduced as a healing act without a caring Body behind it, there is a risk of its being a dead ceremony. It may then be merely the expression of a magical idea of a God who intervenes from outside.[7]

The communal character of the gifts of the Spirit is, as we shall see, of equal importance in respect to the other *charismata* also as a safeguard against the cult of a spiritual elite.

When we follow the history of the church we find that the proclamation of the gospel has rarely been entirely bereft of the witness of some healing ministry. In the second century exorcism appears to be regarded as a matter of course in the life of the Christian community. Irenaeus, speaking of the miraculous gifts of the Spirit still manifest in the church of his day, mentions exorcism, prediction, visions, prophecy, and healing. And Justin boasts in about AD 150:

Many devil-possessed all over the world, and in your own city, many of our men, the Christians have exorcised in the name of Jesus Christ. . . When all other exorcists and sayers of charms and sellers of drugs failed, they have healed them and still do heal, sapping the power of the demons who hold men, and driving them out.[8]

Origen, Tertullian, Cyprian, all add a similar testimony. And Origen's great missionary pupil, Gregory, was nicknamed Wonder-worker because of his ease of exorcism and healing.

But from that time we notice a greater priestly control of this *charisma*, partly out of a recognition of that communal and representative nature of Christian healing which we have already noticed, and partly from the need for order and decency. But by the third century the oil for anointing the sick could only be consecrated by the bishop, though any Christian might apply it. By the fifth century the priests alone were permitted to anoint. The anointing of cases of extreme sickness was intended as a means of healing as late as the days of Bede and, indeed, to anoint those who were known to be dying was regarded as a heretical practice. But by the twelfth century the idea of healing in this way had become obsolete and the practice of anointing survived ironically as the special sacrament of death!

This by no means meant the end of the *charisma* of healing and exorcism in the mission of the church. They reappear again and again in the lives of the saints, and when all the accretions of hagiography have been allowed for there remains too much evidence of health restored and evil influence overcome to be dismissed unless one writes off all such phenomena *ipso facto*, including all the cures in the New Testament and every non-scientific healing of our own day also.

But although the gift of healing has been manifest in the life of the church, albeit spasmodically, throughout its history, for most of the time it has been a very different thing from the *charisma* which we see in the New Testament. The change, I suggest, was due to the determined attempt to institutionalize the Holy Spirit in the life of the church. Instead of being the creative Lord and initiator of all the communal responses of the church, he is treated as a thing – a force to be manipulated, a fluence to be placed at the disposal of bishops and priests and dispensed sacramentally and in no other way. Monasticism which may have started as a protest against clerical centralization very quickly took over the same error, and as Bishop Kirk pointed out,[9] the monks became in some ways the successors of the gnostics, a spiritual aristocracy in the midst of an unenlightened, fleshly majority.

This clerical monopoly over the gifts of the Spirit had the effect of dividing in two something that had at first been indivisible. Life in the Spirit had been both communal and transfigured. It was the life of a new manhood, the life of the new creation, and its hall-mark was the freedom and strength of love. If anything could be called supernatural this was it, only it was seen in fact to be the most natural and truly human life that had ever been experienced. And this Spirit-filled life was known not as an individual attainment but in the relationships of a community. This was the only safe and true context for the *charismata* of healing and prediction and ecstasy.

But as a result of institutionalizing the experience of the Holy Spirit his special gifts were removed entirely from the normal life and witness of the church and limited either to the aristocracy of transformed individuals – the saints and mystics – or to those persecuted minorities which had been forced to develop an abnormal degree of communal solidarity without the discipline of an inner transformation. It is one of the comic ironies of church history that more and more of the spiritual aristocracy exhibited the most striking gifts of the Spirit after they had departed this life, through their shrines and relics, while it is the second type of manifestation, that of the cohesive minority sect, which has mainly caught the attention of Christians for the past six centuries. The Albigensiens claimed to possess healing gifts, and George Fox and some of the early Quakers were credited with power to discern an evil or lying spirit masquerading as godly inspiration and to exorcise it.

And so we come to the present day and the exuberant spread of the pentecostal movement since the beginning of this century. Not all, but a considerable majority of these churches and sects give a prominent place to healing and exorcism. In Latin Ameria, and in Africa south of the Sahara this is often the main attraction that brings new converts into a pentecostal fold either from the traditional religion or from other Christian churches. Professor Bengt Sundkler once called the Roman Catholic Church in Africa an Institute of Grace, the Protestant Churches an Institute of the Word, and the

Zionist movement an Institute of Healing. Samuel Mutendi, for example, who helped to bring Zionism to Rhodesia in the 1920s, 'was believed to have the mystical powers of healing, exorcising evil spirits, granting fertility to women and of making rain'.[10] Turner has described a typical healing service of the Church of the Lord (Aladura) in Nigeria, lasting for five hours after midnight, when consecrated water was used for anointing the sick.[11] And a recent study of Pentecostalism in Chile found that nearly half the people interviewed 'linked their conversion with a cure, not necessarily miraculous, since sometimes it was due to a doctor, but always attributed to God, "who saved me when the doctor thought it was impossible" '.[12] These quotations are typical of the main stream of the movement. But it is not to be associated only with a naive and primitive faith. The reason why so many young graduates in Latin American universities are drawn to the pentecostal healing sects is that they seem to be more relevant to human needs and conditions than the Protestant or Catholic congregations. After all, these students argue, for every person who feels an immediate concern for politics or social change there are ten who feel the need for help in some sickness of body or of mind. And for every person who goes to a doctor there are ten who cannot possibly afford scientific treatment and turn thankfully to the promise of healing through the close-knit effectual fellowship of some pentecostal sect.[13]

The alternative way of non-medical healing today is the individual faith-healer, so-called. Despite their own sincere protestations these 'healers' are looked to as being in themselves the vehicle or source of a superhuman power, rather than the Holy Spirit in the life of the fellowship. So the cult of the uncannily endowed *guru* persists in parallel to the spread of the highly cohesive sects in the two spheres in which the special *charisma* of healing is expected to be found.

It is only gradually and belatedly that a third way is being discovered, or rather, rediscovered. This is a return to the New Testament concept of the Spirit-filled and Spirit-led group living in the continual forgiveness of God the life of the new mankind, and offering a body in which Christ can be incarnate still, to heal and reconcile and liberate. What this ought to mean was illustrated some years ago, in a remarkable experience in a mental hospital in this country.[14] In a unit of twenty-six beds the patients and the medical staff shared the responsibility for organizing all the details of their domestic and social life and for sorting out their personal problems together. In the general atmosphere of frankness and tolerance everyone began to talk freely about problems they had never dared to mention before, and to comment frankly on the unacceptable attitudes and behaviour of others. Staff problems and weaknesses were as readily exposed as those of the patients. As each one became more and more himself, badness as well as goodness emerged more clearly. But whenever a patient was obviously going through a disturbed phase the rest of the group did all they could to try to understand and help towards a solution. The discovery that they could be accepted and forgiven in spite of themselves brought many of the patients, and some of the staff also, a deep and lasting emotional healing, and sometimes physical healing also. The creative power of this healing fellowship is such that it draws out the badness not only from the individual patient but from the wider community. The doctor who described the experiment wrote:

> A unit working in this way has a profound effect upon the whole hospital community. Many of the staff are critical and scornful of what they consider to be a soft, or even immoral approach. They cry out for more discipline, for a tougher approach. . . In this way, the accepting approach calls out the 'badness' of the whole hospital and puts a great strain upon everybody.

For that particular doctor the working of that therapeutic unit was 'a profound religious experience'. And so he turned to the church to see why he had not found this accepting love there; and to the Bible to see what it had to say about it.

> Should not the Church fellowship be a therapeutic community based upon the free flow of Christian love? Should it not be providing the kind of atmosphere in which people are free to be themselves and to find healing in the redemptive nature of an accepting sacrificial love, the love of God, mediated by the members of the Church? Dare we share the life of Jesus together like this in our church fellowships and let this love expose our badness to the full, knowing that he loves us just the same, or must we fall back on the more comfortable path of good works and respectable Christian behaviour?

A missionary doctor doing some research into endemic disease on the coast of East Africa wrote a few years back of a somewhat different experience in words which came strangely from a man of the twentieth century, though his almost clinical manner of speaking about exorcism shows how accustomed he had become to the healing effect upon strangers of a deeply integrated Christian team.

We visited the village of a woman called Bendera who had been demon-possessed at the time of our last visit. We thought we had failed through inexperience. The African pastor who accompanied us before had attempted to deliver her, apparently in vain. But this time she came forward to greet us, free of fear, smiling and full of friendliness; so very different from the fearful possessed woman of two years ago. Another woman in the village who had been insane with demon-possession (she had been maniacal and violent like the man of Gadara) was also quite different; calm, lucid and friendly. She and Bendera and the other villagers listened intently to the Gospel.

More and more practitioners are coming to recognize that the little-known dynamics of our interpersonal relations are the clue to a great deal of healing. We are rediscovering the therapy of touch, which is a sacrament of acceptance and love. We are also learning how much of the healing process consists essentially of releasing the patient's power to heal himself.

Dr Graham Clark, eye surgeon at the Columbia Presbyterian Medical Centre in New York, has described the case of a woman patient. A week after surgery, he says, nothing had changed in the eye. All the tissues were exactly as he had left them at the end of the operation. Ten days later the original condition was beginning to return. At that point he sat down by his patient and said to her 'I'm afraid you are under a misapprehension. I am a surgeon but not a healer. I put tissues together so that they can heal as they could not if they were separated. I cannot heal you. I can merely put your eye back together. Now I must do so again because your eye has come apart again. But if there is to be healing it will have to be yours not mine.' The patient was delighted with this frank personal relationship. A second operation took place the next day and ten days later she was healed.

All this must surely enable us to see in a new way that the arena in which health and disease fight each other is one in which the Holy Spirit as we have understood him – the life-giving Go-Between kindling awareness and compelling choice – is supremely relevant. It is not surprising, therefore, that there is a slowly growing minority of doctors and surgeons who combine the skills of their medical training with prayer for healing and the laying on of hands, with no sense of contradiction. All Christians, but especially those working in cultures that are not dominated by western thought, should keep a scrupulously open mind towards what is commonly called 'faith healing'. The ministry of certain men through whom the healing power of the Christian community seems to be channelled offers incontrovertible evidence not only of a power of diagnosis which is a form of extra-sensory perception, but of processes of restoration, which we have not yet learned to identify or explain, operating in the little known realm of person-to-person interaction in a physico-spiritual universe.

The fact that we have not yet begun to understand the 'laws' which govern these processes tempts both the sceptic and the believer to make hasty, subjective judgments in this matter. If we baldly call the unexplained a miracle, the former is compelled either to disbelieve or to explain it away, while the latter is, for the wrong reasons, predisposed to make much of it. Both, in fact, are making the same mistake in thinking that there is more of God in a healing by laying-on-of-hands than in a healing by surgery. To both of them religious faith, whether they accept or reject it, means belief in a God who is 'other' in the sense of 'extra' – a power to be called in when human help fails. The truth is that God is just as much at work, and just as wonderingly to be praised, in the techniques which man has 'mastered' as in the processes which remain a mystery to him.

*The Gift of Prediction* I have dwelt at considerable length on the gifts of healing and exorcism because these are for most of us the only ones which seem to have a contemporary counterpart of any value and therefore offer an object of intellectual historical study. But from this we have been able, I hope, to identify a certain pattern of development which we can now more easily follow in the case of those other gifts of the Spirit to which the New Testament refers.

One of these which was obviously given a high place in the apostles' scale of values is the gift of prophecy. It is not easy to determine of what exactly this gift consisted. The name προφῆται was of course applied to the great prophets of the Old Testament; but from their various references to contemporary Christian prophets it is obvious that the New Testament authors were not describing an Amos or Jeremiah of the first century A.D. Agabus and his kind were much more like the primitive prophets of the days of the Judges. Although one cannot be certain, the evidence in the first two centuries of the Christian era points to their speaking under some form of direct inspiration, though Paul was at pains to compare them favourably with those who had the gift of speaking in tongues on the ground that the prophets' mental processes were continuously rational and conscious. So it was not a case of oracular trance or hypnosis such as one meets in the pagan soothsayers, and the authors were careful never to use the word *mantis* which was the common name for a pagan oracle. Yet they must have realized the danger of confusing Christian prophets with pagan mountebanks, and this may underlie Paul's injunction 'despise not prophesying'. It is remarkable that Paul consistently ranks the prophets next to, or even with, the apostles in the hierarchy of ministries, and yet they remain almost entirely in the shadows in the New Testament story. Perhaps it is significant that in his lists prophets and teachers are several times paired together. This suggests that these men were gifted with an interpretative insight whereby, intuitively rather than logically, they set down the fundamentals of Christian belief and behaviour as this emerged from the, as yet, unthought-out experience of Christ and his resurrection. I have an idea that the prophets were the authors of the many pieces of rhythmical teaching, usually called hymns, which we find quoted throughout the epistles. This would naturally give them a special place in the ordering of the very spontaneous forms of public worship in those days, and so we read in the Didache that it is the function of the prophet to conduct worship and offer thanks. But together with such an expository ministry, if such was theirs, the prophets of the early church were clearly gifted with powers of prediction also, as we find on both the occasions when we meet Agabus.

Prediction was given much greater prominence in that breakaway revival which bubbled up in the second-century church in Asia Minor, in that very region which in previous centuries had been the breeding ground of the grim orgiastic resurgences of the worship of the earth goddess, Cybele. Montanism, as it was named after its most famous convert, was an adventist movement, living in immediate expectation of the end of the world. Great emphasis was laid upon the accurate foretelling of the last days so that Montanists called their movement 'the new prophecy'. Their prophets, however, unlike those of orthodox Christian groups, operated through self-induced trance.

In spite of the odium which such extravagance naturally brought upon this gift, Christian prophets retained their good repute until the third or fourth century. The goodly fellowship of which we sing in the Te Deum refers to them, not to the Old Testament prophets, and once more ranks them next to the apostles and above the martyrs.

But by this time the prophets had fulfilled their function. Christian teaching had passed beyond the first formulations and become the prerogative of philosophers. Or, if the development of the *charisma* of healing affords a more generally applicable pattern, we may say that the professionals took this gift of the Spirit also into their exclusive control. Teaching, like healing, was no longer the task and the gift of the Christian community as such. Hereafter it is to be found either in the hands of the so-called 'doctors' of the church or else it breaks out in fresh bursts of adventism in close-knit, inward-looking minorities. The anabaptists claimed that their prophecies stood on an equal footing with the scriptures. Ecstatic prediction was a feature of Huguenot refugees in the Cevennes in the last years of the seventeenth century. And prophecy so-called has provided the initial impetus that brought into being a great number of adventist and pentecostal groups since the mid-nineteenth century.

A very typical example is the founding of the Musama Disco Christo Church of Ghana by the prophet Jemisemiham Jehu-Appiah. Five days after his birth in 1883 a stranger visiting the village prophesied that the boy would become a great messenger of God. His parents made great sacrifices on this account to procure a good education for him. As a youth he much impressed another itinerant Christian prophet, Samuel Nyankson. A few years later he began keeping fasts, and during one of these, as he meditated in an easy chair, he fell into a trance and saw three angels holding a crown towards him and placing it three times on his head. He was aroused by the unexpected arrival of one of Nyankson's pupils with the words 'God has made you a great king. On my way here I saw you in a vision dressed like a king with a crown on your head.' On 18 August 1919, while Appiah was praying in an open-air place of worship, he heard the sound of a crowd praising God and saw an angel approaching him with a Bible opened at the tenth chapter of Acts. At that moment he knew he had become a new man and began speaking with tongues. From that time he retreated more and more often for prayer and meditation, he found he could perform miraculous cures, and he preached to ever-larger audiences. His activities could not be contained within the discipline of the Methodist Church of Ghana and he founded what he called a 'faith-society' in 1922, which grew into the Musama Disco Christo Church. Appiah died in 1948 and one of his sons was instated as head of the Church in his place.[15]

A more recent example along similar lines is that of Alice Lenshina, an illiterate village wife who grew up in the Presbyterian Church of what was then Northern Rhodesia.[16] In September 1954 she became ill and fell into a coma. Her own sincere belief, shared by her thousands of followers, is that she was brought back from the dead after receiving a special mandate from Jesus Christ to preach his gospel and recall people from sorcery and protective charms. Two books were placed in her hands, but what they contained and for whom they were intended are matters of some confusion. What is certain is that her revivalism won an enormous following especially from the Presbyterian and Roman Catholic folds and the members of her Lumpa Church surrendered their fetishes and charms as they had never done in the mission congregations. Her main medium of teaching was the hymns she was inspired to compose in which biblical imagery is used with the same originality as in Negro spirituals. The personal impression she made upon me in 1958 was of a simple goodness and commonsense enhanced by an unmistakable personal authority. Her message of revival and eschatology was orthodox, the moral code she imposed was strict, her baptisms were primarily an act of exorcism and protection.

The New Testament evidence does not suggest that the Christian prophets were normally the founders of new churches, unless Apollos was more a man of this type than the philosopher we have imagined hitherto. But the style of these charismatic leaders in Africa and elsewhere today does endorse my guess that the gift of prophecy in the apostolic age was essentially a teaching ministry, oracular and poetic in method, through which the primitive doctrine of the church was formulated and passed on. Naturally it was soon replaced by a more rational teaching method and a more analytical theology, and this must always be the pattern. As the African independent churches make more use of their own or others' theological schools their dependence on charismatic prophets is likely to decline. But may it not be that here among the ruins of an old Christendom, where Christian faith is having to be rediscovered, doctrine will be born afresh, crude and flaming, in the Spirit-moved songs of rock and folk and the runes of the banner-makers?

*Speaking in Tongues* This third seemingly supernatural gift of the Spirit has attracted most attention and controversy in recent times. Even more than the gift of prophecy it puzzles the rational mind with its apparent pointlessness. (Miraculously imparted speech in a foreign language is a different matter and has so rarely been alleged that it does not enter into the argument.) A gift of healing, if we can believe in it, has an obvious use, but it is difficult to see that any purpose is served, for God or the individual or the community, by a flow of words in a non-human tongue. Until some rationale can be found for it in functional terms it is hard to discuss what significance it has for our understanding of the Holy Spirit.

I have had no experience of this phenomenon in myself, but I have a number of intimate friends in Britain to whom it happens more or less regularly, and in Africa I have attended worship at which hymn-singing was 'worked up' until there were people all over the congregation shaking and speaking in tongues. As far as I can understand it, the experience, from the human agent's point of view, is one of surrender and release at a deep level. I am assured that it involves no loss of self-awareness, which is why it is better to avoid calling it ecstatic utterance, and that a person speaking in tongues retains a sense of the general meaning of the sounds – that it is praise or prayer or information – without consciously intending or understanding the words. Nonetheless, to 'let go' the organs of speech to respond to the prompting of some other volition than one's own rationality is to yield control of the most hard-won faculty of our human nature. It actualizes not only a letting go but a being let go, in a remarkable token of inhibition broken down and spontaneity welling up. It speaks of the freedom and of the intuitive communication that are characteristic gifts of the Spirit. But it is not a natural symbol of loving concern, and that seems to be the grounds for St Paul's reservations regarding it.

Loving concern, however, compels one to recognize what a blessed release the gift of tongues must be to people frustrated and defenceless because they are slow of speech. This is a very striking element in the several films that have been made of Latin American Pentecostalism. Not only do the pent-up wells of suffering and joy find release but, as Bryan Wilson writes of the Elim assemblies, 'the ability to get up and speak (albeit in an unknown tongue) in people who normally have never dared to do anything of the kind, or obtrude themselves in any way, to give vent to their feelings and be applauded for so doing, no matter how inarticulately they express themselves, is a newly acquired power'.[17]

The dramatic nature of this gift has inevitably focussed special attention upon it so that it tends to be looked for as a necessary sign of the 'baptism in the Holy Spirit'. Outside the pentecostal churches, those who are accustomed to dealing with the gift of tongues deny that it is to be sought for its own sake or as a *sine qua non*. But, by the nature of things, it is not easy for those who have experienced this particular expression of the liberty of the Spirit to be indifferent to its presence or absence in others. Yet almost all who have described to me their experience of this gift put their emphasis upon the far more vivid awareness it has brought them of God and of Jesus Christ, of the world around and, especially, of what other people are feeling, saying and needing.

Because the pentecostalist movement of this century has focussed special attention on this strange *charisma*, it comes as something of a surprise to find how little reference there is in the New Testament to this gift. Jesus healed and Jesus exercised the gift of prophetic insight and prediction, but there is no hint that Jesus spoke with tongues. The author of Acts specifies only three occurrences of the gift: in Jerusalem on the day of Pentecost, in the house of Cornelius at Caesarea, and when Paul dealt with the disciples of John the Baptist at Ephesus. And it is worth noting that all these were initiatory occasions when some outward confirmation of an essential principle was specially required. Then there is a phrase in the late ending of the Gospel of Mark. Apart from these there is no reference to speaking with tongues outside the First Epistle to the Corinthians.

Father Ronald Knox has suggested that, while other churches to which Paul wrote were threatened by different versions of false teaching, the Corinthian church suffered from that exaggerated taste for supernatural phenomena which has often been a mark of superficial or unsettled faith. 'The supernatural germ of life planted in them so recently', he says, 'is in danger of running to seed, and producing a harvest of ultrasupernaturalism.'[18] Be that as it may, Paul is clearly anxious about the Corinthian's evaluation of the different spiritual gifts which he admits they have in abundance. Their use of speaking in tongues constitutes a problem with which he has to deal like their other problems of disunity, laxity and disorder. Though he recognizes and permits the gift of tongues, his object is to discourage too great an emphasis upon it, to discipline its use and to turn their attention towards more valuable *charismata*.

Speaking with tongues reappears only occasionally in the subsequent history of the church. Eusebius writes with distaste of the founder of the Montanists that he 'was carried away in spirit and wrought up into a certain kind of frenzy and irregular ecstasy, raving, and speaking and uttering strange things', and this was still a feature of Montanism in Tertullian's day. But by the fourth century Chrysostom in the East and Augustine in the West testify that the phenomenon is unknown to the churches of their day. The Middle Ages, despite their predilection for wonders in the lives of the saints, make no reference to the gift of tongues, though, to be fair, one should mention the so-called ecstasy of silence which some of the mystics commended as the summit of the life of prayer. But it would almost seem that ecstatic speech is native to the Protestant rather than the Catholic fringe. After a gap of 1300 years it first reappeared among the persecuted Huguenot peasants of the Cevennes region in Southern France at the end of the seventeenth century. Neither Zinzendorf nor Wesley refer to it, though their revivalist meetings, like the wilder gatherings of the Jansenists in Paris, often induced violent weeping and convulsions, and Thomas Walsh, one of Wesley's preachers, records in his diary for 8 March 1750: 'This morning the Lord gave me a language I knew not of, raising my soul to him in a wondrous manner.' It is not until 1830 that we come upon the next occurrence, when a girl 'prophesying' in a strange tongue in Glasgow inspired Edward Irving to lay stress on this gift in his newly founded Catholic Apostolic Church in London. On at least one occasion the saintly Curé d'Ars seems to have spoken in tongues in a state of mystical exaltation. Since then it has become a very widespread phenomenon.

It seems to me that one can identify two causative factors at work beneath all these manifestations of spontaneity and un-rational response in the long Christian tradition. One of them is negative and the other positive.

On the one hand they are a passionate expression of self-concern. Need is met. Unconscious tensions are released. Loneliness is appeased. Sickness is healed. Uncertainties about the future are resolved. Inarticulate weakness finds rich self-expression. Call it relevance of a kind, and recognize honestly that most of our talk of relevance is a demand for a method which gets results. But basically the weakness of the Corinthian church is that it is self-concerned. It is their egotism which keeps them immature. Professor Christian Baëta makes this penetrating comment at the end of his study of six prophetist churches in Ghana.

> The 'historical churches' have developed away from performing any acts the inherent virtues of which are believed to secure or induce divine benefits, religious or other; whereas the exertions entailed in the exercise of the 'spiritual churches' are understood to be directed precisely to that end. . . The 'spiritual churches' quite definitely assume the efficacy of various techniques for securing the benefits and blessings which they desire. Thus, if looked at closely, their religion is in essence a very different one from that of the historical churches.[19]

I believe that is a true diagnosis, for it coincides with Dr Kenneth Kirk's insistence that 'the systematic quest of ecstasy, or of any other form of "experience", merely for the gratification which will be derived therefrom, is irreligious. Such a quest . . . turns the seeker's mind back upon himself and his own states of consciousness and so induces once again just that self-centredness which it is the whole purpose of religion to annihilate.'[20]

One can only feel confidence in an outward manifestation of the inner working of the Holy Spirit if it clearly results in totally disinterested action of some sort. But before we apply that criterion too stringently to others let us admit how much of our motivation and that of the historical churches as well as the pentecostal has been, and still is, a simple calculation of the dividends.

But, positively, this constantly recurring desire for the charismatic gifts must surely be seen as an insistence upon the wholeness of man. No man, least of all Christian man, can live fully in that protracted paranoia which exalts and idealizes his cerebral life and demotes his instinctual being. True growth is not from the intuitive to the rational, but always towards an integration of the two. We never leave primitive man behind but must learn to travel with him in the company.

Failure to do this constitutes a far greater threat to civilization than any incompleteness in our rational control of things. This is why I am so convinced that the recovery of a full appreciation of the Holy Spirit in the Christian scheme is so vital for the church. For he is both the Spirit of Truth, the enlightener, the bearer of discernment and understanding, and also the Creator Spiritus, the bracing energy, the mighty rushing wind sweeping along all the subterranean corridors below consciousness. The hidden irrational areas of reality must be contained within any faith which claims not only to satisfy but to redeem mankind. Here in the West we may still doubt the necessity for this if we close our eyes to the beat groups and the search for psychedelic states of mind. Anyone who has a concern for the mission of the church to the six continents must come to terms with the fact that the vast majority of mankind is not going to find God through such a cerebral religion as the Christianity it has so far encountered. That is what the revival movements, the Zionist sects, the whole pentecostal third section of the world-wide church, are saying to us. That is why a particular missionary in India discovered that again and again simple villagers were calling him and his wife to come and heal their sick children and relatives, not because they mistook him for a doctor, as he had supposed, but because they knew he was a person dedicated to his religion. They were refusing to have their health and sickness wholly desacralized.

I am not looking for a recovery of exotic supernaturalism, but an extension of the range of our empirical enquiry. Above all we need to learn how to retain the sense of mystery amid all the things we *can* understand. It will be a new capacity, for the mystery of the future can no longer feed on ignorance. Perhaps we shall find that mystery, and can learn to recognize the Spirit of God in action, in the ordinary caring of people and in their relationships to one another, in the fellowship of the forgiven and forgiving church, in the service we can render together to the world. Perhaps in the small new groupings of our scattered secularized church we shall help one another to see the glory incarnate, as it were, in every ordinary thing, and that will be the main object of our common prayer. Two sayings from the Oxyrynchus Papyrus which may indeed be the very words of Jesus, sum up what I am trying to say. The first is the oft-quoted invitation: *Lift the stone and you will find me, cleave the wood and I am there.* The second is a promise: *He that wonders shall reign, and he that reigns shall rest.* Our need is not for more wonders but for more wonder.

## NOTES

1. Bryan R. Wilson, *Sects and Society*, Heinemann 1961, p. 1.
2. Lesslie Newbigin, *The Household of God*, SCM Press 1953, p. 95.
3. Walter J. Hollenweger, *The Pentecostals*, SCM Press 1972.
4. Verses 8–10, 28 and 29–30.
5. Michael Wilson, *The Church is Healing*, SCM Press 1966, p. 119.
6. Ibid., p. 35.
7. Ibid., p. 36.
8. Justin Martyr, *Second Apology*, 6.
9. K. E. Kirk, *The Vision of God*, Longmans Green 1931, p. 234.
10. M. L. Daneel, *The Background and Rise of Southern Shona Independent Churches*, Mouton, The Hague 1971, p. 296. See also the same author's *Zionism and Faith-Healing in Rhodesia*, 1970.
11. H. W. Turner, *African Independent Church*, OUP 1967, Vol. II, pp. 144–7.
12. Christian Lalive d'Epinay, *Haven of the Masses*, Lutterworth Press 1969, p. 47.
13. Walter J. Hollenweger, article in *The Ecumenical Review*, Vol. XX, No. 2, p. 166.
14. Denis V. Martin, *The Church as a Healing Community*, Guild of Health 1964, from which the next two quotations are taken.
15. C. G. Baëta, *Prophetism in Ghana*, SCM Press 1962, pp. 28ff.
16. Dorothea Lehmann and John V. Taylor, *Christians of the Copperbelt*, SCM Press 1961, pp. 248ff.
17. Bryan R. Wilson, op. cit., p. 115.
18. R. A. Knox, *Enthusiasm*, OUP 1950, p. 11.
19. Baëta, op. cit., p. 145.
20. Kirk, op. cit., p. 198.

# II

## LOVING

*Prayer in the Spirit and the Silence of Mission*

Josiah Pratt, the real architect of the Church Missionary Society, said right at the beginning, 'Put prayer first', and his words have been taken as the title for the annual directory for intercession which that society, like most others, makes available to its supporters. It is still a commonplace that prayer for the spread of the gospel and the coming of the Kingdom, with intercession for particular people in their particular needs, is the most important thing Christians can 'do' for the furtherance of their mission. But one cannot, without sounding insufferably bland, repeat these pious injunctions as though nothing had happened to the spirit of man since the early nineteenth century. The experience of prayer will go dead for more and more of us unless we face the truth of ourselves in regard to two facts, one a constant condition of all humanity, the other a special condition of western man today. First: most Christians, like most men everywhere and in all ages, do not find that prayer comes naturally to them and, in fact, pray very little. Second: minds conditioned by scientific empiricism can no longer believe in a god who responds to prayer. This is not atheism; on the contrary, we find it is the very people who have the most profound sense of God's reality who find it most absurd to tell him what needs to be done or to ask him to interfere with the course of events. Their prayer, in consequence, is focussed entirely on their personal communion with God-in-the-world or with God-in-themselves, and the link between such an exercise and the Christian mission is not very obvious.

Basically I agree with their position but I want to come at it in an entirely different way, a way that brings the lost dynamic back into prayer and frees it from our chronic reservations and scruples. For we are forced, as Leonard Hodgson has said, to the disconcerting realization 'that those who wrestle with God in prayer after the manner that we have renounced are growing in a richness and fullness of spiritual life beside which our efforts after self-culture appear intolerably thin and unsatisfying'.[1] So we are driven to the conclusion, I believe, that the only way forward is to repudiate our contemporary 'flat-earthers' – the thinkers who reduce every vertical to a horizontal, all language to the literal meaning of words, all faith to an intention to behave in a certain way, all relation with God to a relation with men. Every conclusion I have reached in this study of the Holy Spirit falls to the ground if we will not re-affirm the 'beyondness' of the beyond-in-the-midst. I have tried to show that in every I-Thou experience an awareness of absolute otherness precedes any awareness of communion. I have concluded, echoing Bonhoeffer, that a true situation ethic can be grounded on nothing but response to the unmediated reality of God. I have argued that the only convincing authority is that which emanates from the intrinsic truth *of*, not from the objectified truth *about*, another being (which is the stuff of scientific investigation). And, above all, I have found the essential meaning of Jesus Christ in his continuous and direct intercourse with the Father. By all means let us find that Father in the here and now of our secular engagement, as I believe Jesus did, but at all costs let him be God. And this means testifying to an experience that is irreducible to any other terms. For, as Martin Buber taught, God is a primary term and there is no substitute for it. 'To put it bluntly', says David Jenkins, 'people believe in God because people believe in God, and if God does not keep people believing in himself, that will be the end of the matter.'[2]

That will also be the end of anything that can truthfully be called Christian faith, since Christians are those who have been given the same experience of intercourse with the Father as Jesus knew, and whose mission is simply to let all men know that it can be their experience too.

'Our Father', we say in the midst of the world, under the buffetings of the whole world, and to that extent in resistance to all the world. To whom? To a non-entity? In actual fact we say it to that which bursts upon unbelief as the mystery of non-entity and strikes it dumb in speechless horror. *That* is what we are permitted to address as Father, because what comes to us from that quarter is not non-entity but through Jesus the voice of the Father, and in that voice the Father himself with outstretched arms.[3]

Bishop John Robinson offered the same testimony during the great *Honest to God* debate.

I do not pray to the ground of my being. I pray to God as Father. Prayer, for the Christian, is the opening of oneself to that utterly gracious personal reality which Jesus could only address as 'Abba, Father!' I have no interest whatever in a God conceived in some vaguely impersonal pantheistic terms. The only God who meets my need as a Christian is 'the God of Abraham, Isaac and Jacob', the God and Father of our Lord Jesus Christ.[4]

Traditional religious instruction has so stressed the importance of prayer that we are prone to lose sight of the fact that Christian prayer was such a new experience for the church in New Testament times that it could properly be ranked as one of the signs of the new manhood of Jesus. The word 'pray' had to take on as much extra weight of meaning as the words 'love' or 'church'. The new experience of prayer was as unprecedented as the new experience of the Holy Spirit. Considering the richness of Jewish liturgy and family ritual, it is surprising to find a far more frequent use of the various words for prayer in the New Testament than in the Old, and this surely reflects a unique emphasis in the life of Jesus. Patriarchs, prophets and kings had from time to time acted as intercessors for the people, and Moses was the supreme example of this. Yet no figure in the Bible before the appearance of Christ seems to have depended upon the habit of communion with God as Jesus did. We tend to read back into the Old Testament and into the devotional patterns of other faiths those meanings which Jesus gave to the word 'prayer', and so conceal the fact that what was so characteristic of Jesus is almost unique amid the formal recitations which are the commonplace of religion everywhere else, including most of the churches. Other faiths have their mystics, but only in Jesus, I believe, can we find such spontaneous and personal communion with God combined with such passionate ethical concern for humanity. Both awareness of God and awareness of the world attain their zenith in him.

Here we reach the holy of holies of the inner life of Jesus, momentarily unveiled by the spiritual insight of the fourth gospel, but implicit also in all the teaching about prayer which we find in the synoptic gospels.

When you pray, go into a room by yourself, shut the door, and pray to your Father who is there in the secret place; and your Father who sees what is secret will reward you. In your prayers do not go babbling on like the heathen, who imagine that the more they say the more likely they are to be heard. Do not imitate them. Your Father knows what your needs are before you ask him. This is how you should pray . . . (Matt. 6.6–9).

And then for the first time, through the quiet tones of human speech, the sound-waves of this world were stirred by that eternal converse which is ever passing between the Father and the Son in the Being of God. And since the third person of the Trinity is himself that communion which flows between the Father and the Son, then the Spirit himself is the very breath of the prayer of Jesus. Immersed in the Go-Between Spirit he cried *Abba!* and knew himself as the Beloved Son. And pouring out that Spirit upon the openness-to-each-other of his friends he shared with them the right to use the same naively bold address: *Abba!*

The prayer of the first Christians was, therefore, simply a reflection of the living Christ in their midst. It was prayer 'in his name'; and by this we mean not that a formula was added at the end of every petition, but that in all their prayer they joined themselves to the prayer of Christ himself, and knew that it was his spirit which prayed in them. The best worship they could offer was simply his self-oblation in them. Praying in that Spirit, the Christian's prayer is immersed in the ocean of the Son's communion with the Father: 'In Holy Spirit praying, keep yourselves in the love of God' (Jude 21). 'Keep your watch with continuous prayer and supplication, praying the whole time in the Spirit: with constant wakefulness and perseverance you will find opportunity to pray for all the Christian brethren' (Eph. 6.18, Wand translation). 'We do not even know how we ought to pray, but through our inarticulate groans the Spirit himself is pleading for us, and God who searches our inmost being knows what the Spirit means, because he pleads for God's own people in God's own way' (Rom. 8.26).

To live in prayer, therefore, is to live in the Spirit; and to live in the Spirit is to live in Christ. I am not saying that prayer is a means or a method which we have to use in order to have more of Christ in us or in order to be more fully possessed by the Spirit. I am saying something simpler and more fundamental: to live in Christ is to live in prayer. Prayer is not something you do; it is a style of living. It is living under the witness which the Spirit bears with our spirit that we are sons of God. Such a witness lays upon us the awful freedom of adult sonship. Prayer is our response to both the privilege and the responsibility whereby we cry *Abba*, Father! To engage in the mission of God, therefore, is to live this life of prayer; praying without ceasing, as St Paul puts it, that is to say, sustaining a style of life that is focussed upon God. This is indeed to engage in the mission of the Holy Spirit by being rather than by doing. To realize that the heart of mission is communion with God in the midst of the world's life will save us from the demented activism of these days.

> The end towards which we strive is not a material, external result, but the unfolding of a Person. A material result we may hope to produce or cause to be: the character, or nature, of the Person of Christ, though we may be agents of its manifestation, we cannot make. We cannot cause it to be. . . We seek a revelation. A revelation is the unfolding of something that is, not the creation of something that is not.[5]

Revelation of that kind is, as we have seen, the *metier* of the Holy Spirit. When we say, then, that prayer is the very life-blood of mission, we are not talking about one of several kinds of resources, like money and man-power and influence, which we muster to aid our enterprise; we are saying that the essential missionary activity is to live in prayer. John Venn, the father of the great Henry Venn, addressing the second Valedictory Meeting of the Church Missionary Society in the year 1806, gave this unexpected description of the character of a true missionary.

> He is one who, like Enoch, walks with God, and derives from constant communion with him a portion of the divine likeness.[6]

This is the real meaning of that approach to mission which has come to be known as 'Christian presence'. It is often confused with that method of approach to people of other faiths which is known as 'dialogue'. Christian presence and dialogue may often go hand in hand, it is true, but they are not the same. One of the purest examples of Christian presence which has ever been demonstrated is that of Père Charles de Foucauld, and of those who have followed in his steps, the Little Brothers and the Little Sisters of Jesus. Yet they have placed themselves under rule not to preach, nor to offer organized works, such as schools or hospitals, nor to employ any of the usual methods of evangelism. They believe they are simply called to live among the very poor of this world – on a house-boat amid the teeming refugees of Hong Kong, around a tiny courtyard high above the sacred waterfront of Benares, in a workman's shack on one of the sloping streets of Kabul, in an Eskimo hamlet in Alaska, a shanty suburb of Kampala, a labourers' settlement near Port Moresby, built on wooden piles above the sea like any other village of Papua. Unobtrusively they keep a routine of communal prayer and silent adoration, but every day they go out in their working clothes to do the same sort of job that their neighbours are doing and to offer them an unstinted friendship in the doing of it. A few years ago one Brother was working with a Muslim shoemaker; a Little Sister had found employment as a housemaid among the households of coloured servants in Washington, and another was employed with 300 other immigrant workers in a handkerchief factory in Sydney. Here again a Brother is working as a mason for a local firm of contractors in the Punjab. Out of sight, out of mind of the church as a whole, way below the poverty line, scattered in their twos and threes across the face of the earth, they do not work for their neighbours, they work with them. Their role is that of prayer and of a silent, hidden presence of love. Such extreme renunciation of all the normal activities of mission would suggest either a lack of concern or a policy of despair, were it not for Charles de Foucauld's ardent passion for evangelism. 'I wish to cry the gospel by my whole life', he said; and again, 'For the spreading of the gospel I am ready to go to the ends of the earth and I am likewise ready to live until the Day of Judgment'. To live thus totally towards God for the sake of the world is a profoundly missionary and, indeed, redemptive way. But only faith can perceive this. In her great book on worship, Evelyn Underhill wrote:

Worship is therefore in the deepest sense creative and redemptive. Keeping us in constant remembrance of the Unchanging and the Holy, it cleanses us of subjectivism, releases us from 'use and

wont' and makes us realists. . . Each separate soul thus transfigured by the spirit of selfless adoration advances that transfiguration of the whole universe which is the coming of the Kingdom of God.[7]

To an activist church engaged in struggle and protest and development, that must seem like an escape into a dream unless one remembers that what a man is towards God he is also towards his neighbour. To worship silently and to communicate the gospel silently, as
the Little Brothers and Sisters do, is some guarantee of their skill
in silent communication in all other areas of human concern. The
link between these two has been beautifully described by Ivan Illich
in a meditation introducing an hour of silent prayer at a course
he initiated to prepare ministers, teachers and social workers for the
Spanish-speaking ghettos of New York. He began with the discovery by linguistic experts that more is relayed from person to
person through the pauses and hesitations of speech than through
its words. 'It takes more time and effort and delicacy to learn the
silence of a people than to learn its sounds.' Then he developed an
analogy between our silence with men and our silence with God.
'The silence of a city priest on a bus listening to the report of the
sickness of a goat is a gift, truly the fruit of a missionary form of
long training in patience. . . In the prayer of silent listening, and
nowhere else, can the Christian acquire the habit of this first
silence from which the Word can be born in a foreign culture.'
But all too often, says Illich, the missionary grows impatient,
failing to see what a gift his enforced silence is. 'The man who
forgets the analogy of the silence of God and the silence of others
and does not seek its growth in prayer, is a man who tries basically
to rape the culture into which he is sent. . . As long as he sees
himself as "missioner" he will know that he is frustrated, that he
was sent but got nowhere; that he is away from home but has never
landed anywhere; that he left his home and never reached another.
He continues to preach and is ever more aware that he is not understood.' Only the very brave, says Illich, dare then to go back to the
helpless silence of being learners and listeners – 'the holding of
hands of the lovers' – from which deep communication may grow.
'Perhaps it is the one way of being together with others and with the
Word in which we have no more foreign accent.'[8]
The simple truth that our manner of communication with God

moulds the manner of our communication with people throws an entirely new light upon the connection between prayer and mission. Yet it follows quite logically from the fact we noted in the first chapter, that awareness is multi-directional, and we cannot be opened towards God without being opened also towards the ticking of the clock and towards all the joy and pain of the world.

That is why we can affirm, as I believe the New Testament does, that every kind of prayer is summed up and included in the basic communion with God which the cry *Abba!* epitomizes. It is not difficult to see how this is the case with the three types of prayer – thanksgiving, prayer for guidance, and intercession – which can be distinguished in the New Testament, apart from the direct, loving regard of the prayer of communion.

In the synoptic gospels there are a number of references to Jesus' praying, particularly drawing attention to the unusually long periods that he spent in prayer, but only two of his prayers are recorded, apart from the exclamations from the cross. So it is all the more remarkable that one of these two is the jubilant outburst of praise: 'I thank thee, Father, Lord of heaven and earth, for hiding these things from the learned and wise and revealing them to the simple. Yes, I thank thee, Father, that such was thy choice' (Matt. 11.25, 26 mg). The fourth gospel adds three more, and one of these also begins: 'Father, I thank thee' (John 11.41). This, of course, was in keeping with the characteristic style of Jewish prayer in which blessing God predominates far more than in the Christian tradition. But whereas the Jewish benedictions are marked by a charming application of formality to domesticity – the Hebrew prayer book contains a thanksgiving on going to stool – Jesus seems to have brought a vernacular spontaneity to even the most exalted worship.

A new way of praying is born. Jesus talks to his Father as naturally, as intimately and with the same sense of security as a child talks to his father. It is a characteristic token of this new mode of prayer that it is dominated by thanksgiving. . . There is a profound reason for this predominance of thanksgiving in Jesus' prayer. A fine saying from Tannaitic times (1st–2nd century A D) runs: 'In the world to come all sacrifices will cease, but the thank-offering will remain for ever; likewise all confessions will cease, but the confession of thanks will remain for ever.' Thanksgiving is one of the foremost characteristics of the new age. So when Jesus gives thanks he is not just following custom. There is more to it than that; he is actualizing God's reign here and now.[9]

The church which entered into Jesus' *abba*-relationship to God and prayed in his name took up that style of prayer in which thanksgiving and communion are one and the same, and its worship was eucharistic from the start. This accounts for the remarkable fact that in the Pauline epistles there are almost as many references to thanksgiving as there are to prayer.

The link between prayer and guidance also does not consist simply in God's response to man's requests to be shewn the right way. Too often the 'Veni Creator' or prayer for guidance with which we like to open our religious conferences and committees scarcely rises above the level of harmless magic or a breaking of the Christians' colours. The night of prayer which preceded Jesus' selection of the twelve apostles was focussed, we must surely believe, upon the kingdom and the power and the glory of God rather than on any short list of candidates. It was communion and submission and adoration, renewing and clarifying the human body and mind and soul of Christ, which led, quite incidentally, to that sure knowledge of the next step he had to take in doing his Father's will. This is how it was at the first determinative annunciation at the start.

When Jesus too had been baptized and was praying, heaven opened and the Holy Spirit descended on him in bodily form like a dove; and there came a voice from heaven, 'Thou art my Son, my Beloved; on thee my favour rests' (Luke 3.21–2).

So he continued to make his decisions in the early period of his ministry.

Very early next morning he got up and went out. He went away to a lonely spot and remained there in prayer. But Simon and his companions searched him out, found him, and said, 'They are all looking for you.' He answered, 'Let us move on to the country towns in the neighbourhood; I have to proclaim my message there also' (Mark 1.35–8).

We read of Jesus withdrawing in this way to dwell on his awareness of God when a new situation was created by the rush of popularity following his first healing mission, and again by the crowds' attempt to make him king. Prayer of this kind preceded his crucial self-revelation to the apostles at Caesarea Philippi and again on the mount of transfiguration. And the true nature of all prayer for guidance is most intimately disclosed in the agonized openness of Gethsemane.

This was the kind of prayer by which the young church felt its way step by step along the path of its earliest mission. The prayer that had preceded the choice of Matthias to fill the place of Judas, like the fumbling solemnity of the choice itself, savoured more of ecclesiastical committee-work than of the free movement of the Holy Spirit (Acts 1.23–6). But after Pentecost there is a marked difference; now we have a community in which communion with the Father is constant (Acts 2.42). After the first clash with authority the young church meets for prayer and thanksgiving and is again made intensely aware of the truth of Jesus Christ through their fulness of the Spirit (Acts 4.23 ff.). When James is executed and Peter imprisoned the response is once again a praying church (Acts 12.5, 12). Communion with God precedes the appointment of the deacons, the first admission of the Gentiles into the church, the sending out of Paul and Barnabas, and their first ordination of a ministry in a convert church (Acts 6.6; 10.9; 13.3; 14.23).

But if these first missionaries found their direction through communion with the Father it is evident that they relied even more upon it for their mutual responsibility in the common task. Jesus had taught them to pray to the Lord of the harvest, and from the beginning intercession was an essential part of their service to one another and to the world. All true intercession is a deepening of awareness towards others rather than a request. So almost every one of Paul's epistles begins with a reference to his prayers and thanksgivings for those to whom he is writing. 'God knows how continually I make mention of you in my prayers' (Rom. 1.9). 'I thank my God whenever I think of you; and when I pray for you all, my prayers are always joyful' (Phil. 1.3–4). 'Greetings from Epaphras, servant of Christ, who is one of yourselves; he prays hard for you all the time, that you may stand fast, ripe in conviction' (Col. 4.12). Nor is Christian intercession limited to the members of the church. 'Brothers, my deepest desire and my prayer to God is for Israel's salvation' (Rom. 10.1).

But apostolic prayer is always give-and-take. No Christian, however high his calling or endowment, may be independent of the help of others. It is the mark of the missionary that he knows how to receive as well as how to give, most of all in the things of the Spirit. 'Brothers, pray for us also' (I Thess. 5.25). 'I implore you by our Lord Jesus Christ and by the love that the Spirit inspires, be my allies in the fight; pray to God for me' (Rom. 15.30).

When we realize that intercession is an exercise in awareness it brings a great change to our understanding of it. When praying for others we allow ourselves to be caught in the current of communication which the Spirit gives between us and another, and most of all between us and God. This is brought home most poignantly in an episode recorded by Archbishop Anthony Bloom from the life of Father Silouan, a Russian artisan who came to Mount Athos to be a monk and was put in charge of one of the workshops where other young peasants from distant villages indented for a year or two to raise a little cash they could get in no other way. For Father Silouan 'management' meant secret prayer for each one:

> In the beginning I prayed with tears of compassion for Nicholas, for his young wife, for the little child, but as I was praying the sense of the divine presence began to grow on me and at a certain moment it grew so powerful that I lost sight of Nicholas, his wife, his child, his needs, their village, and I could be aware only of God, and I was drawn by the sense of the divine presence deeper and deeper, until of a sudden, at the heart of this presence, I met the divine love holding Nicholas, his wife, and his child, and now it was with the love of God that I began to pray for them again, but again I was drawn into the deep and in the depths of this I again found the divine love.[10]

Such a fading of one's awareness of another human being into one's even more intense awareness of God is the surest safeguard against the wish to use prayer as a means to manipulate other lives by remote control – for their own good, of course – which to some people makes the very idea of intercession distasteful. I am convinced by experience that prayer 'makes a difference' not only to the one who prays but to those also for whom the prayer is made. Yet I am equally sure this does not operate through any undiscovered telepathic power – not, at least, if the prayer is moved by the Spirit of Christ. True intercession invokes only one power, the power that 'comes to its full strength in weakness', though that weakness 'is stronger than man's strength' ('I Cor. 12.9; I Cor. 1.25). True intercession places another person more firmly in the arms of the divine love which will never infringe that person's freedom, but which works through bestowals of awareness and recognition, through evocation and response, through the offer of choice and the glimpse of possibility. True intercession in the service of the Christian mission is the purest acknowledgment that the mission is God's, not ours. For this reason it is far more significant that a church or a particular missionary fellowship should be, and be seen to be, a community to which God is a burning, joyful reality, than that it should busy itself with vigils of intercession and lists of names.

Every form of prayer that is stirred by the Spirit, therefore, is in essence a repetition of the love-word *Abba!*, the Jesus word. It should be to the Christian what the syllable OM is to the Hindu, to be uttered not as the exclusive talisman of one religion, but as the password of humanity, establishing in Christ the ultimate truth of everyman. Each time of prayer is an attempt to open ourselves more fully to that direct communion with the Father which Jesus knew, and to realize more deeply our relationship to him as adult sons and daughters. That communion is the primary gift of the Go-Between God and he alone can make it happen.

But, having said that, we have to do our part; and the first requirement is simply to have the nerve to pray. I choose that phrase because it means effrontery as well as fortitude, and both are needed for prayer in these days. Coolly we have to challenge the reported death of God even while we feel in ourselves the evidences of it. We have to defy the habits of thought that tell us prayer is meaningless, remembering that other ages also found it so. But we also need the endurance to learn a long-lost art and recover functions that have started to atrophy.

Some years ago, in a Prism Pamphlet, Alan Ecclestone proposed a simple beginners' technique for those who had forgotten or not known how to pray, and I have not met anything to better it.[11] He suggests that we should take as a starting point those commonly-experienced sudden annunciations which occur day by day and are not specifically religious in content at all. They are, in fact, the same raw materials that I have taken as the basis of this study of the Holy Spirit, though I had not read Alan Ecclestone when I began. He instances first of all the fleeting moments when we are surprised by joy. I immediately think of the morning walk to the underground across a corner of the park where the first almond blossom has burst into flower; or the relief of catching sight of a friend too long awaited, so exquisitely conveyed in a Chinese couplet of the fifth century B C:

> *I saw you coming down the western road,*
> *My heart laid down its load.*

'Praying at this point', says Ecclestone, 'means deliberately prolonging, extending, savouring the expression of gratitude so that it doesn't drop away unused and unexplored. *To pray is to make the most of our moments of perception.* You pause on the thing that has happened, you turn it over and over like a person examining a gift, you set it in the context of past and future, you mentally draw out its possibilities, you give the moment time to reveal what is embedded in it.'[12]

I imagine that the most natural time to do this 'praying' is immediately after the moment of perception, when I dive out of the pale sunshine into the crowded subway, or when I turn for home, my arm linked with my friend's. That is when the little surge of gratitude ebbs away and when I can best prolong it. But as we get better at it, says Ecclestone, that same response of gratitude may be recalled and 'used as the willed basis for praying when we come to sit down or kneel down to reflect upon a day's experience'. The same use, he suggests, can be made of two other types of sudden awareness: 'God help me', even if it means little more than a passing whiff of anxiety, can be the raw material of prayer as we 'begin to stretch it over the whole of life to bind ourselves, our need for help and the Lord together in an unbreakable relationship. And 'God, I'm tired', which again merely marks an all-too-familiar moment of exhaustion, can be 'stretched', with practice, until it grows into that habit of 'letting go and letting God', which is such an important and needful part of prayer.

Sooner or later, however, prayer must advance beyond the cultivation of our own states of feeling and their use as flimsy bridges to bring us to the God we thank or depend on. But it is along the next stage of our re-discovery of prayer that we grind to a halt, either through the tedium of words or the sheer difficulty of doing without words. We need a great deal of help to find our way through both these frustrations.

I am reminded of the two views from the little town of Assisi. To the north-east lies a forbidding landscape of bare mountains. Grey crags and grey sky seem equally empty and remote. Hour by hour nothing moves but the shadows of the clouds. Season by season nothing changes but the fall of snow and its melting. It is a landscape of silence and non-event and naked existence and the only way one can express one's love for it is by simply being there in a stillness that is open to receive it just as it is. The scene hints at the eternal otherness for which man strangely longs with a desire that purges the last vestiges of self-regard. It is fitting that somewhere beyond these grey ranges towers Monte La Verna where Francis received the stigmata.

Now turn the other way and look down into the wide plain of Spoleto. All is mellow and homely. A score of little hamlets are threaded on the twisting string of road; carts rumble out of sight among the vineyards, children's voices babble, and old bells call across great distances. The very different beauty of this scene speaks of the rhythms and changes of life and of the eternal made known in human ways.

There are two kinds of prayer associated with these two aspects of God which I prefer to call the prayer of stillness and the prayer of movement. The classical distinction between contemplation and meditation is no longer obvious from their dictionary definitions, and has been further confused by popular teachers of 'transcendental meditation'. The difference does not lie in subject-matter but in the way in which one looks at it. It is not that in the prayer of movement we choose to dwell upon passages in the Bible or incidents in the life of Christ or the needs of the world, while in the prayer of stillness we seek the vision of God in a direct exposure to the uncreated light. The difference is much simpler than that. In the prayer of movement our mind moves from thought to thought and from image to image as it does most of the time when we are 'thinking' either about God or tonight's dinner, an article in the newspaper or a chapter in the Bible, the Christians in the Sudan or the pack in the Welsh rugby team. But in the prayer of stillness the mind stands still and looks, takes in what is standing before it and gives itself, but does not move from thought to thought.

I can make this clearer, perhaps, by recalling the distinction I have drawn several times between the truth *about* someone or something and the truth *of* someone or something. In the prayer of movement we try to open ourselves to more of the truth *about* Jesus by dwelling on part of the gospel; or to open ourselves to more of the truth *about* the Sudanese church by reading a letter and using our imaginations with compassion. In the prayer of stillness we try to hold ourselves open to the impact of the truth *of* Jesus not in a succession of bits and pieces, but as one whole person; or, aided by such knowledge as we already have about the Sudan, we try to hold ourselves still before the truth of those Christians 'because they are there', open to their reality without thinking any new thoughts about them.

The real difficulty of the prayer of movement is that the words we are given to think with, and the images we are given to picture with, strike us as stale, incredible or emptied of meaning because they reflect a mentality and a situation we left behind many centuries ago. No culture can survive on its old masters alone, and no church can continue to live on 'incomparable liturgies' from the past. New versions of the Bible, contemporary styles of prayer and song, formulations of the faith that speak today, symbols that convey old meanings with the shock of fresh discovery, personal devotion and corporate worship that turn drama and dance, fantasy and play to account and allow more scope to our physical nature and our interpersonal dynamics – none of these can generate the awareness of the living Lord which the Holy Spirit alone can give, but they can at least throw the doors open and allow the Spirit entry.

But all that we have so far learned about that Spirit suggests that our greater need is for a recovery of the prayer of stillness. It can best be understood in terms of presence. We have already seen what the practice of Christian presence means in the lives of the Little Brothers and Sisters of Jesus. It is the direct giving of self without any auxiliary or token giving of words or work. We are back at the scene of the annunciation once more.

> *These neither speak nor movement make,*
> *But stare into their deepening trance*
> *As if their gaze would never break.*[13]

I would offer two reasons for thinking that most of us in the western churches, and not those only who are temperamentally so inclined, need to re-learn the prayer of stillness. The first is that we are all becoming the prisoners of our activism. We speak with the tongues of men and of angels in a dozen different committees; our gift of prophecy and knowledge defeats the politicians at their own game; our faith removes mountains of discrimination; our goods feed the hungry millions, our bodies are burned up in evangelistic zeal. Yet we lack charity, the only quality which makes contagious Christians, from whom others may catch the love of God. And charity comes by adoration.

But the second reason why the prayer of stillness is more likely to become the vehicle of our communion with the Father is that we have grown sick of words. We find it increasingly hard to accept the language of poetry when it is applied to religion. We are, perhaps, afraid of being taken in. The sort of prayers we would like to make, if we still feel able to put prayer into words at all, are those of Charles de Foucauld himself. Something of the desert in which he has died has prompted the gaunt style of his spiritual utterance. The man who became the Prior of the Little Brothers has written:

> If you have read Père de Foucauld's spiritual writings at all, you will certainly agree that it would be difficult to find anything more utterly simple, more completely devoid of conscious style or literary effect. The secret of this is not only that these meditations were written for God and not for publication – that was his way of meditating, and the one thing that mars their intimacy is the fact of their being printed – but that they are an expression of a constant and continuous relationship with Jesus which has transformed the soul of a strong man and a man of learning and culture and ability into the soul of a child.[14]

But today's preference for bare statement in matters of religion is not merely aesthetic. We are less and less at home in the language of symbols and images. Our bent, technological rather than scientific, makes us naive and literal, so that we often confuse the symbol with the thing it symbolizes; and there is no surer way than this of robbing a symbol of vital significance. Every religious affirmation seems to throw us into a panic of doubt, and prayer becomes more difficult than ever because we want to define whom it is we are talking to, as though anyone ever succeeded in doing this; because, taking our own symbolic act literally, we wonder whether 'talking to him' is an appropriate response to such a being, anyway; and because the whole action seems to refer to a realm of supernatural phenomena which we cannot reconcile with our empirical view of the universe. Betrayed by our absurd literalism we go doggedly on rejecting the inner springs of humanity itself.

Yet this wilderness of no symbols may be purgative and creative, 'a dark night of the soul'. Desert sands have always been the seedbed of faith, for the desert is the natural home of the *ruach*, and has more than once been the place from which the church recovered the life of prayer, strange as this may seem. The prayer of the modern secularized Christian, like his mission in the world, will be stamped with unpretentiousness.

So, both because of our activism and our mistrust of words and symbols, we would do well to find the way to God in the prayer of stillness. That is certainly the direction in which the younger generation of the western world feels it needs to be pointed. But it is a way of prayer for which we are peculiarly disqualified. For so long we have worshipped the process of analytical argument and played down every other way to knowledge that our amalgam of brain and body has almost grown incapable of any form of thought except 'one damn thing after another'. We have lost the simple power of attention by which our mind can stand still at one point, doing nothing but taking in what is there. This is the skill which Father Slade's community at Anchorhold, and the Fellowship of Meditation at Guildford, are undertaking to teach again. They have quickly realized that the unceasing movement of our conscious minds, combined with the strain and noise in which most of us now exist, have strung us up to such a pitch of muscular tension that we need some technique, such as Yoga or the T'ai Chiih Chüan, to relax the body enough for the mind to allow itself to rest and stand still.

The next step is to enter into an awareness of some other creature. Father Slade finds it most helpful to focus a loving attention upon some simple object, rich in associations, such as a lit candle, a flower, a glass of water or wine. It is a deliberate attempt to experience the same quality of encounter and mutuality which comes unbidden to each of us from time to time; and if, as I have suggested, it is the Spirit of God who gives us those unlooked-for annunciations, it is he alone who can give the living awareness we seek deliberately in this prayer of stillness. When the current of communion is there between oneself and the candle flame or the water, so that one is aware with every sense of the otherness of it, the truth of it, then one tries, with the minimum of thinking *about* it, to see it as a symbol or embodiment of Christ – the Light, the Living Water – so that one's awareness is of him and it is he who confronts and beckons. The next stage is to shut off the external, visible object in order to bring its presence, its reality which is the presence and reality of Christ, into the heart and concentrate one's whole being upon him there in stillness. And finally the mental image of the symbol should be quietly removed, leaving in its place a space, at the very heart of one's heart, which is filled with Christ.

Because of the difficulty and possible dangers of re-learning these skills of the mind and soul those who undertake to teach them usually do so in groups. This in itself is a protection against any neo-quietism which would be merely ego-centric. It also helps to overcome the resistance of those who find it impossible to make any commitments except corporate ones. It is easy to see how closely this development accords with the recovery of the eucharist in an increasingly corporate form as the main, and in many cases the only, act of worship and prayer in which Christians of the younger generation can find vivid significance. They know intuitively that the Spirit is always the Go-Between, the fire amid the branches of the burning bush, the giver of Christ's presence to the two or three gathered together.

It may come as a surprise to many seekers to learn that the prayer of stillness can be a shared, corporate experience, and that it can be directed towards any other than the pure Being of God. It is enormously important, I believe, to dissociate this direct, wordless prayer from the rarified mysticism to which we think only the saints can aspire. The prayer of stillness is that which most naturally deepens our communion with the Father and reproduces in us the *abba*-relationship that Jesus knew. But the same manner of praying can make Jesus himself more real to us; it is a form of intercession also whereby other people are held in our loving regard and sympathy. It can make us more profoundly aware of the crying needs of mankind and the mysterious bond between ourselves and the physical world.

This richness should make it impossible for us to disregard the many who can find their God only by the same gradual progression as the disciples, first knowing Jesus as a man who draws them humanly and commands their allegiance as no other being has ever done, who becomes the point of reference by which they set their

standards and make their decisions, into whose presence they want
to bring their perplexity and pain, whom in fact they begin to treat
as God long before they have formulated theologically their convictions about him. If this was legitimate for the fishermen of
Galilee – or, rather, if it was illegitimate yet necessary, for them –
may it not be permitted to secular man to treat the man Jesus as his
God even before he can admit that there is any meaning in the
word 'divine'?

> Many a man who rejects the formulae of theological Christology
> because he understands them amiss may yet existentially have a
> perfectly genuine Christian faith in the Incarnation of the Word
> of God. Anyone who contemplating Jesus, his cross and death,
> really believes that there the living God has spoken to him the
> final decisive, irrevocable word that delivers him from all bondage
> to the existential categories of his imprisoned, sinful, death-
> doomed existence, believes in the reality of the Jesus of Christian
> faith, believes in the Incarnation of God's Word, whether or not
> he realizes the fact.[15]

We need not shrink from inviting men to focus their love and
thought upon the historical and contingent elements in the fact of
Christ. Christian mysticism is not centred upon an abstraction but
upon a person – a particular, historical person. Christian devotion
is to this extent vulnerable to historical research and cannot be
emancipated from it without ceasing to be Christian devotion.

It does not matter whether the Christ who fills our vision is the
historical Jesus, or the living Saviour, or the Christ of the Body and
the Blood, or the Logos and Lord of the universe, or the master and
meaning of history, or the Christ in my neighbour and in his poor.
These are only aspects of his being. In whatever aspect he is most
real to us, what matters is that we adore him. For, loving him
whom we think we know, we are drawn to that Lord Jesus who
transcends our knowing. But all too often we have lost him amid
our enthusiasms. What dominates our mind is not the figure of
Jesus of Nazareth but our New Testament studies, not the living
Saviour but the doctrines of salvation, not Christ in the neighbour
but the civil rights movement.

This is not a plea for pietism but for adoration. The Jesus of
history, whensoever we discern him, is not a topic of debate but a
master and brother to be loved and followed. Christ in his poor is

neither a case nor a cause, but a mystery before whom we bow even while we serve. Whatever way of knowing him is valid for us – and it may be simply as the one whose 'give ye them to eat' sends us into the fight for a new world order – we must be in love with *him*, not with ourselves or our schemes. We must find time to let our minds dwell on him. The beauty of holiness in the midst of this revolutionary world belongs to those who set the Lord always before their eyes. *Venite adoremus!*

By the same token, when the prayer of stillness takes the form of intercession, it consists quite simply in allowing the Holy Spirit to make other people present to us and us aware of them. We should try to focus our stilled minds upon them in the same way as Father Slade teaches us to focus our stilled minds upon a candle. Such prayer will probably not feel like a religious act at all. Some years ago I received a letter from a missionary in a rather desolate area of Nigeria. She wrote both from a sense of shame at the ineffectualness of her intercession, and also to share a basic query. 'Let me give an example,' she said. 'There were five boys weighing on my mind at the end of last term as I knew their fees for this year were just hopelessly inadequate. They were pretty constantly in my mind, yet I do not recall that I formulated any prayer for them. However, within a month four of them had adequate financial assistance. A week later came a Christmas gift from my sister and her husband for any student needing help; so that was the fifth! I quite simply regard this as miraculous – the result of God's concern – and I do not see that formal intercession would have made any difference one way or the other.' When someone whose life is simply and sacrificially dedicated to God has any fellow man 'pretty constantly in mind' to the extent that the feeling of concern leads to responsible action, that, surely is the whole of intercession. For a timeless moment it makes one totally present with the other person or persons across the intervening distances, without words and in a manner that goes beyond thought. It is simply a matter of 'being there for them' in a concentration upon the other which obliterates all awareness of self and yet is not strung up but totally relaxed. In that stillness which lies beyond thought we are to let the presence of that other person impinge upon our spirit across the distance, with all his rich reality and all his need and burden. His presence matters more than our own.

So is it also when the other on whom our silent regard is concentrated is once again God himself. For in this prayer of awareness we swing from intercession to worship and back again, we alternate between communion with fellow men and with God, the image of the symbol merges into the image of Christ, without any break in the stillness. This is the gift of the Spirit, the beloved Go-Between, the opener of eyes and giver of life.

A colleague has recently described to me an occasion when a West Indian woman in a London flat was told of her husband's death in a street accident. The shock of grief stunned her like a blow, she sank into a corner of the sofa and sat there rigid and unhearing. For a long time her terrible tranced look continued to embarrass the family, friends and officials who came and went. Then the schoolteacher of one of her children, an Englishwoman, called and, seeing how things were, went and sat beside her. Without a word she threw an arm around the tight shoulders, clasping them with her full strength. The white cheek was thrust hard against the brown. Then as the unrelenting pain seeped through to her the newcomer's tears began to flow, falling on their two hands linked in the woman's lap. For a long time that is all that was happening. And then at last the West Indian woman started to sob. Still not a word was spoken and after a little while the visitor got up and went, leaving her contribution to help the family meet its immediate needs.

That is the embrace of God, his kiss of life. That is the embrace of his mission, and of our intercession. And the Holy Spirit is the force in the straining muscles of an arm, the film of sweat between pressed cheeks, the mingled wetness on the backs of clasped hands. He is as close and as unobtrusive as that, and as irresistibly strong.

## NOTES

1. Leonard Hodgson, *For Faith and Freedom*, SCM Press, 2nd ed. 1968, Vol. II, p. 163.

2. David E. Jenkins, *Living with Questions*, SCM Press 1969, p. 180.

3. Gerhard Ebeling, *The Lord's Prayer in Today's World*, SCM Press 1966, p. 56.

4. John A. T. Robinson & David L. Edwards (eds), *The Honest to God Debate*, SCM Press 1963, p. 262.

5. Roland Allen, *Missionary Principles*, World Dominion Press 1964, pp. 68, 73.

6. Eugene Stock, *History of the Church Missionary Society*, CMS 1899, Vol. 1, p. 85.

7. Evelyn Underhill, *Worship*, James Nisbet 1936, p. 18.

8. Ivan D. Illich, *Celebration of Awareness*, Calder & Boyars 1971, pp. 45–51.

9. Joachim Jeremias, *The Prayers of Jesus*, SCM Press 1967, p. 78.

10. Anthony Bloom, *School for Prayer*, Darton, Longman & Todd 1970, p. 75.

11. Alan Ecclestone, *On Praying*, Prism Publications, reprinted in *Spirituality for Today*, ed. Eric James, SCM Press 1968, pp. 29–40.

12. Ibid., p. 31. The italics are mine.

13. See p. 11.

14. Fr Rene Voillaume, essay in *Jesus Caritas*, Paris 1958, p. 30.

15. From the article on 'Jesus Christ' in Karl Rahner and Herbert Vorgrimler, *Concise Theological Dictionary*, Burns & Oates 1965, p. 241.

# INDEX OF THEMES

*References in brackets show where a theme is implicit*